The Imperial Challenge

The Imperial Challenge

Quebec and Britain in the Age of the American Revolution

PHILIP LAWSON

McGill-Queen's University Press
Montreal and Kingston, London, Buffalo

© McGill-Queen's University Press 1989
ISBN 0-7735-0698-5

Legal deposit first quarter 1990
Bibliothèque nationale du Québec

Printed in Canada on acid-free paper

This book has been published with the help of a grant from
the Social Science Federation of Canada, using funds
provided by the Social Sciences and Humanities Research
Council of Canada.

Canadian Cataloguing in Publication Data

Lawson, Philip
    The imperial challenge: Quebec and Britain in the age of
    the American Revolution
    Includes index.
    Bibliography: p.
    ISBN 0-7735-0698-5
    1. Canada – Politics and government – 1763–1774.
    2. Canada – History – Military administration, 1760–1763.
    I. Title.
    FC2921.2.L39 1990   971.02   C89-090238-0   F1032.L39 1990

For Elizabeth and Caroline

Contents

Preface

The study of imperial issues in the general sweep of Hanoverian history has suffered some woeful neglect over the last generation. The impact of an expanding empire on the mother country has been marginalized, more often than not, into single chapters in texts dealing with the eighteenth century. To make matters worse, these chapters are usually dominated by a brief survey of why Britain lost the American colonies. This tunnel vision is not, however, a fair representation of how the British viewed their imperial adventures at the time. Contemporary observers and commentators fully recognized the critical domestic ramifications of an expansionist policy that resulted in the governance of alien peoples and their cultures. But somehow twentieth-century scholars have lost sight of this fact, and an imbalance in the approach to Hanoverian history has resulted. By examining the challenge posed by the conquest of Quebec to the British, it is hoped that some redress to this trend of trivializing imperial issues may be offered.

The conquest of Quebec set in train a sequence of events in which historical opinion is still polarized. American historians argue over whether it can be seen as a primary cause of the War of Independence, French-Canadian scholars dispute the idea of a decapitation in New French society after 1760, and the British imperial school argues about statesmanship and first and second empires. What is missing from this schema is an explanation of the contemporary British context for the Quebec legislation of 1774. This episode in eighteenth-century history is significant not only to historians of empire but also to those concerned with domestic developments in an era of change and instability. Failure to acknowledge these themes has clouded a fuller understanding of the period in general and the political and social background to the act of 1774 in particular. The genesis of the Quebec legislation produced a lively popular and parliamentary debate that went right to the core of political and philosophical assumptions derived from the Glorious Revolution some eighty-five years before. Religious toleration, the function of representative government, and the meanings of English law all come to the fore in the debate about Quebec. The accent in studying such dynamics in eighteenth-century history has always been on the colonial society concerned, which, in this case, has worked to the detriment of a real appreciation of a unique problem. It seems right therefore to turn the penny over and ask what effect the conquest of Quebec had on Britain. Thus, I have attempted here to treat the debate over Quebec on its own merits, as contemporaries did. The sources used include official documentation and contemporary correspondence, as well as press and pamphlet literature that reflected and amplified the political decisions being taken in London. I have resisted the temptation to weave all the arguments of the period about Canada's future into parallel discussion on Ireland and America. Where the debate overlaps, its importance is acknowledged; but my overriding intention in what follows has been to portray the eighteenth-century debate about Quebec as it was then presented.

A study of this nature always depends a great deal on the pioneering scholarship of others in the field, and to those historians who opened up this subject area I owe a debt. No less important was the financial support for the research that preceded the writing of this study, and this was generously given by the Central Research Fund at the University of Alberta. The book itself has been published with the help of a grant from the Social Science Federation of Canada, using funds provided by the Social Sciences and Humanities Research Council of Canada.

Acknowledgments are also due to the owners and managers of the archival material used in this study, without whose co-operation the production of such a monograph would not be possible. In particular, I am indebted to Countess Fitzwilliam; the trustees of the Bedford estate; Earl Cromartie of Strathpeffer; the Marquess of Bute; the Duke of Grafton, and the librarians and archivists throughout Britain who offered patient assistance with my enquiries. The staffs at the Scottish Record Office and West Register House, Edinburgh, the British Library and Public Record Office, London, and the National Archives, Ottawa, proved invaluable in this regard. In addition, special thanks must go to the following individuals, who helped in various capacities to bring this project to fruition: Karen Philp, Vanessa Radke, Karl Schweizer, and Galen Wilson. As a last word, thank you to all those not mentioned in the text who answered my queries and made helpful comments on earlier drafts of this study. This assistance was much appreciated and will not be forgotten.

The Imperial Challenge

CHAPTER ONE

The Conquest of Quebec and Peace-making 1759–63

The assumption of an easy conquest by British arms over Quebec never appeared in contemporary writing or thought. Failure in this design during the Seven Years' War had become a commonplace, and those in Britain had become pessimistic about the prospect of Major General James Wolfe's expeditionary force taking the city. In August 1758 Henry Bilson Legge, the chancellor of the Exchequer, advised George Grenville at the Admirality that despite many setbacks over the year he yet hoped "we shall give a good account of Canada still before the end of the campaign."[1] The nation held its breath while news of the action on Quebec trickled across the Atlantic. It had all the elements of an epic tale. The press plotted Wolfe's military fortunes to the very point of engagement. The *Gentleman's Magazine* presented the most optimistic view, reporting in September 1759 that "as our commanders are men of merit and approved courage, little doubt can be made of their being in possession of that city."[2] The contemporary diarist and politician Horace Walpole was more sardonic. He told one correspondent on 13 September 1759 that though all the news from North America boded well for the future, he himself could never be sure: "I would keep this letter back for a post, that I might have but one trouble of sending you Quebec, but when one has taken so many places, it is not worth while to wait for one more."[3] In the end, no one would be disappointed. Quebec fell and the floodgates of loyal celebration opened. The fact that it would be another year before Trois Rivières and Montreal (and thus the whole of New France) capitulated cast no shadow over the national rejoicing. The mood of the people was embodied in the City of Nottingham's Address to the King, declaring that the taking of Quebec represented the utter destruction "of the trade and commerce and power of France in North America."[4] The exultation at court matched that in the country at large. Prince George, in particular, held no doubts about the significance of Wolfe's victory; he told his favourite and mentor, Lord Bute: "Heaven be praised for this great news, it puts an end to the French dominion in America."[5]

All this comment tends to give the impression that Britain knew exactly what it wanted from the war. But did it? To talk of destroying French commerce by conquering Quebec was hardly realistic. The economic value of New France appeared minimal compared to the West Indian possessions taken from the French during the war or, to look even further ahead, the cost of defending this new territory against Indian attack and the possibility of a war of *revanche* by France. What sense can be made of a strategy to conquer New France, a possession derisively termed by one minister as "a long barren tract of country," at a cost of millions to Britain when the expected return would be the sum of £40,000 per annum?[6] What is, in fact, known of the fundamental aims behind the strategies employed by the British in the Seven Years' War with regard to Canada? Until the 1980s such questions had not played much part in the debates on the course of the hostilities. Narrative histories of the period 1756–63, in particular, exhibit some enduring but often misleading generalizations about British conduct of the war and the ensuing peace negotiations. In short, the picture has emerged of Britain's war efforts being wholly reactive: one thing simply led to another. The war machine fed itself. Then as initial failure turned to rampant success during the "annus mirabilis" of 1759, the schemes grew more aggressive and expensive until George III, assisted by his pacific ministers under Lord Bute's leadership, called a halt to the policies of aggrandizement in late 1760. This view has dominated histories of the war over the last generation and it has prompted one leading scholar in the field to declare that, voluminous though this literature might be, it is "in large part now outdated."[7] What has emerged over the last decade is more searching analysis of the European and colonial background to the Seven Years' War, revealing new perspectives on the aims and aspirations of the leading nations involved and their political representatives.

In turn, this revisionism presents a much clearer view of each stage of Britain's involvement in the war, from the diplomatic revolution in Europe following Britain's participation in the Convention of Westminster in 1756 with Prussia to the detailed peace negotiations in the period from 1760 to 1763 in which crucial decisions about future continental and colonial priorities were taken. No less important, the role of individuals within this process can be better evaluated. During the war years 1756–60, for example, it is now possible to appreciate how the first lord of the Treasury, the duke of Newcastle, was instrumental not only in raising finance for operations abroad but also in formulating strategy.[8] By implication, such re-evaluations of the personalities in the wartime government have downplayed the traditional view of William Pitt the elder as the great leader, a dominant figure of the war who single-handedly snatched a British victory from the jaws of defeat in 1759–60.[9] More light has been shed instead on the growing concern of the nation and its parliamentary representatives that war would never end. By 1760 enough voices were being raised against continuing hostilities with France to show that Pitt's policies of unfettered expansionism did not have universal approval. Opposition came from all quarters, the most compelling proving to be the polemic by Israel Mauduit, *Considerations on the Present German War*, which enjoyed phenomenal success after it was published in 1760. The piece contained a simple message: end Britain's involvement in the continental war and its subsidy payments to Prussia and drive a hard bargain with France over possessions in other parts of the world. In other words, separate the European theatre from the war elsewhere. The former was not in Britain's best interests, but the latter was. Opinion about the significance of challenges like that of Mauduit has remained remarkably constant. One contemporary observer at court, Lord Egmont, observed that Mauduit's argument gained credence "in a very surprising manner," and two centuries of reflection have hardly dimmed this assessment. [10] When he examined the literature of the Seven Years' War in the 1960s, Spector commented, of the growing pacifism, that *Considerations* ... "had no small part in shaping this public opinion at the end of 1760." Indeed, as Schweizer has shown, the piece by Mauduit offers a fine example of how the press debate over the war influenced the politicians. When the duke of Bedford moved for the Lords to adopt a resolution "that the German war is in every circumstance prejudicial to the interest of their nation, and that the troops destined to carry it on should be recalled" on 5 February 1762, his supporting speech contained passages lifted directly from *Considerations* ... [11] The reception accorded Mauduit's piece displayed little sympathy or understanding of the importance of the Prussian alliance in tying down French resources in order to make gains elsewhere. Nevertheless, neither Pitt nor Newcastle could stem the rising doubt about British strategies and the desire for peace revealed in the sentiments surrounding Mauduit's tract. Behind all the bravura over the victories against France lay a body of opinion giving thought to the consequences – good and bad – of extensive territorial conquest.

Quebec would play a unique part in this debate. The enthusiasm that greeted the conquest in 1759 was part and parcel of a genuine relief in Britain that three years of disappointment had been reversed. But in the subsequent three years any desire for more conquest wore thin as the nation wearied of war. There were many facets to this disillusionment, which spread over the whole theatre of operations. In terms of Quebec, however, it began immediately after Wolfe's victory on the Plains of Abraham. In the first place, the taking of Quebec City did not herald the immediate downfall of the rest of New France. Occupation of the rest of the French colony took another year and proved no easy task. In fact the city of Quebec itself could have been retaken by the Canadians in the winter and spring months of 1759–60, as much of the correspondence coming back to Britain from Canada made clear. In the duke of Newcastle's papers there is a diary of a serving soldier on Quebec

duty and it reflects the desperation experienced by British forces there. On
1 May 1760, after a defeat outside the city walls, the entry for that day runs:
"the garrison employed in adding works and preparing to make a vigorous
defence."[12] James Murray, who took over the command of the Quebec
garrison in the early winter of 1759, wrote similar letters to his brother, George,
in Scotland. One missive in particular, on 25 May 1760, embodied the hope
that the British, after surviving many desperate moments during the French
counter-offensive, had in the taking of Quebec at last achieved something concrete. The siege had been lifted, thanks to the intervention of the Royal Navy,
and Murray declared: "the happy consequences we hope will please our
countrymen, as we have given at least uncommon proofs of fortitude of mind,
and patience in the most laborious and critical situations that British forces
have seen in our time."[13]

Murray's wishes came true to the degree that ministers in Britain accepted
his view that a corner had finally been turned and that French affairs were
"quite over in that part of the world."[14] Yet not until the final articles of capitulation were signed on 8 September 1760 by General Amherst, commander-in-
chief in North America, and the marquis de Vaudreuil, governor of New
France, could the British rest easy. The capitulation was indeed cause for
further celebration, and much press comment took on a familiar ring to justify
the whole campaign. As the editor of the *British Magazine* put it: "If prior
discovery can give a legal title to a whole country, the English are certainly
possessed of this claim to Canada."[15] At the very moment of success, however,
the acquisition of such vast territory in North America came under scrutiny
and question. On 25 October 1760 George II died, and the heir to the throne
took a view of the conduct of the war entirely different from that of his grand-
father. The young prince, supported by his chief adviser and confidant, Lord
Bute, favoured peace and an end to the strain and expense of an ever-
enlarging theatre of war. On succeeding to the throne, there is no doubt that
George intended to initiate the political changes that would bring his pacific
politics into fruition. It is also important to remember that these policies were
popular in the eyes of a war-weary nation.[16] What was to come in the new
reign can be traced in the prince's correspondence over the Quebec campaign
in 1759-60. Compare, for example, George's letter to Bute on 19 October 1759,
in which he calls the conquest of Quebec City "great news," to his reaction
on 5 October 1760 to the news of Montreal's fall. Vaudreuil's capitulation,
evokes a more sober response, for George now sees it as giving encouragement to Pitt's policy of unfettered expansion, rendering the prospects of a
durable peace less likely. "I wish my Dearest Friend joy of this success," the
prince wrote only three weeks before becoming king, "but at the same time
I can't help feeling that every such thing raises those I have no reason to love."[17]

These prejudices and preconceptions about the war naturally led into a
second phase of doubt about Quebec, concerning the role that the conquered

territory would play in any future peace negotiations. The common view gleaned from most texts on this period is that, once taken, Quebec would never be used as a gambit at the peace table. Such notions unfortunately obscure a truer picture of events over the period 1760–63 in which a complicated debate over Quebec and all other conquered territories took place. Within this discussion, furthermore, Quebec did surface in the guise of a bargaining counter to be used in securing predominance in other areas of British interest around the world. The crucial fact here is that although the war in New France ended in September 1760, hostilities with France and Spain continued until the fall of 1762. By this time the major players, Pitt and Newcastle, had resigned. Those who waged war would not make the peace; and this changed the whole nature of the debate about the thrust of the military campaign in the later stages of the war and what should be sought in the peace negotiations. The heady celebrations of 1759 had, by 19 January 1762, given way to the cynical realism of those forced to pay the piper. To Richard Rigby (MP for Tavistock), a privy councillor, and Charles Townshend (MP for Harwich), the secretary at war, the policies of global expansion had turned sour. "Canada gave us only furs," Rigby told the House of Commons, and he wished "not to keep our conquests, and put an end to a ruinous war." Townshend was equally blunt; an unchecked expansionist policy, in his opinion, could only lead to a position in which Britain "would sink from a dream of ambition to a state of bankruptcy."[18]

A fascinating aspect of this reappraisal of wartime strategy and priorities after George III's accession is that it took place not only in the government's inner councils but also in the press. Remarkably little was said about Canada in parliament during the years 1760–63, after the initial Addresses of Thanks "on the Conquest of *Canada*, with circumstances so much to the glory of this nation."[19] What knowledge MPs gained of events after the taking of Quebec was gleaned from the mass of accounts submitted to parliament while hostilities continued. From these sources, it is easy to see that the government made bureaucratic mistakes from the start. The most notable occurred in the spring of 1760 when two departments, the Treasury and the Victualling Office, took responsibility for fulfilling the same provisioning order for the Quebec garrison. "By this means," as Pitt put it, "there is ten times as much provisions there as the present garrison want for a year."[20] James Murray, now governor of Quebec, only knew of the Victualling Office contract and, in early June, refused to let those provisions from the Treasury contractors be unloaded from the supply ships. The disappointed contractors, Sir James Colebrooke, Arnold Nesbitt, George Colebrooke, and Moses Franks, refused "to stand the loss" and petitioned Newcastle, the first lord of the Treasury, for redress. In late August 1760 the papers reached Pitt, who urged an immediate remedy, and in October Newcastle's board approved the claim for damages "reasonable and proper." On 11 December the House of Commons, in turn, approved a payment of £50,000 to the contractors contained in the "account of extraordinaries."[21] No record of what the contractor's agent in Quebec, P. Bellivier, did with provisions "sufficient for ten thousand men for eight months" survives in these papers. It is likely, however, that due to its "perishable" nature most of it ended up in the St Lawrence as fish fodder, an expensive casualty of administrative duplication. No censure arose at Westminster, for members only saw the raw figures in the accounts. Such tales, nevertheless, fuelled the criticism of those profiting from government war contracts that appeared in popular literature after hostilities ceased.[22]

On the broader strategic front, the politicians assembled at Westminster remained equally silent during the remainder of the conflict, but the press did not. Over the whole period from 1759 to 1774, newspapers, magazines, and pamphlets informed the eighteenth-century public, and informs historians today, of British views on Quebec, and what priorities were adopted in the construction of policy. The striking feature of the peacemaking era, 1760–63, is that press debate on Canada mirrored a wider discussion on the war. It ranged from the enthusiasm of officials at Westminster to a strain in English thinking that challenged the whole thrust of imperial policy to date.

Of the British reading public having been well informed about Quebec, its people, religion, trade, and topography, there seems little doubt. After the conquest, numerous descriptive articles appeared, especially in the monthly magazines, with splendid maps and illustrations to support the text.[23] The *British Magazine* went a step further, embarking on an ambitious educational project by serializing a book on the history of Canada. The first instalment appeared in January 1760 and others followed monthly for the next two years. No other topic in that journal would receive such comprehensive treatment in these years. Perhaps this interest and attention is not so surprising in view of past events. The public had been informed through the press of the planned invasion of Canada in 1746, and of the argument that developed at Westminster the following year over the rivalry between France and the Hudson's Bay Company. The latter in fact led to a parliamentary inquiry into the Company's activities that sat from April to August 1748.[24] What this attention helped to engender among the British, including the politicians, was the impression of Canada as a distinct entity amongst the colonies of the Atlantic empire. The newspapers and magazines acknowledged this identity by their physical presentation of reports on Canada after 1759. With few exceptions, news items about Quebec were never classed with reports from the thirteen colonies to the south or published in the familiar column of this period headed "Plantation News." The reasons for this seemed innocent enough. From the knowledge gained of New France over the previous one hundred and fifty years, especially its warring relations with the Americans, informed observers realized from the beginning that here was a part of the empire with unique problems of culture and religion that demanded careful handling.

Assimilation into the imperial structure would be no easy task, and several writers and correspondents in the press doubted it could be ever done at all.

Such fundamental questions about Canada's place and value to the empire received a good airing well before the politicians sat down to finalize the preliminary articles of peace in 1762. The touchstone of this public debate was the phenomenal success of British arms in 1759–60, for those victories forced people to think about terms in any future peace negotiations. The discussion generated plenty of heat, with over sixty pamphlets, apart from numerous newspaper and magazine articles, appearing in the next two and a half years Canada's future came under scrutiny. The overwhelming message behind this output was that Quebec should be retained, though with certain guarantees affecting other areas like the Newfoundland fisheries and the West Indies, while a minority canvassed the view that the best means of achieving a durable peace settlement would be to let Quebec remain French in exchange for favours elsewhere. It is unjust to say that this pamphlet war centred on a straight choice at the peace table between Canada and Guadaloupe, the prize French sugar island captured by the British; but, unfortunately, this is the myth that has grown out of studying these publications. Eminent scholars like Namier, Sosin, and Labaree have done their best to dispel the misrepresentation first put forward by Alvord and Beer in the first two decades of this century.[25] Yet the fantasy has taken root, and still appears in high-school texts and popular histories of Canada.[26] Even the literature itself fails to support the simple Canada-versus-Guadaloupe controversy. This idea of surrendering conquests in North America for a West Indian sugar island was expressed more often than not as a catch-phrase, to attract attention to a more serious analysis of Britain's imperial future in the North Atlantic. Moreover, few authors said in such simple terms that Britain could have one conquest and not the other. Opinion ranged from those who said to keep everything taken from the French, thus smashing their colonial designs once and for all, to those who believed that Britain should only concern itself with expanding trade abroad, not with territories, and, that by necessity, all conquests should be restored.

A close look at any of the pamphlets written in this period reveals all these themes. Those involved in this debate who favoured retention of all North American conquests had more authors at their disposal and acquired a head start in the argument. As early as 1760, for example, strategic priorities emerged uppermost in the minds of those wishing to keep Quebec at the peace. The author of *A Letter to the People on the Necessity of putting an immediate end to the War: and the Means of Obtaining an Advantageous Peace*, in particular, spent much time explaining the global implications of the decision to keep Canada and how Britain should avoid "haughtiness" in its dealings with France over the peace to come. An economic comparison between the superior Caribbean possessions and conquests in North America occupied little space in this analysis, for it went without saying that in monetary terms one was worth more than the other. Nevertheless it was quite obvious to the author that in the broader context of securing a lasting settlement at the end of hostilities, immediate gain could not be considered paramount. Quebec had to remain British not "on account either of its trade, the number of inhabitants, or the fertility of its soil; the principal objection that appears to me against giving up any part of Canada is the danger we thereby run of giving occasion, in a few years, for another war."[27]

The most sophisticated and famous exposition of this school of thought appeared the following year, 1761, in a pamphlet by Benjamin Franklin entitled *The Interest of Great Britain Considered with Regard to her Colonies and the Acquisitions of Canada and Guadaloupe.* This piece represents a cogent vision of the future of colonial expansion. Franklin raised and demolished the same arguments that would so trouble the politicians in the peace negotiations with France, such as the fear of depopulating the mother country to settle the newly acquired territories. In response to this fear, Franklin asked a simple question: did the growth of the American colonies cause this to happen? Of course not, he replied. "The objections I have heard, that if we had *Canada,* we could not people it, without draining *Britain* of its inhabitants, is founded on ignorance of the nature of population in new countries."[28] Franklin's political connections, founded on his job as a colonial agent, were impeccable, and he knew that the winds of opinion in cabinet were blowing towards an expansionist position. With an impressive mixture of strategic and economic argument, he hammered home the point that the rule of Old France in Canada should end. To exert British control over the Canadians, he asserted in his pamphlet, would solve three fundamental problems: friction between the French and the northern colonies of America; Indian disputes and conflicts; and the "border problems." With Canada in British possession, there would no longer be a physical or spiritual barrier to the growth of the American colonies. The whole continent would prosper, and the mother country would reap the economic rewards.

The argument for keeping Quebec on strategic and economic grounds was taken to its logical conclusion by other writers. They pointed out that, although backward now, Quebec possessed infinite potential for growth and could eventually become a major consumer of British manufactured goods.[29] Such analyses portraying the colonists as future mass consumers of British products have been interpreted by some historians as representing a fundamental shift in eighteenth-century thought about the role of colonies. In its crudest form, this interpretation sees the British abandoning the old idea of plantation settlement and staple trade in favour of outright exploitation of cheap labour in Britain and raw materials from the colonies. Beer's work popularized this view, but a reading of the pamphlet literature hardly reinforces the idea that such rigid economic determinism drove Britain to retain

Quebec. One notable feature of this and other contemporary theories in favour of ridding North America of the French was the fact that Canada was initially seen as a catalyst to a coming change of status further south. Canada would be the guarantor of a secure and prosperous future for the Atlantic empire. The tone of this argument emanated from a purely European voice. The taking and retention of Canada became a means to an end seemingly unrelated to that part of the American continent. There was no discussion in this literature of what would happen to the population of Quebec or of the future of the Canadian economy and government.

These matters were earnestly addressed by the opponents of territorial aggrandizement. A pamphlet appearing in 1760, entitled *Some Account of Remarks on the Letter addressed to two Great Men*, proffered an opinion about Canada quite at odds with prevailing thought. New France might not be given up by the French court, the author wrote, and it should not matter if this was so, for trade should be Britain's priority in peace-making, and there were far richer pickings in the West Indies. Several reviewers greeted this heresy with derision.[30] But such tracts could not be ignored entirely, for those writers who challenged the certainty of retaining Canada at the peace table raised fundamental questions about its value to, and effect on, the future of the Atlantic empire. The editor of the *British Magazine* expressed a certain admiration for the argument in *Some Account of Remarks ...*, commenting in his review that "this pamphlet is written with great elegance, spirit and moderation."[31] Indeed it would be wrong to insinuate, as is often the case, that these dissenting voices represented only a pinprick to the main body of opinion. Commentators took note of their views because they explored crucial issues ignored by the imperial expansionists.

The primary target in the early stages of the debate was the strategic case for retaining Quebec. The author of the pamphlet discussed above, for example, pointed out the weaknesses evident in hoping that the retention of Canada after the peace would offer security for the American colonies. The French would still be in Louisiana and along the Mississippi, he wrote, making the chance of further conflict highly likely. Talk of detaching the Indians from French allegiance and banishing French fishing vessels from North American waters he considered foolish. The future would be far more secure with agreement on a definite boundary for Quebec and Acadia that would cover the hinterland and erase doubts about territorial rights and sovereignty. So the choice about leaving France in North America was not the simple one put forward by the expansionists, and which historians have often repeated. Possession of Quebec itself did not eradicate the whole French empire in North America. Even the most hostile readers of such remarks as those in *Some Account of the Remarks ...* had to wrestle with the question, as the politicians would do later, whether whatever was not within the boundary of Quebec was to be considered Louisiana. The only solution proposed to overcome this problem was a military one. As "A True Briton" wrote in the *Gentleman's Magazine* of March 1761, the situation "more strongly requires the reduction of Louisiana to his Majesty's dominions to the state and condition of the more northern province ... and I still hope it is designed."[32] It proved a vain hope. Those favouring yet more and more expenditure had fallen into the trap laid by the writers giving more serious thought to the future and yielded to the mood of the country at home. Not even Pitt could find sanction for another campaign, as he discovered to his cost in October 1761.

The greatest fillip to those questioning the unbridled global war of conquest came from the groundswell of popular feeling for peace engendered at George III's accession. Of the many tracts appearing after this event, the most stunning piece of analysis against conquest for its own sake was *The Reasons for keeping Guadaloupe at a Peace preferable to Canada explained in five letters from a Gentleman in Guadaloupe to his Friend in London*. The title suggested that the author would concentrate on a straightforward explanation of Guadaloupe's value to the empire. In part this was his aim, but the pamphlet also revealed a great deal about a contemporary strain of thought that deplored unchecked imperial expansionism. This writer had looked closely at the nature of the conquered territory in North America and could see no benefits to Britain in its retention. His argument asked how great a revenue or profit would accrue from taking over an economy based on the fur trade. New France had been a constant drain on the treasury of the parent nation, he pointed out, and it was not surprising that the French offered the colony up as a gambit in the peace negotiations. He also reinforced the argument, expressed by earlier writers, that removing the French from the north would not dissolve their ties with the Indians or with the southern settlements on the Mississippi. In terms of broader strategy he was far more perceptive and emphatic than other writers. The people of New France, he wrote, were an alien race, with a different culture and religion that would demand special handling. Their allegiance would forever be suspect, and the only hope of securing a loyal population rested with a permanent garrison of troops in the main areas of settlement and trade. The point was well made: the support of civilian authority by military government not only offended English constitutional sensibilities but also cost a great deal of money. The issue would be discussed during 1762 by two members of the cabinet, the duke of Newcastle and the earl of Hardwicke, in identical terms. Only the recommendation differed.

Unlike several other critics of the government's approach to the peace, the author of *The Reasons* ... did not leave the debate in its negative state. He wished to return Canada to the French, for he held a vision of the British empire based firmly on trade, not territorial aggrandizement. It was a mode of thought later referred to as a "little Englander" mentality, and its leading proponent during the peace negotiations would be the duke of Bedford, who would represent Britain in Paris during the final stages of the treaty settlement. Sosin has described Bedford's ideas as "ludicrous," but this seems quite unwarranted.[33] The arguments of the little Englanders did not lack a genuine conceptual thrust; rather, they lacked appreciation of the dynamic state of the American colonies. At the core of their thought on Canada's future in the peace lay three interlocking assumptions. First, the American colonies had exceeded their original function and dependent trading relationship with the mother country, and would continue to do so until Britain took remedial measures. Second, as a first step in reversing this process and securing a loyal colonial empire in America, it would be far more beneficial to leave a profitless, alien Canada in French hands, "to be a check upon" the colonists.[34] This done, it would then be imperative to retain the conquered West Indian islands, especially Guadaloupe, and draw the eastern seaboard of America into a revamped trading community: "Thus by a prudent and timely increase of your territory or possessions in the West Indies, you not only double the trade and shipping of Great Britain, but you bind America larger and firmer to her dependence upon England, by establishing a more equal balance betwixt America and the West Indies."[35] It was an ingenious plan. The inclusion of France in a North American settlement would guarantee the loyalty of the colonists; the exclusion of France from trade among the rich West Indian islands would encourage the ascendancy of British economic might.

The characteristic undertone of this pamphlet and other literature sceptical of Canada's value to the empire was certainly a tendency to treat "our colonies in North America with rather too much contempt."[36] Yet, as events unfolded over the next fifteen years, this pessimism about American loyalty and the problems to be faced bringing Quebec into the empire proved well founded. These writers highlighted points of concern about the nature of imperial expansion over alien peoples that would be used not only in the North American context but later with respect to conquest in India. Such conquest would come to be seen as posing a threat to constitutional liberties in the mother country.[37] The author of *Reasons for keeping Guadaloupe* ... laid the base for later debate in a discussion on the merits of building empires. The process took the form of an historical analysis of the Greek, Roman, and Spanish experiences. Of the latter, he observed that "Spain grasped at conquests in a foreign country in the new world, so far above the extent and ability of the mother country that she dispeopled herself: and though she conquered those countries, the inexhaustible fountain of those precious metals the world hunt after with so insatiable an appetite, yet she gradually declined from those mistaken maxims to the state she is now in." Britain need not follow this path in the New World, he concluded, because "she has more there already than she can manage to any profitable purpose."[38]

Why did the argument in Britain so overwhelmingly favour Canada's retention despite these powerful counterweights? The answers offered by historians ranged over a mixture of factors, none of which are mutually exclusive. Two are worthy of note. The most popular recent explanation is that the decision came as a result of some intensive lobbying by a powerful group of West India merchants and planters at Westminster, led by men like William Beckford and Alderman Sir William Baker. These men feared the retention of the French sugar islands, as opposed to Canada, because it would result in a flood of cheap sugar on European markets, undercutting their vested interests in the English exporting plantations like Jamaica. The weight of opinion favouring this argument naturally accepts the sheer volume of pamphlet and newspaper material sympathetic to West Indian interests as proof of the potency of the Caribbean lobby. It has also been pointed out that Beckford and Baker had the ear of William Pitt and the duke of Newcastle. What weakens this thesis is that Pitt and Newcastle, the ministers seen as most receptive to this lobby, were out of office by May 1762, before any final decisions had been taken. Furthermore, of those ministers remaining after May 1762, like Hardwicke, none found Bakers's or Beckford's entreaties particularly persuasive. To accept the West Indian lobby as the all-conquering force driving Britain to the decision on Canada implies that very powerful voices in the government, like the duke of Bedford, were ignored. His little England philosophy may not have been popular, but it was certainly not dismissed out of hand. The other theory favoured by historians is the strategic argument, which again found expression in many of the articles and pamphlets that appeared on Canada in the early 1760s. Ministers and those with similar views in the press saw the reduction of New France as the crucial factor to the future security of the sea-borne Atlantic empire. There were few preconceived economic, or (in one amusing case concerning the duke of Newcastle) geographical motives behind the decision to keep Canada.[39] The idea simply evolved during negotiations that giving up some of the conquered West Indian islands would be the means to achieving greater ends on the mainland. Of late, this theory has gone out of fashion, for it harbours no clear motive. Without a degree of economic determinism, it has been assumed, the strategy argument appears an empty shell as an explanation for retaining Canada. Such criticisms are not without foundation, for all ministers had some thoughts on trade and empire and none operated in an environment devoid of crude imperial theorists and thinkers.

The time seems ripe for a new synthesis based on a combination of the salient points in these arguments, settling, once and for all, the Canada-versus-Guadaloupe controversy. This synthesis could certainly be reinforced by an examination of the behaviour of the politicians during the peace negotiations of 1762–63. Namier and Sosin highlighted this possibility in their work, emphasizing the need to examine the decision-making process as the key to understanding why Britain favoured the retention of Quebec in contrast to conquests elsewhere. Some of their conclusions, however, do require revision. To say that the press discussion of the Anglo-French position prior to the peace negotiations misconstrued the argument over imperial priorities is one thing; to assert that it did not mirror the political decisions being taken is quite another. Few of the pieces appearing in this public debate represented the work of great thinkers, but many expressed serious thoughts about Canada's future role in the British imperial structure. More important, the pamphlet literature, in particular, contains all the doubts and anxieties about what should be done at the peace table later experienced by the politicians: the debate was nothing less than a dress rehearsal. Most of the work written in the years 1760–63 appeared anonymously, but a great deal of it would have been written by either the politicians or hacks in their employ. The political world was simply not that disinterested; to produce over sixty pamphlets took a great deal of official encouragement.[40]

The political initiatives culminating in the Peace of Paris, 1763, went through three stages: the 1760 "Hague Conversations"; the exchange of "Memoires" or Stanley-Bussy talks in 1761; and the successful negotiation of 1762–63. The facts are well known and each stage of the talks has been subjected to varying degrees of critical dissection.[41] Over the years historical judgments on the peacemakers have fluctuated. From Hotblack's disapproving examination of the politicians in 1908 to Hyam's view in 1975 that ministers "were muddled in theory and misinformed in fact," verdicts have swung between toleration for politicians doing their best in difficult circumstances to hard-nosed condemnation of lost opportunities on Britain's part.[42] Of late, however, these black and white opinions have been revised. Recent scholarly work on the treaty negotiations from 1760 on is pointing the way to a better understanding of the whole process of Anglo-French rivalry, hostilities, and, later, peace. Of particular importance have been a thorough examination of Lord Bute's papers covering his political career from 1760 to 1763 and the publication of the duke of Devonshire's political diary for the period 1759–62.[43] Research of this type has revealed new perspectives on both the strategic imperatives governing Britain's bargaining positions in the negotiations, in particular the Anglo-Prussian alliance, and the complicating domestic political factors influencing the formulation of long-term goals for peace. Definitive judgments on figures like Bute, for example, are now rendered very difficult indeed, for it is clear that his strategic thinking changed from hard-line to conciliatory in the summer of 1761.[44] No less important, the question of the Prussian alliance remained a constant factor in all deliberations with the French, especially in the failed negotiations of 1760, and cannot be ignored in future discussions of the peace process.[45] More pertinent still in this context, all the revisions being undertaken at present not only make it possible to recast the major themes of the post-war period but also illuminate specific factors, such as the role that Quebec played in the peace-making process.

The standard and most widely accepted view of Canada in these negotiations states quite simply that, from the conquest, Quebec was not a negotiable item in any future peace. The British had tidied up the map of North America with possession of the eastern seaboard, from Newfoundland in the north to Florida in the south. Quebec had opened the door to this achievement, and one historian has gone so far as to say that Wolfe's death alone had made "the retention of Canada a necessity."[46] Yet could the decision on this one point have been so cut and dried? If it was, it flew in the face of normal conciliatory negotiating procedures in the eighteenth century and took no notice of the cut and thrust of the public debate on the war. Unconditional conquests had been an unknown quantity in European conflicts over the previous seventy years, where captured islands in the West Indies, factories in India, and forts in New France and Nova Scotia had changed hands in post-bellum settlements.

In this instance, however, it does seem that in the lead-up to the Hague conversations in 1760 Britain was determined to retain Quebec. Wishing to retain the conquest and doing so once negotiations and counter-proposals began, on the other hand, were two different things. As it happened, the British would get their own way over Quebec, but they achieved this goal because of factors not entirely under their control. In 1760, for example, it is clear that both French insistence on making a separate peace with Britain without its ally Prussia, and Pitt's "Carthaginian terms," meant that the war would continue with the British more determined than ever to hang on to and even increase their colonial conquests.[47] Two other neglected factors are also worthy of note with regard to Quebec's place in the initial negotiation, for both would play a part in the outcome of the war and the final territorial settlement.

The first concerned Spain. The Spanish crown expressed unease at the British gaining so much power in the Americas even before the news of Quebec's fall reached Madrid.[48] Throughout the peace negotiations of these months the Spanish held grievances against Britain over its claim to the North Atlantic fisheries, British piracy and interloping in Spanish waters, and log-cutting in Honduras. Failure to redress these grievances by 1762 would play its part in driving Spain into an alliance with France, and eventual declaration of war that prolonged hostilities another year. Try as it might in 1759–60, diplomacy could not conceal the Spanish crown's anxiety about the expansion of Britain in North America after the fall of Quebec. In consequence, the British became highly suspicious of Spain's protestations and her political and familial links with France in late 1759 and 1760. This distrust proved an important factor in the failure of the Hague initiative. In this period the cabinet moved from a position of temporizing over Quebec in 1759 – as Pitt put it in October that year, "As to Quebec, Montreal and Louisbourgh they were points to be treated of and given up for nothing" – to a mood of intransigence towards the whole issue of making peace at all nine months later.[49] Continuing British military success and the failure of French attempts to make a separate peace in the Hague without Prussia hardened the resolve of ministers in London to expel France from North America once and for all – an outcome quite at odds with Spain's original motive for mediation in the Anglo-French war, and one ending in near disaster for Spanish interests.[50]

To be fair to the Spanish crown, the behaviour of France towards Quebec's fall did not help the Spanish cause in the years 1760–63. Indeed, a second crucial factor contributing to Britain's resolve to keep Quebec in 1760, and one usually absent from accounts of this episode, concerns the French motive. The common assumption about the peace negotiations is that they opened on the basis that, given a chance, France would take back its lost colonies in America. This is a mistake, for France did not want Quebec returned. It is apparent from an examination of the French manuscripts pertaining to this episode by Eccles that doubts about the worth of keeping New France began as early as 1748, when the governor-general of the colony, the marquis de Glassonière, reported to Paris: "we should never delude ourselves that our colonies on the continent ... could ever rival the neighbouring English colonies in wealth, nor even be commercially very lucrative."[51] This encouraged a dim official view in both France and Canada of the colony's prospects, leading to a defeatist mentality by the outbreak of the Seven Years' War. This mood afflicted the highest command. In 1757, the marquis de Montcalm, commander-in-chief of the North American theatre, wrote: "If Canada was to be ceded, it would not be an irreparable loss." Securing a post for the fishery alone would, in his opinion, "be as favourable to us, as Canada would be unfavourable to the English."[52] Such thoughts also pervaded the recommendations of one minister of marine during the war, marquis de Capellis, who favoured relinquishing control of Canada in any future peace talks. It is hardly surprising that on hearing of Quebec's fall the French foreign minister, Choiseul, faced with such negative advice, said the colony should be sacrificed for considerations elsewhere.[53] Thus the imponderables of 1759–60 – the Prussian alliance, Spanish grievances, and French strategy – cast their shadow over British aspirations in the peace negotiations. Whether they liked it or not, the British were stuck with Quebec and would have to force the colony back on Old France at the peace table.

The cabinet came to know of Choiseul's position on Quebec during the second stage of negotiation, the exchange of memoires, in the summer of 1761.[54] After France and Britain failed to reach a settlement, the Board of Trade drew up a paper for leading ministers outlining options in North America. In this document the fact of Quebec's not being returned is taken for granted: "the French for several years past have set no great value upon Canada, – Their ministry on several occasions have had thoughts of totally abandoning that inhospitable region, and of transporting the inhabitants to strengthen and better people Louisiana – That such is their view at present."[55] This realization then cast Quebec in a peculiar role during the final stages of the negotiations of 1762, as the sole certainty in the outcome. By April 1762 all that was being discussed about Quebec was the time to be allowed for those French colonists who wished to leave the conquered territory.[56] Nevertheless, it would be wrong to assume that some of those involved in the talks did not consider forcing the issue. Quebec became enmeshed in a fascinating contemporary British debate over the question of territorial expansion. No one was willing to adopt the extreme postures of the pamphleteers, of either giving Canada back to the French or keeping all conquests. But some politicians did adopt qualified positions akin to these ideas, and ministerial in-fighting reflected the themes raised in the public debate. In government the most interesting question asked about Quebec came from those least enamoured of territorial expansion and most in favour of peace. This body of opinion centred on the duke of Bedford and his associates, especially Lord Gower. Their strength lay in the fact that Bedford had the ear and sympathy of Bute and George III. In cabinet they made up what Bedford himself called "we that were the pacifick party."[57]

In 1761 this group had influence in the government's inner councils because the desire for peace had gained such momentum, and Bute's change of views in the summer of that year gave "the pacifick party" great encouragement. As Walpole, no friend of the Bedfords, declared on 10 April 1761, "Blessed be Providence! We are going to have peace; I do not regret it."[58] Bedford himself saw the peace overtures of 1761 as a heaven-sent chance to put the warmongers to shame. During the run up to the general election of 1761, the earl of Buckinghamshire asked Bedford to intervene in Exeter on behalf of his relative, George Hobart. Bedford refused, but declared that he "should be glad to have it in my power to conduce to the reestablishing peace, so essential to the well being of a trading and manufacturing city."[59] Bedford saw the practical benefits of an early peace and remained optimistic during the exchange of memoires in the spring. In May, for example, he was still weighing up the merits of a peace that secured territorial conquest relative to one that looked after Britain's trading interests. In a letter to Newcastle on 9 May there appeared a clear hint that Bedford's money had been paid to those pamphleteers sceptical of conquest in North America.[60] The inter-cabinet rivalry and conflicting viewpoints are explicitly portrayed in Bedford's prose. "The rock we may split upon," he told Newcastle, "will be the demanding terms ... which ... will be inadmissable by France." There were two sides: "the one demanding to keep all or a greater share of our conquests over her, than she can possibly be prevailed upon to part with"; the other opposed to the idea of Britain's being "overloaded with foreign possessions should Canada and Guadaloupe be ceded to us." Indeed, Bedford went further, echoing much press comment when he wrote that, although it seemed inevitable that Quebec would become British territory, "I don't know whether the neighbourhood of the French to our Northern American Colonies was not the greatest security of their dependence on their mother country, which I fear will be slighted by them when their apprehensions of the French are removed." These proved prophetic sentiments in view of what happened over the next fifteen years, and Bedford had confronted a problem that others wished to avoid.

It did him little good. Bedford may have been powerful and have had the king's sympathy, but he could not carry his vision of the peace in cabinet alone. He needed the support of other ministers besides Bute and Newcastle, who appeared most in favour of an early peace. It never materialized. During the important cabinet meetings of May 1761, Bedford's position weakened as he was surpassed by the ministerial hawks Pitt, Temple, and Halifax, seeking stiffer terms from the French. Two difficulties arose initially: the epochs or *uti possedetis* clause, and compensations. The former was a clause aimed at fixing certain dates for the end of hostilities in the different theatres and opening negotiations on the basis of what each country controlled on those dates.[61] The latter point concerned what the British could gain in compensation for France's conquest of Minorca. On the surface these seemed simple obstacles, but they encapsulated the contrasting views of how to negotiate. The hawks saw France down and wanted to prolong the agony to extract better terms for Britain. Bedford and his friends, on the other hand, believed this sort of approach would not secure a lasting settlement. The internal wrangling continued on into July 1761, with Bedford becoming increasingly despondent. Gower attempted to rally the cause on 3 July, reminding Bedford of the priorities to be pursued in cabinet: "do not insist upon their holding out their throats be cut. Ask what is reasonable, the enemy must give you and you may maintain it. But demand what is beyond all bounds and things will be left to the future decision ... France will take the first opportunity of breaking through her engagements or even the rest of Europe may not care to see your naval and maritime monopoly."[62]

This represented fine advice in light of the fact that, as early as April, Pitt began proposing that France be excluded from rights to the fisheries in the Gulf of St Lawrence and off Newfoundland.[63] Bedford took heart and tried to achieve his "pacifick" ends in cabinet throughout the really crucial ministerial gatherings of July and August. On 9 July he wrote out a definitive statement of his aims in the negotiation for Bute's benefit. It had four parts. First, he believed that the losses of another year of battles would far outweigh the anticipated gains. Second, the success of the Martinique campaign looked very doubtful. Third, he did not foresee France being so accommodating about Canada and its boundaries if the war continued. Last, but by no means least in Bedford's views, he pointed out that there existed a general aversion to continuing "a bloody and expensive war" in the country at large.[64] These words must have rung a bell in Bute's mind, for it was the very wording of the clause that had Pitt struck out of the draft of George iii's first speech to parliament as king on 17 October 1760. The phrasing "just and necessary" was the expression later used instead.[65] Indeed, Bute's reply to Bedford offered support and enthusiasm for his prospectus.[66] What was said in private and what was said in cabinet, however, were two different matters. After several stormy sessions, culminating in a rancorous meeting on 25 July, Bedford threatened never to attend cabinet again.[67] In a rage of indignation, Bedford told Gower of his defeat and frustration in a letter of 31 July.[68] Oddly enough, the cession of Canada had been the one area of agreement, and Bedford had had his way on the important boundary question. Agreement was reached, he wrote to Gower, on "the total cession of Canada, without setting boundaries betwixt that and Louisiana, there being vast uncultivated countries inhabited only by savage nations, which are the natural boundaries betwixt them." The rest was acrimony. "The warlike party, Mr. Pitt and his brother," not only wished to exclude the French "from any fishery at all, even that which is allowed to all other nations in the world" but also to "incapacitate them from being any longer a naval power." The means to this end would be another campaign "of 16 millions," which Pitt considered "buying it [French defeat] very cheaply." Bedford was utterly dismissive of the temporizers in cabinet like Halifax and Bute, whose behaviour "can be ascribed to nothing but the fear of Mr. Pitt." It must have been quite a scene, for, as Bedford said, "I left them at 1/2 past 5 hammering at a dispatch upon the middle system of civilly desiring the French to lie down quickly to let us cut their throats."

To all intents and purposes, Bedford had relinquished control of the negotiations to his enemies, Pitt and Temple. In this instance, however, they were given too much rope, and by October 1761 had hanged themselves with it. Their eclipse began immediately after Bedford had stormed out of a cabinet meeting on 14 August, for after his departure his colleagues drew up a sort of ultimatum for France, embodying Pitt's belligerent position on the contentious issue of fishing rights, fortifications on the French coast, and East Indian possessions. The French responded with their own ultimatum "drawn in very strong terms," resisting all moderation on the points at issue and, quite out of the blue, saying no peace could be arranged without accommodating Spanish grievances.[69] The cabinet met on 19, 20, and 24 August to hammer out its next move. Pitt and Temple had their way in the wording of the response but not entirely in the clauses, for in this initiative the French were to be allowed access to the Newfoundland fisheries. It proved too little too late. Choiseul returned the proposals in early September, indicating that the war would continue and was now likely to include Spain as a second hostile party. Pitt's time had come, and on 18 September he and Temple delivered a paper to the king recommending "that orders be forthwith sent to the Earl of Bristol to deliver a declaration [of war on Spain] and to return immediately to England without taking leave."[70] Pitt and Temple believed that the existence of the Bourbon alliance vindicated their hostile attitude to the negotiation, and demanded that their colleagues support a pre-emptive strike against the

Spaniards. They refused: as Walpole put it, "The Cabinet Council were for temporizing. This is not *his* style."[71] Ministers did not oppose war with Spain in the future: they simply favoured Bute's approach of using it as a threat in the first stage of seeking negotiations. The cabinet rejected the strike proposal on 2 October and three days later Pitt and Temple resigned.

In a strange twist of fate, their exit from the government had little immediate effect on strategy. The restructured ministry, with Bute, Newcastle, Halifax, and the earl of Egremont at its head, soon found itself sanctioning hostilities against Spain in the best Pittite manner, hostilities which would eventually lead to the fall of Havana in the summer of 1762. At root, however, Britain's strategy in the negotiation did change, reflecting the court's pacific outlook. The initiative for change did not just come from the top either. In October 1761 few ministers shed any tears over Pitt's departure, not even George Grenville, who remained as leader in the Commons and was broadly sympathetic to Pitt's hard-line policy of territorial expansion.[72] A dis-illusionment had spread among Pitt's colleagues during the summer, leading to a conviction that there could be no peace with Pitt at the helm. The problem centred on Pitt's demeanour as a negotiator. In July, Hans Stanley, the government's chief envoy in Paris, made no secret of the fact that Pitt's "manner of negotiating spoilt the peace."[73] Even Hardwicke, the most disinterested and objective minister involved in the peace process, recognized the shortcomings in a man fit to wage war but not to make peace. He remembered the summer as a time of "disunity," in which Pitt's *"spirit of Hauteur"* reigned supreme.[74]

The reasons for this disenchantment with Pitt had nothing directly to do with Canada itself, but rather with the philosophy behind endless territorial gain in which Quebec played a major part. For Pitt and his allies, bigger was better, and this was the way they approached strategic questions. They did not stop to look at the interlocking factors of domination on the North American continent as Bedford had done. Up to July 1761 Pitt gave no serious consideration to the future role of France in North America because in his scheme of things France would play no role. When Pitt unrolled the map of the Atlantic empire he saw the reality of British power in possession of the whole American-Canadian eastern seaboard and the principal sugar islands of the West Indies, and the exclusion of France from its "nursery of seamen" in the fishing grounds off Newfoundland and in the Gulf of St Lawrence. The growing desire for peace in the nation at large or the anxiety over the bur-geoning costs of the war did not touch him. It is impossible to analyse Pitt's views about Canada in the same fashion as those of the "pacifick party" because he does not appear to have had any. The conquest of Quebec, in Pitt's eyes, was part of a larger operation to drive the French to ruin by denying them the benefits of a lucrative colonial trade. In this grand design and eventual negotiated peace, no quarter would be given. To Pitt the question of Quebec's future being in doubt was simply a *non sequitur*.

And thus it would be in the final peace talks of 1761–63. There are good contemporary records, both published and unpublished, of the third stage in the negotiations, all of which shed light on how the underlying problems in Anglo-French relations were resolved.[75] One such useful unpublished source can be found in Granville's papers in the Public Record Office.[76] In this document, dates of each letter exchanged with France, first through the Sardinian envoys, Viry and Solar, and then through duc de Nivernois, are noted, as well as the subject matter concerned. Quebec warrants not one mention throughout. The simple explanation for this omission is that the talks were reopened on the basis of the previous year's discussion about Canada: "On the 8th April, Lord Egremont transmitted to the Duc de Choiseul thro' the channel of Count Viry and Baille Solar, a Declaration proposing to France to resume the negotiation on the foot of the last ultimatums of the two courts." Under this rubric, the fate of Quebec was sealed. The cabinet decisions of August 1761 took it for granted that Quebec would be retained, not least because of the attitude of France. The papers of those involved in the negotiations of 1762 reflect this assumption. The only outstanding problems perceived in London concerned the boundaries of Louisiana and the fisheries. This is certainly evident in the cabinet records of these months. On four occasions, in March, June, July, and October 1762, Canadian matters came under consideration. But they received only the most cursory attention in *pro forma* resolutions, during the many hours ministers spent discussing the preliminaries clause by clause. One of the government's most influential legal officers, Lord Northington, demonstrated this attitude when he drew up a memorandum in early 1762 highlighting the issues facing Britain in the negotiations. The entries on Canada were short and sweet: "All Canada surrendered, no lines of division fixed to Louisiana ... That all Canada together with islands in the Gulph be ceded."[77] His views were not exceptional. The papers of the government's other leading legal officer, Lord Mansfield, contain many queries on clauses of the treaty being drawn up in 1762 but none on Canada.[78] Perhaps the best witness of all, however, is the duke of Bedford. On 21 August 1762 the king named him the chief plenipotentiary to the French court, responsible for negotiating the final articles of the treaty. He carried out the task without once mentioning Canada in his extant correspondence. The matter had been cut and dried since August 1761, and Bedford said of his mission: "I could not do better, nor did I ever imagine I should have been able to have done so much."[79] His was the last laugh.

The Peace of Paris was ratified by the French and British crowns on 10 February 1763. The clauses regarding the outstanding problems about fishing rights in the Gulf and the Louisiana boundary caused no difficulties. The task had been handled ostensibly by Egremont in the summer of 1762, but it was Hardwicke who guided the policy. On 25 April 1762 he wrote to Egremont pointing out the weaknesses of Britain's negotiating position, and, by implication, Egremont's failings too.[80] The first point concerned possessions in the

Gulf. "As to the cession of Canada," Hardwicke wrote, "and what relates to the fishery of the Gulf, your lordship refers to the last memorial i.e. the ultimatum of France and accepts it. Your lordship will observe that, at the end of the fifth article France makes a dispute about the word *Dependencies* and requires an explanation of it. Should not something be said about that?" Sure enough, Egremont did seek an explanation of the term dependencies; and article IV of the final treaty read: "his Most Christian Majesty cedes and guaranties to his said Britannick Majesty, in full right, Canada, with all its dependencies, as well as the island of Cape Breton, and all the other islands and coasts in the gulph and river of St. Lawrence, and in general, everything that depends on the said countries, lands, islands and coasts."[81]

The second discrepancy that Hardwicke spotted centred on the Louisiana boundary, and again arose from a misreading by Egremont of the French ultimatum. The words "The limits of Louisiana, and the *Nations Intermediaries*," in particular, troubled Hardwicke. "Should not something be said upon that ... in the course of the negotiation?" he asked Egremont.[82] Obviously it was, for the confusion was cleared up by the time of signing the final peace. Article VII of the treaty drew such a clear east/west dividing line that no mistake could be made over areas of influence in the south-east. The French retained New Orleans, but gave up Mobile, the right of sole navigation on the Mississippi, and all possessions east of the river, "fixed irrevocably by a line drawn along the middle of the River Mississippi, from its source to the river Iberville."[83] The third and most technical point at issue concerned a definition of what future role the French fishermen could play in the Gulf. Hardwicke reminded Egremont that Britain's ultimatum of August 1761 proposed to "restrain the French *from fishing* upon any coasts of the continent, or islands in the Gulf belonging to Great Britain," whereas the French ultimatum of September had offered only to be restrained "*from drying their fish or leading or drawing their nets* upon those coasts." As Hardwicke put it, this is "a different proposition, your lordship will consider whether it is necessary to take any of that."[84] As before, Egremont did as he was bid. Article V of the treaty clarified the issue in France's favour, allowing French fishermen the right to catches in the Gulf and off the coasts at designated distances from the shore.[85] This represented a final concession on the original ground staked out by Pitt in the negotiation of 1761.

With these loose ends tied up, the entry of Quebec into the British empire had been achieved: "the proper thing," as Newcastle put it in 1747. Contemporary argument over the peace proved as disputatious as the historical one today. Lord Lyttelton, for example, told his brother in December 1762 that he was very happy with the events of late: "we have got *peace abroad*, and I think, on the whole, a *good one*."[86] Lord Chesterfield, on the other hand, wrote to his son that little pleased him about the peace: "We have by no means made so good a bargain with France; for, in truth, what do we get by it, except Canada, with a very proper boundary of the river Mississippi, and that is all."[87] The political debate at Westminister reflected some of these disappointments, with Pitt and Temple working hard to embarrass ministers for being soft on France, as the peace preliminaries passed through parliament in the fall of 1762. The duchess of Bedford was moved to comment on their activities: "Lord Temple and Mr. Pitt are moving heaven and earth to prevent the Peace. There are such lies as you cannot Conceive."[88] MPs, however, had no sympathy with the opposition, voting the preliminaries through with large majorities. The well-documented press campaign was equally lively, with a mass of literature, often paid for by the politicians, reflecting doubts on both sides of the question.[89] Yet on one point consensus did exist. Throughout the controversy all manner of clauses and articles in the treaty negotiations came under attack: all, that is, but those concerning Canada. The conquest of Quebec was deemed beyond reproach, with an enthusiastic ignorance and naïveté about the problem of governing Quebec in the future that was truly remarkable. The pertinent questions about bringing this alien society under imperial rule, hinted at by the pamphleteers in 1760–61, had never really been addressed by any leading politicians. No one stopped to think of the magnitude of the task facing the government, and, if past precedents of British dealings with French colonists in North America were anything to go by, such neglect did not bode well for the future.

CHAPTER TWO

Policy and Mythology 1763-64

If the decision to keep Quebec had been difficult, the framing of policy to govern the province proved no less thorny. Quebec presented the sort of social, economic, and constitutional challenges that defied an empirical palliative. At the root of British discomfort with the province in the immediate post-war period lay an inflexible political ideology, seemingly incompatible with the practical realities of governing seventy thousand or so French Catholics. The legacy of the Glorious Revolution of 1688-89 for mid-eighteenth-century Britons manifested itself in constitutional forms ill equipped to deal with the demands of retaining the loyalty of the king's new Canadian subjects. The Anglican church, an active newspaper press, the English civil and criminal court system, and, most important, a representative government formed an orthodoxy in Britain completely unknown to the residents of Quebec. Yet after the French and British ratified the Peace of Paris in February 1763, the government in London found itself charged with marrying two contrasting cultures into an administrative whole, closely scrutinized by interested observers outside the hallowed walls of Westminster. It proved an unenviable task, for many of the legislators and commentators on the Quebec issue became victims of their own rhetoric about the events of 1688-89, unable, or even unwilling, to mould their ideology around the special needs of the situation in Quebec.

The initial perception of the problems posed by integrating Quebec into the imperial structure did not run very deep. The public debate showed little appreciation of the intricate policy decisions required to ensure the security of an alien people under the British crown. At Westminster the immediate concern with Quebec went no further than rudimentary accounting related to the cost of victualling garrisons, and a first mention for the vexed issue of debts due to the Canadians by France, or, as it became known, the Canada Bills controversy.[1] In the latter days of French rule in Quebec a chronic lack of specie had been met by paper currency that still circulated after the conquest. The British government naturally wanted these bills redeemed at the best possible price so as not to denude the Quebec economy of all liquidity, and it became locked into an interminable round of talks with the French over the next three years to settle this issue.[2] Such differences were not the stuff to spark a fiery debate, but were the reasons for the public passivity towards those clauses of the peace affecting Quebec.

In the press, attention focused on two concerns: patronage and trade, both central to imperial expansion in the eighteenth century. On the former subject, some copy proved serious, some less so. Cryptic comments were made about the collapse of the parliamentary opposition to the peace, which many viewed as an abandonment of Pitt's glorious conquests to Britain's enemies. How could this have happened? asked "Quidnunc," one correspondent to the press. Simple, came the reply: "for these *smoaky* Gentry might have been bought off with a few pence, or a few pots of porter whilst *other* champions of the Opposition require no less than the Government of Canada, and the Bishopric of Quebec."[3]

More earnest comment over appointments to the new government in Quebec did appear in the *Gentleman's Magazine*. A long article in the fall of 1763 listed the qualities that a governor would require to make a success of his posting.[4] Top priority was given to being a good soldier because of the constant wars expected with the Indian nations. Also important, the future governor would need to be an astute politician, as he "will sometimes be called upon" to mediate not only between the province and the Indians but also between the various colonies in North America, racked as they were with internal jealousies. Last, but by no means least, the governor should not be a petty despot, rather a man who "WOULD NOT ONLY REVOLT at acts of cruelty but even at whatever has the least semblance of severity, oppression or tyranny." The punch line to this sanctimonious piece came with the author's recommendation of the person fit to assume this saintly role as governor – none other than the incumbent, James Murray. That Murray should have someone protecting his interests in Britain is hardly surprising, owing to the nature of colonial appointments in the mid-eighteenth century. An able performance alone was not sufficient to secure preferment. Great deeds had to be reported to great men or promising careers could come to naught.[5] What is surprising in this report about the future of Quebec's government, and others like it, is that dealing with the Canadians themselves did not figure in anyone's prospectus. Quebec in 1763 was a conquered territory containing thousands of French souls still living under military government, and yet the questions this raised about assimilation had not intruded themselves upon the thoughts of any contributors or correspondents to the press.

The reasons for this omission are not that easily explained. Plain ignorance about the size of the Canadian population and the magnitude of the task facing the legislators certainly existed. In addition many observers simply believed that worries about what Canadians might think of British governance were neither here nor there. The abundant confidence in British institutions and culture supporting the territorial expansion in North America embodied many chauvinistic prejudices. One prevalent notion of the time taught that any Frenchman in possession of his senses would seize on the conquest as a chance to be liberated from an *ancien régime*, with all its repressive trappings in law, religion, and politics.[6] The British, as Burt put it, "rather nourished the hope that Canadians might be brought to see the light."[7] The unflinching nature and intolerance of such eighteenth-century perceptions about the primacy of the British way of life are striking to twentieth-century eyes. But popular assumptions with respect to French custom rested on certain tenets, especially the belief that Catholicism and despotism represented synonymous moralities. The Gordon Riots in 1780 would illustrate the passions that could be stirred when such prejudices came under threat. As a result the newspapers could publish the most preposterous snippets on Quebec and have them received matter-of-factly by the readership. In the *London Evening Post*, for example, it was reported that "letters from Quebec advise that some priests of the Romish persuasion having abjured their religion, and turned Protestant, the example has had so great an effect upon many of their disciples, that proselytes are daily coming over to the reformed religion."[8] Reports of this kind simply reinforced existing misconceptions about the nature of French society and made the task of the legislators that much more difficult.

A last and more tangible cause for the inability of the press to address the problem of the Canadians under British rule rests with the fact that other matters took pride of place. The press played a multifarious role in eighteenth-century national life. It informed and educated on all manner of subjects, including the one aspect of Britain's economy vital to its national survival, overseas trade. A brief examination of the newspapers for the 1760s and 1770s reveals an amazing variety of pieces concerning the most trivial matters of trade abroad. Why this was so has been explained by John Brewer in his work on the commercialization of politics.[9] The engine that drove imperial expansion through this period may have been steered by generals and statesman but it was fuelled by thousands of small investors up and down the country. These citizens wanted investment information about overseas trade and found it in the columns of the newspapers. Quebec figured in these reports right after the conquest, and speculation about its economic future always took precedence over anxiety about forms of government in the new colony. Indeed, the news about trade to Quebec proved optimistic from the beginning, and this underpinned British confidence in dealing with the Canadians on other fronts. The onward and upward progression of the economic propaganda can clearly be seen in a newspaper like the *Public Advertiser*. Its columns are peppered with news on trade to Quebec from 1760 onwards. In 1763 after the peace was signed, there were tentative reports on ships leaving for the new province and what cargoes they contained – mainly gunpowder, ammunition, and spirits, at this stage. By October a more definite air permeated the copy, as correspondents talked of good exchanges with the Indian nations involved in the fur trade and the fine land to be had in the province. "I make not the least doubt," concluded one piece, "but this will, in a few years, be a flourishing colony."[10] This confidence about Canada's economic future received its most impressive, and, for the historian, illuminating, fillip in December 1763 when the paper reported that the iron mines at Trois Rivières, whose development the French had constantly encouraged to little effect, were "now in the hands of an English Company and turn out beyond expectation."[11] Here in a nut-shell lay the public confidence to deal with Quebec, born out of a simple superior view of British commercial expertise, which in turn was nurtured by uniquely beneficent constitutional forms and religious principles. On this foundation lay Britain's greatness at home and overseas, in eighteenth-century eyes.

Did the bureaucratic decisions after conquest mirror this public confidence? Not by any stretch of the imagination. The reason for this was that official expectations about the future value of Quebec to Britain's trading empire never matched the optimism expressed elsewhere after 1760. The ghostly arguments of those opposed to retaining Quebec after the war had come home to haunt the administrators in London by 1763. It was not that reports from Canada themselves expressed pessimism in the years between the conquest and the peace, or, as Neatby has stated, that the Quebec problem was ignored.[12] In October 1760 Murray prepared a long report for Pitt on his view of the conquered province, and made some generous statements about the skills of the inhabitants and the trading possibilities in the St Lawrence River: it was "The finest in the Universe," in Murray's view; "the navigation is easy and now well known. Its banks produce hemp, flax, tar, pitch."[13] This glowing reference and Murray's early sympathy for the Canadians would exercise an enormous influence on the military government of Quebec, which lasted until 10 August 1764. The experience of Quebec under the military government has been well documented by Canadian historians, but opinions vary considerably on whether it proved good or bad. Seen from a nationalist French-Canadian viewpoint, Murray's sympathy was tempered by a lack of imagination and a blind obedience to his British traditions. His narrow Anglocentric attitude to the problems confronting the military government wreaked much havoc, especially in the application of justice.[14] Seen from the other side of the fence, Murray's "humanity and justice" ensured that the introduction of British rule to Quebec enjoyed an easier passage than might otherwise have been expected.[15] There is no easy resolution of these differences in approach to Murray's role in the history of Quebec. Some brave souls have attempted to steer a middle course, seeing good and bad in the first governor's policies.[16] Others see the judgment on Murray as irrelevant. Quebec history begins with the simple tenet: how can a conquered people ever be free?[17] The question never asked in this context, however, is what the bureaucrats in London thought of reports like that prepared by Murray, for more often than not the assumption has been that Murray and the bureaucrats are interlinked, even interchangeable.

Murray may have been optimistic from the beginning, and to a degree he was supported in this by Burton and Gage, the military governors of Trois Rivières and Montreal. But their opinions, and all the reports from Canada, underwent a metamorphosis in London, supervised by administrators who saw Canada in a completely different light. Among the manuscript collections in the British Library and Public Record Office there is a great deal of documentation on Quebec in the early 1760s. Some pieces represent official observations on the problem of incorporating the new province into the empire, some are general statements about Quebec's worth to Britain and its potential. Nowhere in the official manuscripts is the ebullience of the public debate on Quebec's economic promise reflected. The best examples of these decidely restrained appraisals of the province can be found in the Liverpool papers, which most likely once belonged to Charles Jenkinson, a leading figure at the Treasury and policy advisor in the early 1760s. The salient feature of all these reports is their Eurocentricity.

One particularly withering critique prepared in early 1763 examines Quebec as though Murray had never put pen to paper.[18] Its account of the history of New France and its economy and development, for example, was taken almost verbatim from a French text by Pierre F.X. de Charlevoix, *Histoire et description généal de la nouvelle France, avec le journal historique d'un voyage dans l'Amerique*, published in two editions in Paris during 1744. It is impossible not to conclude that Charlevoix's work took on biblical proportions in the British administrative mind, for his ideas infuse the ideas of all those looking at Quebec in the early 1760s. This is not really surprising in view of the amazing scope of Charlevoix's work on travel and natural history in the eighteenth century. He wrote not only on North America but also the West Indies, Japan, Paraguay, and Europe generally. His detailed knowledge of Quebec undoubtedly had very definite repercussions in the official view of the province, by the very fact that Charlevoix frequently painted an unflattering picture of life in New France as seen through old European eyes. This can be shown by just looking at a section from his critical précis on the economy. Charlevoix wrote a damning evaluation of French attempts to make New France a profitable colony. Nothing had worked, in his view. The Canadians were only interested in the fur trade and this drained the colony of skilled labour and produced insufficient revenue in ratio to the crown's investments. The cost of producing and transporting goods was also prohibitive, with the result that "les merchandises en Canada, sont au double de ce qu'elles valent en France; cela paroit exhorbitant."[19] Without the pensions and administrative salaries sent directly from Paris, Charlevoix concluded, the colony would have been sunk without trace long before the mid-eighteenth century. "La Canada n'enrichit point la France," he wrote, using the words of an intendant from 1725.[20]

Such pessimism would take some eradicating from the official British psyche. The good things said about Quebec's future in the public debate and the reports emanating from Canada itself swam against a tide of administrative scepticism that threatened to engulf all before it. There existed doubt on every front as to Britain's ability to make Quebec a prosperous member of the imperial community, which offered a stark contrast to newspaper predictions on this score. The report adumbrated above, for example, sought some way to be positive about perceptions of the Quebec economy, but Charlevoix's shadow loomed large.[21] In terms of providing bulk commodities, ran the report, "Canada produces only the peltry," which was certainly not considered adequate to keep the economy viable. Indeed, the report predicted with some accuracy that over the next fifty years the fur trade would meet its demise, making it imperative to seek a different economic base for the province's future prosperity. Of the alternatives, the author realized that the natural resources in Quebec offered the best prospects of wealth, but, as caveat, he also pointed out that if transport costs were too high profits would be negligible: "whatever may be the quality of the country, commodities of this kind can never well become the proper objects of commerce unless freightage is cheap." The British had learned this lesson the hard way over the previous one hundred and fifty years in competition with the Dutch. Low transportation costs, carrying fees, and insurance formed the bedrock of British trading wealth, and the crucial role of the keeping down of these costs in Britain's economic advance was stressed repeatedly in one of the most influential economic tracts published in the eighteenth century by Sir Josiah Child, *New Discourse of Trade*.[22] The one hope of making commerce from Quebec viable, a goal which the French had never attained, was seen to be the welding of Quebec into the New England economic system. Such a move would give the province and its goods year-round use of all-weather ports and access to larger markets, while cutting its transportation costs considerably. These terms appeared the best that could be offered at the time as a basis for Quebec's future prosperity. The general aura of the official debate found expression in the last line of this 1763 report, which concluded that in transferring the sovereignty of Quebec, France lost nothing and Britain gained very little.[23]

These contradictions between the public and private statements on Quebec reveal the blurred policy perspective confronting the British after the peace was signed in 1763. Thinking affecting the province over the next ten years or so would be characterized by doubt and indecision, reflecting the differing views about Quebec's future that were evident from the very moment of conquest. The problem was exacerbated, however, by two factors fundamental to the emergence of an overall policy for the province; a bureaucracy without the power to act on its own cognizance, and confusion over the philosophical assumptions supporting decisions on Quebec.

It is worth dealing with the problem of the bureaucracy first, as this structure had such a profound effect on policy during 1763 and early 1764. Policy decisions governing the colonies in the mid-eighteenth century emanated from an administrative process with several branches. Dependent upon the imperial problem afoot, information that led to the formulation of orders in council or parliamentary legislation arose from different sources. This web of intelligence involved disparate individuals and bodies such as the colonial agents and merchants trading to the colonies. But the bedrock of the supply of intelligence centred on the Treasury and Customs Board, the Board of Trade itself, and the government's legal officers.[24] No colonial office existed at this time to oversee an empirical approach to imperial government. Power lay in the hands of senior ministers when it came to constructing colonial policy in the mid-eighteenth century, and procedures in this exercise resembled decisions on any domestic issue. In fact, in terms of parliamentary government the procedures were exactly the same. Imperial topics came before cabinet or ministerial gatherings in the same way as domestic issues, very often in no particular order, and frequently with no special treatment being given to the colonial problem at hand. The introduction and application of British institutions and customs, whether in Manchester or Murshidabad, was perceived through British eyes and tackled from the same assumption of right.

The difficulties in this way of proceeding have been well documented elsewhere, and its symptoms are clearly evident to historians.[25] At the top level, rivalry developed between the secretaries of state and the Treasury for influence over policy, and, more important, patronage. The situation then became more complicated after 1763 when the first lord of the Treasury sought to extract revenues, for which he assumed sole responsibility, from the empire. At the lower level there was often an unhealthy competition between advisory bodies, like the Board of Trade and Customs Board, to direct the course of policy and even to frame clauses in specific legislation.[26] To confuse matters further, the Plantations Committee of the Privy Council retained effective, but to many contemporary observers rather nebulous, powers to control colonial affairs and issue edicts governing the behaviour and development of imperial governments around the world. Just what the limits of these powers were became a matter of dispute in the 1760s and 1770s. Indeed, in two instances the dispute led to major governmental crises. In June 1766 the Rockingham ministry was brought down after a cabinet dispute on formulating policy for Quebec by edict, and in early 1774 the earl of Dartmouth had to present the Coercive Acts to parliament after losing a battle over what the Privy Council could and could not do in the creation of American colonial policy to punish the perpetrators of the Boston Tea Party.[27]

In view of these internal conflicts, the genesis of a policy for Quebec in 1763 and 1764 becomes more comprehensible. The first priority of the British government after February 1763 was to bring the military regime in Quebec to a close and provide a framework of civil government. The major players and their reports in the evolution of this policy are now well known. Shortt and Doughty opened the door to an understanding of the process in 1907 when they published a series of manuscripts from the Public Record Office relating to the establishment of civil governments in the territories ceded to Britain in 1763 – the Floridas, Grenada, and Quebec. The authors suffered no doubts about the importance of this documentation, asserting that "the papers contain an account of the steps taken ... to provide a suitable construction and policy of administration for Canada ... They furnish the basis for the Proclamation of October 7th, 1763, as also for the Commission and the Instructions of the same date given to General James Murray."[28] This represented something of an overstatement, and further work on the lead-up to the Proclamation by Humphreys and Crane in the 1920s uncovered a broader context for the pressures affecting policy on Quebec in the months before October 1763.[29] These avenues of investigation have since been widened in the general texts by other scholars such as Burt and Neatby, with perhaps the most pertinent contribution coming from Marshall in 1971.[30] Marshall drew the previous body of research together through an illuminating essay that explained, in brief, policy-making on Quebec from the British point of view.

It is generally accepted that the Proclamation emerged from three main stages of bureaucratic activity. Lord Egremont set the ball rolling on 5 May 1763 when he forwarded a report to the Board of Trade on the situation in North America, demanding, in return, suggestions on the economic and political future of the province. The report itself was probably the work of Henry Ellis, whose stint as the governor of Georgia from 1757 to 1760 had given him first-hand experience of colonial government, albeit over transplanted Britons.[31] The Board of Trade's reply, written under Lord Shelburne's supervision, appeared on 8 June 1763. Its principal clauses contained recommendations for establishing boundaries and civilian rule in all of Britain's new possessions. Each case received pragmatic attention. For Quebec the recipe for civil harmony and successful integration into the empire consisted of one main ingredient as far as civil authority was concerned: "a Governor and Council under Your Majesty's immediate commission and instructions."[32] The official debate then died away until the flurry of cabinet meetings of the Grenville administration prior to the Proclamation in October. In the interim, Egremont had died and Shelburne had resigned as president of the Board of Trade. By late September, however, the boundary question and western settlement had led to an Indian uprising under Pontiac, placing the security of the area around the Great Lakes in jeopardy. Faced with this crisis, the government was forced to deal with outstanding governmental problems in the new possessions when it might well have preferred more time to consider its course of action. Indeed, in light of what the Proclamation ordered in relation to the government of Quebec, it would appear that Halifax, the new southern secretary, should have spent more time examining certain clauses in the Board of Trade's report of 8 June. While seeming to accept the boundary suggestions and economic prognosis, Halifax gave the recommendation that Quebec should have a governor in council short shrift. The government abandoned the pragmatic approach to each new possession in favour of an ominous empirical commitment to representative government: "So soon as the state and circumstances of the said Colonies will admit thereof, they shall with the Advice and Consent of the Members of our council, summon and call General Assemblies within the said Governments respectively, in such Manner and Form as is used and directed in those Colonies and Provinces in America which are under our immediate Government."[33]

What can be made of these policy revisions? Historians have argued over whether or not the commitment to an assembly in Quebec represented some discontinuity in the British approach. The traditional view, espoused initially by Humphreys, asserts that the Proclamation can be seen as progressing from earlier policy statements.[34] Marshall, on the other hand, denies this, believing that that school of thought pays little attention to the consequences attendant upon the promise of an assembly.[35] In many respects it is a phantom controversy, which really misses the point. To talk of the existence or non-existence of continuities is surely unrealistic. Before Halifax came on the scene the whole decision process about Quebec in these months was characterized by internal disagreement and contradiction. The best example of this confusion was certainly the vexed decision on a form of government for the province. Henry Ellis had originally suggested to Egremont a type of government modelled on the representation in Nova Scotia and Georgia, with legislative powers confined to the governor and council. Shelburne then turned this around into a recommendation that dispensed with an assembly and gave sole power in the province to a governor in council. Halifax, in turn, came along and promised a full-blown representative government with an assembly, styled on existing bodies in the thirteen American colonies. This was not the only dispute to develop, either. In July and early August, Shelburne and Egremont differed completely in their views of how the hinterland should be policed and regulated, a disagreement which crucially affected the decision on territory to be annexed to the new province and its government.[36] In the case of revenue for Quebec, something Egremont had asked about on 5 May, Shelburne simply refused to answer, saying that the relevant Treasury papers were not available to the Board of Trade. The list of disagreements was considerable, with consistency being the least prominent feature of these discussions over policy.

Thus, the message for historians from the official debate on Quebec in 1763 is that the proposals encompassed in the documents before 7 October were not written in stone. The road to Halifax's decision on the Proclamation was pitted with large craters that made consistency of approach impossible. First there were the petty jealousies of the bureaucrats and their departments. Shelburne wanted to be the principle influence over the direction of North American policy in the early months of 1763. Throughout his short term as president of the Board of Trade, from 23 April to 17 September, he clamoured for increased power over patronage and decision-making. Both Halifax and Egremont resisted the pressure, arguing that Shelburne desired a seniority that did not become his office or board. In other words, this seniority would draw power away from their departments. This was somewhat disingenuous, for, ironically, Shelburne only sought the trappings of office that Halifax had enjoyed as president of the Board of Trade in the 1750s. Shelburne did not know, however, that even when Halifax briefly held cabinet rank in the previous decade, control of colonial appointments had not raised the Board of Trade to the status of the southern and northern departments.[37] Antagonism at this practical level hardly aided unity of purpose in the policy-making process.

Second, Halifax's personal views about colonial policy must be taken into account. In some areas of imperial policy he relied on the informed advice of his subordinates; in others, like Quebec, he took his own counsel.[38] Halifax's colleagues saw in him someone who could blow hot and cold over policy and this trait aroused a good deal of hostility. For example, Henry Fox, the retired paymaster-general, summarized his character in 1763 like this: "vain and presumptuous, aiming at the highest degree of power, and secure in his own mind of universal applause, taking no connections seriously, or that may bind him whenever they became in the least inconvenient to his views, and parting with no connections which he thinks may one day serve him, however they may be offensive or injurious to those he acts with ... Insincere, regardless of his word to a supreme degree, and regardful only of what may serve his vanity and ambition, which are without bounds."[39] Harsh words indeed, but they were certainly borne out by Halifax's experience in the Grenville ministry from 1763 to 1765. Halifax had several disagreements with his colleagues on North American policy in these two years, even with Grenville himself. Sometimes he got his own way, sometimes not. The cabinet met in September 1763, for example, to discuss western settlement and the boundary line limiting expansion in the interior. Grenville queried the recommendation of Halifax's department on this point but found himself overruled – a rare recorded instance of an eighteenth-century premier suffering such a defeat.[40] In January

1764, however, Grenville gained his revenge, when the two debated the question of paying the salaries of colonial officials directly from London. Halifax urged the policy strongly, but Grenville would have none of it, leaving Halifax "extremely heated and eager."[41] Halifax clearly knew his own mind on colonial issues and possessed the rank to ensure that in most cases his will prevailed.

The gel that bonded Halifax's bureaucratic jealousy and personal ambition into an overwhelming force on Quebec policy was a keen sense of power-broking. Despite all the reports and recommendations flying between Quebec City, the Board of Trade, and the Southern Department, senior ministers retained, and had to be seen to be retaining, ultimate control of the big imperial decisions. At times this jealousy on the part of senior ministers went further than a simple desire to ensure that the junior departments, like the Board of Trade, remained in their political subordinate place. There is also evidence to show that senior politicians lacked confidence or trust in the ability of these boards to produce what they considered sensible political solutions to imperial problems. The two facets of this case were most strongly put by Lord Chief Justice Mansfield in March 1763. Mansfield was undoubtedly the most respected jurist of the time and would play an important advisory role in the evolution of Quebec policy, as it constantly raised difficulties of legal interpretation and precedent. His general influence on the direction of imperial policy is well known, of course, and culminated in the landmark judgment in the case of *Campbell and Hall* (1774), which delineated the rights of inhabitants in settled and conquered colonial possessions.[42] Mansfield proved to be more than an eminent lawyer in this period, however, for he was also a politician of the first rank and power, enjoying a special relationship with the king and consulted by both government and opposition over the whole breadth of parliamentary affairs.[43]

On the issue of what to do about the new imperial possessions in 1763, Mansfield had very definite views. In conversation with the king in the middle of March, Mansfield found out that ministers intended to be guided by the advice of the Board of Trade in settlements for the new acquisitions. Mansfield found this intelligence quite disagreeable, and it is worth citing what he said to the king at length, for his words express succinctly the realities of imperial policy-making at this juncture: "that he [Mansfield] was of a quite different opinion; that schemes ought instantly be form'd then sent round to those consulted in the public affairs, that when consider'd by them and the properest plan fixed on, then the Board of Trade should be writ in a public letter for their advice (but privately instructed what they should say); for otherwise that the Board of Trade would probably send from want of lights, a plan that would be improper which would be a very unpleasant affair."[44] This insistence on firm ministerial control and a hard-nosed attitude to the government's advisory boards has a very modern ring to it, but the procedure developed into a fine art under the "effective Cabinet" of George III's early reign.[45] Mansfield's sentiments were echoed elsewhere in the administration's inner councils, most notably by Barrington, secretary at war from 1765 to 1778. He prepared a report for Shelburne in 1766-67 in which doubt was cast upon the ability of the Board of Trade to produce a sensible policy for the interior policing of North America.[46] In fact, his reflections were a severe indictment of the whole thrust of bureaucratic thinking that had produced a system of forts and out-posts guarding the western boundary. At one point Barrington even suggested that the reports from Sir William Johnson, superintendent of Indian affairs, were neither "clear" nor "conclusive," and should be treated with caution. In effect, this was one advisory body accusing another similar body of ineptitude, which could only have confirmed the opinions about the necessity of ministerial control over imperial affairs that Mansfield expressed in his state-ment to the king.

Halifax's decision on the Proclamation of 1763 certainly reflected these political realities. Advice had flowed thick and fast into the Southern Depart-ment by the time of Egremont's death in late August, and it is unlikely that Halifax had time to assimilate all this information before the Proclamation of 7 October. Perhaps he never intended to; the Proclamation has all the ap-pearance of a hasty public compromise. It is instructive to note, for example, that the Board of Trade itself did not formally take the 1762 reports from Burton, Gage, and Murray "into consideration" until 28 October 1763.[47] On the general points of boundaries, settlements, and records for the officers and troops engaged in the campaign, Halifax accepted an amalgam of recent ad-vice. But on the fundamental issues of government and the law for Quebec, Halifax took his own line. Having battled long and hard to secure the per-quisites of ministerial office, he required little encouragement to act on his own initiative; and there seems no doubt that that is just what he did on the commitment to an assembly and system of English justice. On the question of an assembly. Halifax was a whig of the old school. Of all the recommen-dations about forms of government in the province, the idea of a governor in council stood least chance of being accepted. It affronted the spirit of the representative traditions inherited from the events of 1688, and would pre-sent a fine opportunity for the government's critics to exploit the mythology of Stuart despotism raising its head again. The judicial decision flowed from the same assumption about the primacy of British institutions. In political and, as will be shown below, constitutional terms, it was inconceivable for Halifax to tell parliament that English law would not prevail in Quebec over British subjects.

Halifax had to sell the settling of the new possessions in a public debate that would satisfy everybody's expectations and hopes of future success. An assembly and English law provided the key to this pitch. Settlers from the colonies to the south would be attracted by a familiar political environment;

merchants would move in and invest because of the chance to have a say in the running of the province, while also enjoying access to English legal processes. Most important, a future commitment on these grounds did not offend tender constitutional sensibilities in Britain itself – or so it was hoped. When the promised representative assembly did not materialize over the next two or three years, objections arose in Britain to complicate the search for an equitable solution to the problem of two or three hundred Britons governing seventy thousand Frenchmen. Considerations of this nature caused no ripple of doubt to surface in ministerial thinking of 1763. Action had been required on Quebec and the government had been seen to respond, no matter how many inadequacies and mistakes the Proclamation contained. Past judgments on the motive and impact of the Proclamation have ranged from "casual" to "defensible," but this does not really tackle the point at issue. [48] The pertinent question here is whether anything else could have emerged from the philosophical imperatives of the eighteenth-century whig mind. Halifax was a prisoner of his own political rhetoric, and the Proclamation, in turn, was a product of the ascendant whig traditions in mid-eighteenth-century life.

Having made a decision for the future that made no sense in Quebec, but that appeared infinitely reasonable in the British context, Halifax left others in North America to pick up the pieces of an almost insoluble puzzle. The trouble ahead would make James Murray's breezy prediction that "two years may do the business" look ridiculous. [49] It can be seen in all the hurry and scurry of September and October 1763 how little time was given to considering precedents to the action taken on Quebec. Far more effort, in fact, was allotted to separating the parts of what are now Newfoundland, Nova Scotia, and New Brunswick from the province of Quebec, which became its own entity. Historians have spent much time pondering over earlier English constitutional decisions that may have affected the new province. This exercise has included examples from the medieval period of English government in France, the acquisition of Minorca at the Treaty of Utrecht in 1713, and the less salubrious example of Acadia in the decade preceding the Proclamation. Each example has been assessed its role in the background and lead-up to Quebec policy, although British advance in Ireland and India is notably lacking in these accounts. Surely too much has been made of precedent with respect to the immediate declaration of principles embodied in the Proclamation of October 1763, or even the governor's instructions that followed. In the first place, all these precedents merely show that the British had been pragmatic, rather than consistent, in dealing with their overseas possessions. [50] More important, however, the only precedent Halifax utilized in making up his mind on the Proclamation was the lesson learned from the events of 1688. This is not to say that the Glorious Revolution had no immediate relevance to the development of a colonial empire in the eighteenth century. On the contrary, it had very definite repercussions, seen in the rise of ministerial and, ·

in turn, parliamentary power over all aspects of the legislative process.[51] No area of policy, domestic or imperial, proved immune from these profound developments, and Quebec offered its challenge at a crucial moment in the "reconfiguration of politics."[52] The manner in which the British reacted after 1763 to the special claims of the new territory revealed the confused notions of polity that stemmed from fundamental constitutional change.

The ten months following October 1763 provided ample evidence of this confusion. The only outstanding administrative problems perceived in Britain following the Proclamation concerned the designation of a governor, and providing him with a job description. James Murray, the incumbent, secured the post of "Captain General and Governor in Chief of the Province" – not of governor-general, as is often assumed and written – and his commission was issued on November 1763.[53] There was nothing untoward in the combination of civil and military powers granted Murray in this instance. Quebec would be under a military government until August 1764 and the king's representative would normally retain such authority.[54] One aspect of the appointment that also requires revision concerns the impression that Murray's promotion was a foregone conclusion. Murray himself certainly did not see it that way, and his doubts seem justified in retrospect. His rise to the governorship of the province derived from a happy mix of luck and shrewd political management in London. Of the former Wolfe's death and the eagerness of Townshend and Amherst to leave Canada for England proved most propitious, to say the least. Over the latter, political management, Murray exercised more control, but good fortune again served as a timely ally. The Elibank family enjoyed good connections in ministerial circles, and Murray obviously did well when William Pitt held senior ministerial rank. Murray boasted to his brother in July 1761 that he asked "nothing from anybody but Mr. Pitt and the King."[55] And so confident was he in this protection that he added as a rider to this boast the following year, "I think it my duty to do all I can to reestablish the poor Canadians and I am sure I can make them as good and as faithful subjects as any belonging to the British Empire."[56] After Pitt's resignation in October 1761, however, and the ministerial instability that ensued, Murray's confidence was shaken. He then had to rely on his only other ally at Westminster, James Oswald, the MP for Kircaldy and a minor office-holder. Oswald possessed considerable talent and a connection with two powerful figures in the new reign, the earl of Bute and George Grenville. Fortunately for Murray, Grenville's star was in the ascendant in early 1763, and the connection to Oswald secured Murray's future at that juncture. Grenville and Oswald were political associates of long standing, and, when the Grenville administration took office in April 1763, Oswald lobbied successfully for Murray's continued service in Quebec. Given the way in which Grenville's administration operated, convincing Grenville was as good as securing Egremont's approval of the arrangement.[57] Murray recognized the machinations behind his appointment and thanked Oswald profusely on 12 November 1763, commenting, "the success was doubtful it is true, but your kind endeavours to procure it were, always certain; I have no words to express my gratitude."[58] Murray's lucky streak in patronage did not last, for it is well known that securing the prize appointment proved easier than remaining *in situ*. Almost as soon as Halifax established himself at the Southern Department after Egremont's death, the walls of Murray's defence system in London were breached. Grenville was never able to exert the same power over Halifax that he had exerted over his brother-in-law, and it was from this point on that Murray's fabled troubles with the London authorities began.

In the fall of 1763, however, Murray saw only good times ahead for the province. He had received his commission on 23 October, and told Gage on 2 November that, although he did not know "what form of government we are to have," prospects for the province appeared good.[59] The immediate plan of government was taking shape in London, and appeared on 7 December 1763 under the simple title "Instructions to our well beloved, James Murray." This proved somewhat misleading, for the formidable document ran to eighty-two clauses, and would provide the very basis of the civil government, beginning on 10 August 1764. The Proclamation in comparison to this manuscript appeared a rambling aside, though it would be true to say that both documents shared the failing of being quite inappropriate for the task at hand. In short, their contents reflected assumptions at Westminster on policy for the province utterly removed from the reality of life in Quebec. Had the politicians or administrators in London not read the dispatches from Canada, or were they simply guilty of insurmountable ideological prejudices? Their actions certainly lent weight to the old adage that there are none so blind as those who do not wish to see.

The Instructions to Murray encompassed every aspect of colonial life considered of importance by the government at Westminster, and the order of priorities revealed much about the workings of the eighteenth-century political mind.[60] It is striking, for example, that the initial clauses laying down recommendations for the establishment of civil governmental and legal procedures were followed by two lengthy passages on where the responsibilities and power over patronage lay. The very core of eighteenth-century political practice was laid out in these two clauses on a Quebec government that did not at that time exist. Only when this basic issue had been settled did the critical problems of religion, future settlement and surveys of the province, and, finally, relations with the Indian nations receive attention. The whole was rounded off with further orders regarding trade, naval policy, and what matters Murray must report to the Board of Trade in the future. With this package the government hoped to ensure a smooth passage for Quebec into the imperial system controlled from Westminster.

It does not take a great deal of effort to dismantle the premise upon which many of these instructions rest. The clauses dealing with government, law, and religion, in particular, appeared fraught with difficulties. From the British point of view, it came as no surprise to see that the Instructions maintained a commitment to an assembly. This commitment did not stem simply from the sinister ideological implications of ruling by executive edict but took priority because without an assembly no monies could be voted to support the intended civil establishment. As Murray and then the government found to their cost, the continuation of duties on imported wines and spirits from the French regime could not be used as a surrogate form of taxation. After several lawsuits and protracted disputes, the government was obliged to abandon attempts at enforcing old duties in 1769. This fixation on creating an assembly represented absolute, orthodox constitutional thought in mid-eighteenth-century Britain. Nevertheless the implementation of the theory lacked one important practical ingredient: who on earth would sit in the assembly? It could not be the Canadian Catholic population, who were disqualified in clauses twenty-eight to thirty of the Instructions from taking part in representative government while retaining their faith. Nor, for obvious reasons, could it be the few hundred Protestants in the province, though many did show willing in the future to undertake the creation of what would have been the most exclusive and vindictive representative body known to the British constitution. The only hope of success for an assembly, therefore, depended upon attracting thousands of new Protestant settlers to the province from Britain and the American colonies. As Burt so ably described it, this ridiculous "miscalculation" was bound to backfire and, when it did, "a constitutional miscarriage in the province took place."[61] The mass of the population was denied a say in its own destiny.

A similar "miscarriage" looked likely over the proposals governing the practice of Catholicism in Quebec. The most prominent concern arose from clause thirty-two in the Instructions. It stated: "You are not to admit of any Ecclesiastical Jurisdiction of the See of Rome, or any other foreign Ecclesiastical Jurisdiction whatsoever in the Province under your Government." Again, this clause represented the standard approach in Britain to the (mythological?) threat of popish interference in the religious life of the state. On this count alone the policy was wholly inappropriate for Quebec, but the situation looked worse still from the fact that, since the death of Bishop Pontbriand in June 1760, the province's Catholic church had lacked a physical and spiritual figurehead. If the Instructions were applied rigorously, moreover, there would be little chance of securing one, a fact which held grave implications for the renewal of the priesthood. The prospect of successfully establishing English legal procedures looked equally depressing. On small points trouble loomed: who would sit on juries if Catholics were debarred and who would serve as JPs throughout the province? On the larger front the problems seemed intractable. In essence, how could the French Coutume de Paris be swept away and English civil and criminal courts be established equitably in only a matter of months?

This was the scene confronting Murray as the establishment of civil government approached in August 1764. The new governor-in-chief would have to have been something of a deity to avoid trouble. The tools provided to bring Quebec under British rule clearly did not match the problems to be tackled. Murray's declared ambitions seemed noble enough, and his personal application to the task of governing Quebec in what he considered an even-handed manner cannot be disputed. The personal letters and official reports that he sent to Britain testify to an honest endeavour to come to terms with the alien people and institutions under his supervision. Murray's own preconceptions about French society and religion hindered this process, but, at root, this proved irrelevant in the formulation of policy in London for Quebec. Murray's difficulties with the Canadian way of life were nothing compared with the abject ignorance displayed by the politicians in England. To secure the successful integration of Quebec into imperial structure, the old pragmatic practices of the past would have to be resurrected. The policy decisions of 1763 displayed a singular lack of sensitivity and foresight, born out of the particular political circumstances and mistaken assumptions in which post-war policy evolved. The press frequently displayed a similar lack of understanding of the practical necessities required in producing a workable scheme of government for the province. This doubtless reinforced existing prejudices amongst the politicians, and yet in the last analysis the press was not charged with the responsibility of governing. This job fell to the politicians and only an urgent change in ministerial thinking about Quebec looked likely to save the situation from utter deterioration. In its absence, the instruction to Murray would simply open the way to destruction of the delicate balancing act in existence between conqueror and conquered since 1760.

CHAPTER THREE

A Troublesome Task: The First Year of Civil Government in Quebec

In the fall of 1764, Governor Murray commented to the auditor-general, Robert Cholmondeley, in England that "Hitherto our time has been employed in settling the civil government of the province which I find a very troublesome and difficult task."[1] This observation could probably have qualified for the prize understatement of the year. A civilian government had only been in existence for three months in Quebec and already the future for the emerging forms and institutions of British rule appeared shaky and uncertain. The first year after martial law proved traumatic for Murray and the whole Canadian population. A cursory look at the Colonial Office papers and Board of Trade journals reveals a huge outpouring of distrust and frustration on the part of the old French population and new post-conquest settlers. Hardly one aspect of life under the new regime escaped censure. Law, religion, land tenure, taxation, and the constitution were just some of the fundamental issues that caused immediate problems for Murray. The trials and tribulations of these months in the history of Quebec are no mystery; they have now been well documented. But what remain less clear are the attitudes of the British to these teething troubles of the civil government. The blithe political and philosophical assumptions that can be found embodied in the Proclamation and in Murray's Instructions suddenly came under pressure in 1764 and were found wanting. The unbridgeable gulf between the hopes of theory and the realities of practice would never be more evident than in the attempt to Anglicize Quebec during the initial period of civilian rule.

It would be naïve to believe that it could have been any other way. Creating the institutional fabric of British rule and cultural hegemony in Quebec was bound to involve a painful transition period – one, indeed, that might never end. In the application of Murray's Instructions, all sections of Quebec society suffered some unexpected repercussions. The dichotomy here for historians who look at these developments is well known. The impact of civilian rule on the habitants, for example, was very different from its impact on the Protestant mercantile body in the province after the conquest. Unfortunately the British government proved less sophisticated than modern scholarship in its perception of Quebec's needs under its changed sovereignty. In 1764 the commitment to mould Canadian society into a near image of that of Britain stood firm in the minds of Halifax and the officials at the Board of Trade. Any delimitation between the needs of the old and new Canadians was purely coincidental to the overall intention of bestowing the benefits of English civilization on Quebec over the next generation. This dream, carried in the Proclamation and the Instructions to Murray, failed miserably, as the customs and traditions of New France could not be cast away like so much flotsam and jetsam on the tide of British imperial expansion. Nevertheless it is instructive to examine the assumptions which spawned this intent, for they not only reflect much about the nature of British aspirations in the development of a colonial empire but also divisions within the body politic at home on crucial religious, legal, and constitutional issues.

In this context the stipulations governing the practice of the Catholic faith and law would have the most immediate impact upon the Canadian population, and proved the most difficult problems for the administrators in London to solve. To understand why this was so it is best to start with an examination of the religious issue. Catholicism in mid-eighteenth-century Britain was, to official eyes, not simply a spiritual matter. Confessed religion determined what role a citizen played in the political, social, and, often through these, economic life of the nation. Between 1780 and 1829 the question of Catholic toleration was raised many times and the debate was frequently attended with violence. Good examples of this are offered by the terror and panic caused by the Gordon Riots in London in 1780 and the disturbances in the 1807 general election, both of which showed the raw emotion surrounding the issue on the streets. For the political élite this inflammatory problem was perfectly summed up by one of Peel's correspondents in 1827. The Catholic question, he wrote, "was mixed up with everything we eat or drink or say or think."[2] The problem arose in part from two hundred years of prejudice and official proscription. Legislation against Catholic participation in national life began under Elizabeth I, with especially strong measures being enforced in the 1580s. The severity and scope of anti-Catholic legislation then fluctuated under the Stuarts of the seventeenth century, depending on the particular domestic circumstances of the time. This *ad hoc* approach continued until the 1670s when, in the wake of a popish plot, systematic exclusion of Catholics from office began. The Test Act of 1673 required all MPs and office-holders to take an oath against transubstantiation, and in 1678 the act was extended to cover peers of the realm, making it the first time that Catholics had been barred from the Lords. The theoretical supremacy of the Protestant constitutional world was completed with the revolutionary settlement in 1689. In the Bill of Rights an innovatory clause, clearly born out of the anti-popery sentiments of the time, restricted succession to the British crown to Protestant heirs. The ancient maxim of the people following the faith of their sovereign was abandoned and remains so to this day.

It was this tradition of antipathy and exclusionism towards Catholics that pervaded official thinking in 1763 and 1764 when the Quebec settlement came up. In the long run the narrow-minded approach to the question of Canadian Catholicism did not survive. But the distinction needs to be drawn between an initial period of trial and error reflecting established mores on this point, and the revision of thought that took place between 1765 and the passage of the Quebec Act in 1774. When the important colonial administrator William Knox wrote a panegyric on the Quebec legislation in 1774, he stressed the role that precedents had played in the religious settlement for the province. He had Ireland particularly in mind, and what he believed was a most regrettable state of affairs where a minority of Protestant subjects enjoyed ascendancy over the majority Irish Catholic population.[3] Fine words in the circumstances, yet they represented justification after the fact, clouding the actual stages of development in the religious policy for the province. And there is no doubt that this misconception about British motives has been echoed in many texts on the period vainly looking for a more enlightened side to imperial expansion.

The position with regard to precedents on religion in 1763 was not clear cut, for there were none that quite suited the case of Quebec. Where Britain had taken over alien populations in the recent past, as in Minorca or Acadia, the numbers and priorities defied a deliberate policy of Anglicization. The only legal guidelines on Catholic rights in the colonies rested on a rag-bag of interpretations from older and often unrelated cases. Two in particular stand out. The first, Calvin's case, was heard before King's Bench in 1608. It concerned the rights of aliens to seek protection under English law. Or, to put it another way in this instance, did the laws of England apply to a citizen born in Scotland before the union of the two crowns, whose action arose after James VI became monarch of both kingdoms? In the mind of one of the leading jurists of that time, Lord Ellesmere, the answer was straightforward. It mattered not whether Calvin was born in England or Scotland, for after 1603 the rule of law between the two kingdoms became indivisible. "Shall a foot breadth, or an inch breadth of ground make a difference of birthright of subjects borne under one king?" Ellesmere wrote in his tract on the case. "Nay, where there are not any certain bounds or limits known at all, but an imaginary partition wall, by a conceited fiction in Law?"[4] The assumption derived from this case could only be that, unless specifically exempted in legislation, English laws applied to all parts of the sovereign's dominions, including colonies.

In practice this meant that Elizabethan legislation against Catholic priests in England could be applied in North America *in toto*. Or did it? In 1705 a second landmark decision on this issue was presented by Edward Northey, in response to a query over Lord Baltimore's religious policy in Maryland. In this case the lawyers decided that the anti-Catholic legislation of Elizabeth's reign applied only to colonies under English rule at the time of its passage. Doubt existed on the legitimacy of these laws in dominions acquired after the enactment of the legislation.[5] This spelled trouble for Catholicism in Maryland, a colony originating in the 1630s, because in the reign of William III (1689–1703) anti-popery legislation was renewed, which, after Northey's decision, implied no part of the king's existing dominions could claim exemption.[6] Through this slightly confusing constitutional nicety, sense can be made of what at first appear as striking inconsistencies on the part of the government's legal officers over the Quebec problem. For it is clear some lawyers, and maybe one or two politicians, understood these precedents while others did not. For example, it explains why the attorney-general and solicitor-general declared Catholics in Quebec "not subject, to the incapacities, disabilities, and penalties to which Roman Catholics in this kingdom are subject by the Laws thereof," on 10 June 1765.[7] It also justifies the decision of Northington, the lord chancellor, to resign from the cabinet in June 1766 because the government wished to revise Quebec's legal and religious structure by order in council and not through parliamentary legislation. Northington has always appeared the spoiler in histories of this period, but in the strict terms of legal interpretation and precedent at that time right was on his side.

What of Quebec in 1763, however, immediately after the peace? The situation initially looked quite unpredictable. No specific legislation governing religious policy in the province existed. Yet there was a promise in the articles of capitulation, later embodied in article IV of the peace treaty, "that Roman Catholic subjects may profess the worship of their religion according to the rites of the Romish church, as far as the laws of Great Britain permit."[8] Herein lay a conundrum for the British administrators and politicians charged with bringing Quebec into the empire in 1763. At first they thought that the wording of article IV represented an enacting clause, making the Canadians subject to all the proscriptions suffered by Catholics in Britain. Only when the government's legal officers applied their brains to the particularities of the situation in Quebec did they recognize a constitutional error. Article IV did not enact but merely reflected an evident tension between conquerors and conquered that demanded careful treatment before hopes of a lasting cure could be fulfilled.

The progression of official thought on the Catholic issue can be traced from the manuscripts of the leading players and institutions in this drama. The most influential protagonist was Lord Shelburne, the first politician to give serious thought to the problem of a religious settlement in Quebec. As president of the Board of Trade in May 1763, Shelburne drew up a memorandum "on the Subject of Religion with respect to Canada."[9] It represents a fascinating insight into the official eighteenth-century mind on one of the thorniest subjects in the period. Shelburne gave the matter serious consideration, dismissing in his opening paragraph a popular fallacy "that *The Influence of Religion or rather Superstition is confined to a certain latitude*, and that *Nothing is to be feared from its effects in America*." Shelburne displayed deep prejudices, derived from what he had seen in Europe, about the unregulated practice of the Catholic faith: "Canada, it must be remembered, whose many thousand people are now become the subjects of Great Britain, who were neither born or bred such, and whose religion when operating in its enthusiastic form, naturally tends to the destruction of Governors and the worst species of Anarchy." These were strong words indeed, and Shelburne had an equally strong political remedy for the perceived threat. As he put it, British political interests came first: "The Regulations therefore with respect to Religion in Canada must not be deduced from our own credo and unregarded Feelings of it *here*, nor from the *plausible and candid professions from an enemy just conquered*, but from the possibility of what may happen, should the times change, should *their* strength increase, and *ours* diminish."

The practical manifestation of this policy would be draconian on several fronts. "All *Regulars*, the convents of men and women, all canons, Priors, Deans should be *totally abolished*," with strict penalties if they should try to return after the interval given for the disposal of their property. What would be left of the old theocratic structure would be "no other Priests but the *Secular*," strictly licensed and limited in number, and, where possible, of Canadian birth. Responsibility for their appointment and dismissal would lie with the governor. The priests themselves would be under the spiritual supervision of the bishop, but his appointment had to be approved by the king, and he would receive his honours and revenues "by Grant from the Crown, revocable at pleasure." The bishop could not excommunicate anyone without the governor's consent, and would not be able to exercise any influence or authority over the province's Protestant subjects. This strong political control over spiritual matters in Quebec allayed Shelburne's fears about the anarchy he feared from zealous Catholicism. In the rest of the memorandum, Shelburne simply laid down very specific recommendations on the collection of tithes and who would be exempt. Near the conclusion some friendlier sentiments appeared towards the Canadians, in the instructions "to prevent everything intolerant or contemptuous which may be offered to this Religion by the Protestant inhabitants." There was a sting in the tail, however, for Shelburne also wished to instruct the governor to show himself outwardly worthy of his office, and "with respect to the Religion of his own Country, he should, by a proper *external decency* in himself and his dependents avoid that absurd though fashionable *indifference*, which in such a motley society as that of Canada, must be most *contrary to sound politics*, as it will necessarily tend to lessen his character and in that his authority."

This document is fascinating reading on two important levels. First, though it appeared harsh towards many aspects of the religious infrastructure in Quebec, the memorandum did not contain an ideological assault on Catholicism as a series of conflicting, even treasonable, principles under a Protestant crown. There was nothing like the repressive medicine dosed out to the Irish apparent in this recipe. True, Shelburne, an Irish aristocrat himself, was somewhat more broadminded than some of his contemporaries in government or the country at large. Yet his perception of the practice of Catholicism as a problem of political control, as a threat to the state's security that had to be neutralized, represents a clean break with the siege mentality of the previous seventy years. Other high-ranking politicians shared his views on this issue. The earl of Hertford, Britain's ambassador to France, expressed a similar concern over the political control of Catholicism in Quebec.[10] He believed that the answer lay in good leadership by a bishop whose loyalty to the British would be unquestionable. For, like Shelburne, he feared that the large French population represented a potential fifth column in any future struggle, and religion would be a deciding factor. Hertford thought he had discovered just the man for the job in one Abbé Joncaire, a native-born Canadian, anxious to occupy the vacant see in his old country. He fulfilled all the criteria Shelburne and Hertford considered vital to the task – in particular, loyalty to the British crown and a keen awareness of the need to educate the Canadians about the realities of the new political order.

Though more work needs to be done on this subject, it appears that the train of thought set in motion by figures like Shelburne and Hertford was a tentative first step on the road to acts of toleration and eventually emancipation that the next two generations so warily trod. It did not require a quantum leap of logic to progress from Shelburne's position to the provisions for practising Catholicism in Quebec embodied in the legislation of 1774, or, for that matter, to the first Catholic relief act in Britain of the eighteenth century in 1778.[11] Further investigation, beyond the scope of this study, may well reveal that English attitudes to Irish Catholicism also began to change in this period, and the legislation of 1778 in Britain prompted a sister bill for Ireland, and a later one for Scotland.[12]

Shelburne's memorandum was of significance on another level, in that his proposals went much further than they need have done in recognition of the Catholic presence in Quebec. The trouble was that Shelburne's proposals stayed in London, and the bigots went out to Quebec and took charge of policy in London after he left the Board of Trade. The people who arrived in the province during 1760 to 1764 did not want a tolerant recognition of Catholicism but rather the sort of deprivation and exclusion of papists from social and political life they were used to seeing in Britain and the American colonies. In fact, they were led to believe that the proposals on religious practices in Murray's Commission and Instructions would effect such exclusion.[13] These clauses not only contained the intended political control over the Catholic church that Shelburne sought in his memorandum but also a definite commitment to spreading the Anglican gospel and church in the province – something that Shelburne had stopped well short of. This evangelical side to the administration of religious life in Quebec put a different gloss on Murray's role as civil governor, and it was one he did not like. Redistributing Jesuit estates and closing convents (though not all) was one thing, creating a Protestant ascendancy was quite another. Murray's spirit rebelled against this, and by October 1764 he was in a quandary, urging the authorities in London to retreat on this front: "I cannot be the instrument of destroying, perhaps the best and bravest race on the globe, a race, that have already got the better of every national antipathy to their conquerors, and could they be indulged with a very few privileges which the Laws of England do not allow to Catholics at home, must in a very short time become the most faithful and useful set of men in his American Empire."[14]

Murray displayed an astute recognition of the imperatives behind the deep-rooted prejudices in Britain. There would be a political price to pay for showing leadership in the face of anti-papist sentiment. Nevertheless, he believed that it would not be too high: "If the popular clamours in England will not allow the humane Heart of the King to follow its own dictates, and the Popish Laws must be exerted with rigour in Canada, for God's sake procure my retreat, and reconcile it to Lord Bute, as I cannot be witness to the misery of a people I love and admire." The traditional view of Murray's role in the religious life of the province since Burt's study of the period has not been flattering.[15] He is frequently painted as an avid Protestant, plotting the downfall of the Catholic church in Quebec. There seems little support for this view in the extant manuscripts. He certainly saw the necessity of political control, but he was exasperated by the notion of exclusion on the British model. Murray saw the truth of the situation that would develop over the next decade: Britain would have to adapt to the Canadians and their way of life or British efforts at governing would fail miserably.

The reason for Murray's determination on this point was readily apparent. A satisfactory way of dealing with religion lay at the very heart of his ability to govern the province effectively. Hardly any problem arose that did not reflect this fact, from worries over the "matrimonial distemper," in which British officers marrying Canadian Catholics might, as in Ireland, be "ipso facto dismissed from the service," to the question of representative institutions.[16] Without a clear indication of Catholicism's legal status in Quebec, every other aspect of government in the province was under a cloud of doubt, especially in regard to the legal system and the possibility of an assembly. Shelburne, Murray, and one or two others realized this in 1763 and 1764, but it took more than a year before the light dawned on the rest of the administration in London.

The agony experienced over establishing courts of law in Quebec certainly bore out the importance of settling the Catholic problem. When Halifax cobbled the Proclamation of October 1763 together, the assumption of English law being applied in the province was implicit in the passage containing the words "to erect and constitute ... Courts of Judicature and public Justice within our said colonies for learning and determining all Causes ... as near as may be agreeable to the Laws of England."[17] As well as the ideological commitment to replace all repressive things French with the trappings of a free British constitution, Halifax had the force of legal precedent on his side to justify this order. Judgment in a case of 1722 relating to Barbados found that "Where the King of England conquers a country ... the conqueror by saving the lives of the people conquered, gains a right and property in such people, in consequence of which he may impose upon them what law he pleases."[18] Clauses sixteen and seventeen of Murray's Instructions certainly echoed the intent to impose an English legal system on Quebec, and all seemed set fair to achieve this end by August 1764. Murray, however, thought otherwise. His experience of administering justice under the military regime had been a reasonably happy one. Dealing with all manner of legal cases in military courts had allowed him a flexibility and dispatch unthinkable under civilian rule. Canadians had more often than not been heard in their own tongue and judged according to local custom. This had done much for Murray's reputation and that of his officers, but he doubted whether the Instructions would allow this state of harmony in legal matters to continue. Charged with tearing down the old legal structures of New France based on the Coutume de Paris, the governor in chief baulked at wholesale demolition.

This is not to say that Murray blocked the application of English legal procedures or even wished to do so. His ordinance of 17 September 1764, establishing civil courts, consisted of explicit directions for the introduction of the English civil and criminal system of justice to Quebec.[19] Nevertheless, there were one or two modifications of Murray's own making that reflected a more mature awareness of the realities of the province's old legal procedures than was shown by the authorities in London. Murray actually sent a copy of the ordinance to the Board of Trade with his own marginal notes on the modifications, and these jottings highlighted the crucial areas in which concessions would have to be made.[20] In retrospect, his suggestions appear eminently reasonable. First priority was again the question of religious proscription. To circumvent their complete exclusion from the legal processes, Murray proposed a fundamental adjustment that would allow Catholics to be impanelled for jury service. He justified the policy with unerring logic: "As there are but two hundred Protestant subjects in the Province, the greatest part of which are disbanded soldiers, of little Property and mean capacity, it is thought unjust to exclude the new Roman Catholic subjects to sit upon juries, as such exclusion would constitute the said two hundred Protestants perpetual judges of the lives and property of not only eighty thousand of the new subjects but likewise of all the military in the Province." If this was not enough, Murray finished with two other telling points. He warned that without this concession on juries many of the king's new subjects "will emigrate." Then, in conclusion, he added that he saw the policy as a "temporary expedient, to keep things as they are until His Majesty's Pleasure is known on this critical and difficult point." This represented a clever move on Murray's part, for it put the ball on the religious question finally back into the politicians' court in London. Murray presented them with a *fait accompli*; it would be extremely difficult for the administrators not to ratify his actions on this "critical and difficult point."

It seems fair to assume that Murray never seriously considered being contradicted, for the other clauses in this ordinance embody further breaches in the wall of Catholic exclusionism. Two proposals in particular warranted written support from Murray. One concerned the creation of a Court of Common Pleas in the province, and the other was a proposal to allow Canadian advocates and proctors to practise in this court. The reasoning behind these concessions again proved sensible and straightforward. On the first, Murray argued that it would be the least painful method of acquainting the new subjects with "our Laws and method of procuring justice in our courts," while protecting them from "the attempts of designing men and the voracity of hungry practioners in the law," whose only achievement, he feared, would be the alienation of the Canadians from "our Government and Laws." On the second, Murray commented with commendable bluntness: "We thought it reasonable to allow Canadian advocates and proctors to practice in this Court of Common Pleas only (for they are not admitted in the other Courts) because we have not yet got one English Barrister or Attorney who understands the French language." This statement showed admirable restraint in the circumstances, and may have been made tongue in cheek. To oversee the administration of justice in Quebec, the British government appointed William Gregory as chief justice and George Suckling as attorney-general of the province. Neither knew any French or had any knowledge of Canadian law. They then proved so embarrassingly bad at their jobs that the government was obliged to withdraw them almost a year later.

The scope of these proposals did not encompass radical reform by any means, and yet it took some courage on Murray's part to meet popular and institutional prejudices against Catholics head on. What prompted Murray to use his discretionary powers in this manner? Part of the explanation must necessarily be more nebulous than the other. Murray's own views on his role as governor in the province and, more important, his own impression of how to win the minds if not the hearts of the new subjects over to the British crown played a crucial role. Whatever Murray's shortcomings in his personal dealings with critics and detractors, his lack of malice and prejudice towards Canadian Catholics seemed genuine enough.[21] Many facets in Murray's background could have brought this attitude about. He was raised in an aristocratic Scottish household, as part of an élite within which there existed a long tradition of affinity to French culture, language, and custom. This could most obviously be seen in Murray's own bilingualism and his willingness to learn about Canadian society, as well as in an utter disdain for the men of trade and the counting house. The more tolerant and humanistic opinions arising from the Scottish enlightenment may also have strengthened Murray's feelings of largesse in dealing with what he considered a basically innocent peasant society under threat. At a more practical (cynical?) level, it must also be allowed that making concessions on the religious issues rendered Murray's job of governing that much easier. It was his duty to keep the transference of power to British rule and institutional government as smooth as possible, and small favours to the Canadians on fundamental points proved an acceptable, even desirable, means to this end. A last practical factor influencing his course of action concerned the question of right to act in the manner appropriate to the situation. A passage in the Instructions had actually pointed Murray in the direction of concessions. After outlining the governor's power to create "Courts of Judicature and Justice," clause 16 stated that useful models might be found "in our other Colonies in America, more particularly in Our Colony of Nova Scotia."[22] In Nova Scotia after 1755, a potential problem with a minority Protestant faction deciding the fate of the majority Catholic population had been avoided by a liberal interpretation of the Test Act. In practice this had enabled the remaining Acadian population to take an oath of allegiance and perform some limited official functions and duties. This sort of compromise looks exactly like what Murray had in mind with the ordinance of 17 September.

Unfortunately, Murray failed to gauge the depth of feeling amongst the small Protestant community in the province against conceding ground to Catholics. His policies on the practice of Roman Catholicism and the legal system struck right at the heart of popular anti-papist sentiment, and reactions came quickly. By the fall of 1764 Murray found himself beset with complaints and petitions – some sent to Quebec City, others to London – sowing the seeds of his eventual recall. The governor became the classic victim of trying to be all things to all men and finally pleasing no one. The response to his ordinance from the Grand Jury of Quebec on 16 October 1764 epitomized the sensitivity of the nerve endings exposed by his religious policy and was in many ways a foreshadowing of what would happen in England after the 1778 Catholic relief acts.[23]

The main thrust of the jury's presentment sought to undermine the core of the argument upon which Murray's discretionary actions were founded. The grand jurors took aim at the Courts of Common Pleas, for example, calling some of the enacting clauses "unconstitutional." The failure to make sure that the "Laws of the Mother Country for the due observance of the Sabbath" were applied also warranted complaint. The concluding section then questioned the whole policy of allowing Catholics to be impanelled on juries and to serve as advocates in the lesser courts. Citing the statute 3 James I c. 5, the jurors stated: "We therefore believe that the admitting persons of the Roman Religion, who own the authority, supremacy and Jurisdiction of the Church of Rome, as jurors, is an open violation of our most sacred Laws and Libertys, and tending to the utter subversion of the Protestant Religion and his Majesty's power, authority, right and possession of the province to which we belong." A blunter challenge to Murray's hopes could not have been offered. Of course, the Grand Jury had misread its legal history, for statutes from James I's reign did not apply to Quebec, then under French, not British rule. Nevertheless, until the point was resolved by the government's legal officers on 10 June 1765, the outcome hung in doubt. The presentment was sent to London, leaving Murray to wonder which way the lawyers would lean in an eventual judgment.

Another vital issue to come out of the presentment, which to that point Murray had been able to avoid, concerned a representative body for Quebec. In clauses nine and ten of the document, claims were put forward by the jurors to "be considered at present as the only Body representative of the Colony," and, as such, to be consulted before any laws could be passed or taxes levied "for the necessary expenses or improvement of the colony." This looked more threatening to Murray's position than any other issue, for an assembly had been promised in the Proclamation of 1763 and Murray's Instructions the following year. The Grand Jury was simply assuming its right to that role and had hit on the simple eighteenth-century yardstick of an assembly's constitutional power: approval of money grants. What a dilemma for Murray, and how he must have wished for a return to military rule where his word was law! How could he call an assembly that represented all the people of Quebec until the religious issue was settled? However much he wished to deal initially with law and faith, Murray could now no longer dodge the issue of an assembly. The claims of the jurors and Murray's procrastination on the issue would now be laid bare before the authorities in London. Worse still, so would the arguments against the presentment, submitted by spokesmen of the French population. Not unnaturally they supported Murray's policies of involving the Catholic population in the legal system of the province, and made an impassioned plea for the government to support their governor in the fight against exclusion: "En effet que deviendroit le bien genéral de la colonie, si ceaux, qui en composent le corps principal, en devenoient des Membres intuiles par la différence de la religion? Que deviendroit la Justice si ceaux qui n'entendent point notre langue, ny nos coutumes, en devenoient les juges par le Ministere des Interprètes? Quelle confusion? Quels frais mercenaires n'en résulteroient-ils point? de sujets protégés par votre Majesté, nous deviendrons de véritables esclaves."[24] Such feelings provided Murray's confidence with a timely boost, but the only impression all these conflicting reports left in

London was one of confusion, and perhaps a governor losing his grip on the situation.

Fuel was added to the fire in London by a continuing stream of complaints concerning many other aspects of civilian rule under Murray's governorship. Initially only the government's administrative bodies had knowledge of rivalries in Quebec. By the summer of 1765, however, news of discontent had reached the ministerial level and the columns of the newspaper press. Of all the problems and detractors facing Murray, the most menacing were in the mercantile communities of Montreal and Quebec City. On 12 December 1763 the Board of Trade reviewed its first complaint against Murray from the merchants in London trading to Quebec, who, after prompting from their contacts in North America, expressed the view that Murray's governorship to date had proved detrimental to the country's economic interests.[25] From that moment on until Murray's recall in the fall of 1765, the minutes of meetings at the Board of Trade and Privy Council alone bear witness to many man-hours spent deliberating about Quebec's internal difficulties.[26] In fact, there developed very quickly in the first year of civil government a pattern of vicious claim and counter-claim between the ruler and the ruled. The English merchants wrote to London with their grievances, drawing an immediate riposte from Murray. After finding this inadequate, the Quebec merchants then hired a London lawyer, Fowler Walker, in the spring of 1765 to present their case to various government departments or, as it happened, anyone of note prepared to listen. In like manner, Murray determined to fight fire with fire. In addition to his many stinging letters of rebuke sent to London to fend off his critics, Murray had dispatched in the fall of 1764 a personal representative, H.T. Cramahé, to defend the record of his government before the British authorities. Cramahé was a man of real ability who understood Canadian customs, and, more important, could find an entrée into ministerial circles.[27] Thus the structure for a power struggle by proxy evolved very rapidly, and was found to work with remarkable precision.

The initiative always appeared to lie with the merchants, whose campaign against Murray was cleverly managed. Hopes of success lay in co-ordinating attacks between merchants in Quebec and London. The latter group gave credit to the former, and it was in the financial interests of the London group to ensure that the Quebec merchants maximized profits no matter what the social or political cost. The highlight of the merchants' campaign against Murray came in April 1765 when the mayor and four aldermen from the city of London, supported by four MPs, presented a "Memorial and Petition from the Merchants and Traders of the City of London trading to Canada, on behalf of themselves and others" to the Board of Trade.[28] Not only did the memorial hit out at Murray's supposed failures in legal and religious policy but it deliberately linked the whole together as a threat to economic success: "And tho' your Petitioners are far from presuming to dictate in this matter, yet they are in hopes your lordships will in your great wisdom discover that a military government is entirely incompatible with the spirit and genius of commerce, and that a civil administration, with a regular House of Representatives is the only means to make this infant colony flourish." Part of this statement on military government was an outright fabrication. In the fall of 1764 Murray had been deprived of his military command. Though he had clearly wished to retain total civil and military power, claiming that none of the French subjects would ever respect him without the combined authority, the British government respected normal constitutional practice on this point by dividing civil from military jurisdiction.[29] General Gage received overall military command in North America. A junction of the civil and military powers in Quebec had been perceived in London as a wartime measure, but Murray never appreciated this fact and saw the division as a personal slight. Furthermore, the memorial represented a potent mixture of the economic and constitutional, designed for the widest possible appeal to the delicate political sensibilities of an English audience. Indeed all the petitions against Murray followed this line of combining grievances in their attacks against his governorship. The petition of the Quebec merchants in London gained that little edge, however, through the fact that the MPS and aldermen who signed appeared to have no direct contact with the trade. Their signatures were to be seen as a matter of earnest principle, to "crave an effectual and speedy redress."[30]

The net result of all these complaints appeared as a growing consensus, first among the merchant community in London, then within the political world at large, that Murray lay at the root of all the problems with Quebec. In many respects this was hardly surprising when individual grievances are examined, for most were characterized by venomous antipathy to Murray's way of governing the province. A moderate view of his actions in 1764 described the governor as possessing "a rage and rudeness of language and demeanour, as dishonourable to the trust he holds of your Majesty as painful to those who suffer from it."[31] Even people Murray tried to help turned against him. Simon Mackenzie, a general merchant in Quebec after the conquest, had first run foul of the authorities for debt but had had his property retrieved in 1763 at Murray's discretion, pending a decision on the case from London.[32] Meanwhile, Murray recommended Mackenzie to the Board of Trade for the position of agent in the event that "the forge and iron mines at St. Maurice" underwent development.[33] This charitable act did the governor no good at all. The development never took place and in 1765 this same Mackenzie petitioned Lord Bute in London for redress, citing Murray's behaviour as not only an offence to his own future but, by implication, a threat to the country's economic future in the region.[34]

These incidents may have been unfair but they were facts of everyday life for the governor. On occasions too there was no doubt that Murray proved his own worst enemy. He seemed to be completely unable to view the conduct of the merchants without contempt. Their pursuit of profit, he wrote in a report to the Board of Trade in March 1765, stemmed from "private motives which influence their conduct." When they were checked, Murray added, the merchants "display all the malice and envy which the most bitter rancour can dictate."[35] The governor's disdain sprang directly from the old-world aristocratic prejudice against the class of people who enriched themselves by trade. In a society whose future prosperity depended entirely on successfully integrating itself into the imperial trading systems, Murray's prejudices look to the twentieth-century eye naïve and sadly out of place. To cap it all, Murray was appalled at the anti-military sentiments of the merchants in Quebec, on which he commented conclusively, "the merchants hate those who despise them."[36] Needless to say, where the ethos of the mercantile groups met the governor's aristocratic prejudices from the British social and political milieu, a potential for conflict always existed.

To be fair to Murray, which is not usually done on this issue, it should be pointed out that others who lived in Quebec during this period shared his views of the merchants, and they were not all soldiers either. One very perceptive traveller, who left Montreal in 1765, drew up a report on the state of the province on his departure. Of the merchants and other new arrivals he had this brief comment: "The British inhabitants as yet settled in Canada, are the scum of the earth."[37] Several observers shared Murray's opinion that his difficulties with the merchants arose not from questions of constitutional principle but from the simple fact that, as he put it, "I could not make them magistrates, nor allow them to oppress the new subjects," so lacking in ability were they as a group.[38] His case to the government was simple: he had prevented the narrow interests of one segment of society from harming the natural well-being of the majority. From the merchants' perspective, the picture appeared a little different. Murray had not only obstructed them in their pursuit of legitimate economic concerns, the very reason Amherst had first invited them to the province, but had also contravened their rights and liberties as British subjects. The whole dispute crystallized around certain events in which the military and civilian populations clashed. This was especially true of Montreal: in late 1764 and early 1765 riots took place there, and troops of the 28th regiment made a particularly nasty attack on Thomas Walker, a JP unfortunate enough to have to deal with disputes between soldiers and citizens while trying to establish the civil authority. The significance of the Walker affair to Quebec society after the conquest is documented, but its symbolic importance tends to be overlooked.[39] In essence, the events surrounding the attack encapsulated the merchants' case against Murray. His attitude to the new arrivals had percolated down to the ranks and led to the assault on Walker. Worse still, such prejudice had led to a situation where it proved impossible to apprehend the attackers even though their identity was known. This behaviour the merchants viewed as tyranny by the military, which had no place in the eighteenth-century constitution but rather belonged to the rhetoric and mythology of Stuart despotism. This message underlay the very strong case made in London by the anti-Murray groups.

By June 1765 it had become pertinent to ask how long Murray could survive this onslaught. Seen through the eyes of the administrators and politicians in London, Quebec's problems were cause for concern. Comments in the minutes of Privy Council and Board of Trade meetings testify to the fact that the mud slung by the merchants on both sides of the Atlantic had begun to stick. Nevertheless, it should not be assumed that Murray's recall was inevitable, far from it. Murray maintained impeccable connections with the inner circles of the Grenville ministry, and as long as the government remained unaltered the governor had every reason to be optimistic about his tenure. Murray's sister, Mary, did not exaggerate when she told him on 19 February 1765, "as you are the darling of your countrymen and in high favour with the present ministry we have reason to hope that everything that is disagreeable to you will be removed."[40]

There were sound reasons for the ministry to be content with Murray's performance to date. Most important, the governor performed well in the one area of policy closest to the Grenville ministry's heart: revenue. Murray followed Grenville's example and instructions on coming to office by cracking down on smuggling, methodically surveying all possible sources of revenue for the crown in the province, and collecting taxes to defray the costs of civil government in Quebec, including the Stamp Duties in 1765. His thoroughness was much appreciated by a government under a first lord and premier attentive to the finer details of Treasury policy. Murray's proposals for the prevention of smuggling of 27 September were being used by the Treasury for developing policy over a year later.[41] His meticulous preparation of accounts covered the period both immediately before and immediately after the conquest, the first report being sent to Pitt in 1759 with the information that revenues in 1757 for the province stood at £13,961:12:10-½.[42] These financial reports were also used in the argument over the declining income from the peltry trade, when in June 1763 it was estimated that the income had reached a rock-bottom figure of £1,497:3:0, and various remedies linked to the anti-smuggling policy were proposed.[43] In fact, Murray almost managed the impossible dream in colonial policy of the early 1760s, by paying the costs of his administration in Quebec out of revenues from old French duties on wines and spirits continued in the post-conquest era. Unfortunately, the British government's ambiguity on this point in the Instructions had led to several lawsuits being filed in Quebec against the collectors of customs. Much to Murray's relief, the government's legal officers, Fletcher Norton and De Grey, had declared the governor's policy admissable on 6 August 1764. The judgment, however, possessed a sting in the tail. The governor could continue the old duties in so far as such levies "should be found sufficient to answer the expenditure of government." But the lawyers warned that in the province's "present state," the crown's "prerogative" could not be used to collect further new taxes.[44] This was a clear reminder that only parliament could legislate in money matters, and it proved enough to encourage the merchants in Quebec to continue legal action and force the governor to send the Quebec attorney-general into court to defend the case, hoping that the legal decision in London would, as he was assured it should, hold up in a Canadian court.[45]

Another factor in Murray's favour was the realization, certainly at a ministerial level, that behind the rhetoric of the merchants' protestations lay a good degree of self-interest. On the Canada Bills issue, for example, the governor's damnation of the new arrivals in Quebec received a sympathetic hearing from Lord Sandwich, the northern secretary. Sandwich was charged with negotiating a settlement of the affair between August 1763 and July 1765, and he recognized that one enormous stumbling block in the talks with the French government was the greed of the Quebec merchants and speculators, in what might be called the futures market. Many of the new arrivals had bought up considerable quantities of paper money from the old subjects and wanted to convert this "investment" at the most profitable exchange rate. As Sandwich put it: "there has been very great villainy used in Canada by selling their goods at ten times the real value when the payment was made in paper and since in the buying up these bills at an immense discount."[46] Ministers also realized that several land sharks had arrived in the province after 1760, causing consternation among the old subjects in their property dealings. The targets of their operations were those Canadians refusing to take the oaths of allegiance to the new king. Those buying up land maintained (echoing the restrictive property laws in Ireland) that these Roman Catholic subjects should be considered aliens without rights to inherit a transfer property to others under the new reign.[47] Again the government's law officers were called upon to give judgment in this murky affair, and the speculators suffered another reverse when the attorney-general, Fletcher Norton, reported to the Board of Trade on 27 July 1764: "I conceive that the definitive treaty which has had the sanction and been approved by both Houses of Parliament meant to give, and that it has in fact and in law given to the inhabitants of those ceded countries a permanent and transmissable interest in their land there; and that to put a different construction upon the treaty would dishonour the crown and the truth, and it would be saying that by the treaty they were promised the quiet enjoyment of their property but by the laws were to be immediately stripped of their estates."[48] If the government wanted to go down the path of restrictive and oppressive property rights then it would require an act of parliament for Quebec alone. Yet another group seeking private advantage from the conquest had fallen foul of misinterpreted legal and constitutional precedents.

The favour shown Murray, therefore, arose from a good understanding of the intricate problems facing the new regime in Quebec. Murray's stress on the centrality of the religious issue to his difficulties in creating a British-style administration in the province had, by the fall of 1764, begun to revise ministerial thinking. Apart from the governor's personal dispatches, Murray's personal emissary, H.T. Cramahé, played an important role in these changes. Soon after his arrival in London, for example, he seems to have been able to gain access to Lord Mansfield's influential ear. This was done through an intermediary, George Ross, a wealthy Scottish politician and friend to both Murray and Mansfield. Murray had always realized the importance of bringing the great lawyer to his side, and Cramahé's job was to explain the inadequacies of the governor's Commission and Instructions with regard to the law. The task was executed well: Cramahé told Murray in January 1765 that Mansfield's "opinion of matters, I believe, coincides pretty much with your own sentiments," adding, with perceptive insight, "He is always consulted, but avoids shew."[49]

Reports of this kind helped Murray justify in his own mind the intent of involving the Canadians more widely in the legal process that was embodied in the ordinance of 17 September 1764. More important, however, Cramahé was able to put in perspective the violent protest in Quebec and London against Murray's action. Mansfield certainly gave the governor and his representative a good hearing, and, to their delight, appeared to accept the case for a more tolerant approach to the legal and religious problems of the province. On 24 December 1764, Mansfield wrote to Grenville, the prime minister, "Is it possible that we have abolished their laws, and customs, and forms of judicature all at once? – a thing never to be attempted or wished. The history of the world don't furnish an instance of so rash and unjust an act by any conqueror whatsoever: much less by the Crown of England, which has always left to the conquered their own laws and usages with a change only so far as the sovereignty was concerned."[50] This outburst settled any doubts about the government re-examining its legal settlement for the province, as Grenville was not one to ignore the advice of Mansfield on any judicial point at all. Indeed, there is a hint in Mansfield's statement that he considered that the ordinance was too much of an interference in Canadian life, and that the hapless Murray had not gone far enough in his concessions to the old subjects. But, in essence, the message behind the ministerial response to the governor's problems appeared to be an encouragement to carry on running the administration of Quebec along the same lines. The best example of this certainly came on 3 June 1765 when the Privy Council considered a religious settlement for the province entitled "Heads of a Plan for the Establishment of Ecclesiastical Affairs in the Province of Quebec."[51] Though Murray was not to see the plan through, he could take credit for the thrust of the document, which built upon his ideas of toleration and those of Shelburne in 1763. The blunt truth of the matter for the politicians in London was that the

Catholic Canadians, not the two or three hundred Protestants, represented the potential fifth column in the North American empire. If Murray's policies could neutralize the former, the government might tolerate complaints from the latter. Cramahé saw this mode of thought etched in the government's attitude to Murray's administration. Ministers accepted the governor's policies "in a right light," he observed, "and are disposed to give the people content[ment]."[52]

Thus by the spring of 1765 Murray still had a firm backing in Britain for his tenure as governor. Yet how quickly the situation would change over the course of the summer months! The man who had done so much to initiate a change in ministerial thinking would not be in a position to enjoy the fruits of his labours. Even at the height of his power in the spring of 1765, rumblings of discontent with his leadership had begun to be heard outside the normal confines of mercantile pressure groups. The press had finally caught on to the fact that relations between the governor and the old and new subjects in Quebec were far from ideal. The unhappy incidents of Walker's assault and the billeting riots in Montreal, for example, were discussed in the *London Magazine* of April 1765, with a clear implication that the governor did not have complete control over troops and civilians. Furthermore, the Board of Trade, which never displayed the sympathies for Murray's position expressed at ministerial level, lost faith in the governor over this matter. In the absence of Murray's long-delayed report on Walker's case, the board drew its own unfavourable conclusions, recommending to the Privy Council "That Governor Murray, and Lieutenant Governor Burton, did not upon this occasion conduct themselves according to the duty of their several situations." The privy councillors considering this issue on 21 June 1765 did not sanction the board's rebuke, but neither did they disown it. Murray was told of the council's "surprise" at his lack of co-operation in the matter and ordered to provide "an immediate and particular account" of the official action taken in Walker's case.[53] This episode did nothing for the governor's reputation or position, but worse was yet to come. On 9 July 1765 the bedrock of Murray's support crumbled when the Grenville ministry was dismissed from office and all the governor's high political connections dissolved. The new administration under Lord Rockingham's leadership meant a change of personnel that threw not only Murray's future into doubt but also the policies for Quebec being at that moment so patiently revised. On the eve of the first anniversary of civilian rule, the governor's prediction that settling Quebec's government would be "troublesome" had proved disturbingly accurate. Public and politicians alike could see little achievement beyond the piles of dissenting documentation from the initial months of Murray's endeavour. The confident assumptions behind the Proclamation and Instructions lay in dust, and the hope of a smooth transition from French to British rule in Quebec remained just that in the summer of 1765.

The True Spirit of a Lawful Sovereign: The Rockingham Ministry and Quebec 1765-66

The appointment of the Rockingham ministry in July 1765 looked about the worst possible move in the search for a solution to the problem of governing Quebec. The contemporary judgment of the new and inexperienced ministers proved harsh. Members of the "lutestring" government, as it became known, had a reputation for administering racing at Newmarket rather than the nation's business. The MP for Clackmannan, James Abercromby, commented wryly that "since New Market jockeys were employed, he was in hopes to be, sometime or other a minister, as he had the same kind of education."[1] On the shoulders of these ministers rested both the future of Murray and the tenor of his administration. The governor himself was not so pessimistic, despite the demotion of his patrons and friends in Grenville's administration. He adopted a more realistic view of the situation, pointing out to one correspondent that "the new rulers cannot possibly give less attention" to Quebec's affairs than Halifax and his boards had done over the previous years.[2] In this assumption Murray proved accurate. Unfortunately, he could not predict that his career and the troubles in the province would become inextricably linked in the minds of the new ministers. Under Grenville, Murray and his measures had been perceived as separate entities, but Grenville's successors made no such distinction. Barely three months into the new regime, Murray was ordered to prepare to come home to explain himself. A fresh approach to Quebec's problems would be inaugurated without the central figure in the drama of the province's early history under British rule.[3]

It is not certain that the Rockinghams entered office with the express intention of weeding Murray out of the governor's post. The initial impression to be gleaned from the change of government is not of new approaches to Quebec policy but rather of change in responsibilities in the way colonial policy was administered. The principal players in the direction of policy under the new government were Henry Seymour Conway, southern secretary, and Lord Dartmouth, president of the Board of Trade. There had been a considerable shift of political emphasis with these appointments, for Dartmouth secured a place in the cabinet with his office, raising the profile of the Board of Trade to a more senior level. The previous president, Lord Hillsborough, had encouraged Dartmouth to insist on such a move so as to avoid the frustrations he had suffered, surveying all the information on Quebec but only able to recommend rather than initiate policy for the province at ministerial level. "Without this [power]," Hillsborough wrote, "Lord Dartmouth will suffer continual disappointments and too probably undergo undeserved disgrace."[4] So far so good; if the transition worked smoothly, and Dartmouth could emulate Halifax, who had enjoyed a similar status in the late 1750s, policy decisions might be expedited, for the most knowledgeable minister on Quebec would be involved in the executive function of government. There is no doubt too that from the beginning Dartmouth took the problem of Quebec's future seriously. As early as 6 August 1765 the cabinet met, probably at Dartmouth's behest, "to come to a determination" on the subject, owing to the disorganized state that the province's affairs appeared to have sunk to in the eyes of administrators in London.[5]

Though it can be more rewarding to look at the Board of Trade records for clues to Quebec policy under Rockingham's administration, caution is also advisable. Dartmouth did not obtain all the perquisites of senior ministerial rank. No colonial patronage came his way, nor did any of the powers traditionally vested in the Treasury and Admiralty over the colonies. Hillsborough had found this lack of discretionary power particularly galling, and he had urged Dartmouth in vain to rectify the matter. Dartmouth's personality also lent weight to the contemporary view that here was a collection of ministers far too inexperienced to survive an arduous parliamentary session. After examining Dartmouth's experience at the Board of Trade between August 1765 and May 1766, one experienced politician and observer, Lord Chesterfield, wrung his hands in despair, for he believed that a seat in cabinet had changed nothing. The senior secretaries had jealously retained all their ancient powers of patronage and influence to what he considered the detriment of sensible decision-making on colonial matters. Chesterfield exhorted Dartmouth to do more, and ask for the establishment of a separate secretaryship for America if necessary. The trouble lay in faint-heartedness. "Lay aside upon this occasion your natural timidity and diffidence," Chesterfield urged, "in my zeal for the success of this affair, I protest I consider the public service much more than I do yours."[6]

This sort of irresolution and inexperience coupled with the lack of room for manoeuvre in decision-making has done little for the Rockinghams in historical analysis. Their reputation as fumbling political amateurs provides the perfect backdrop for the leading scholar on the first Rockingham ministry to comment that, when faced with Quebec's problems, the ministry's reaction "was predictably one of concession and surrender."[7] This judgment, however, seems severe and unfair. True, information and decision-making on Quebec continued to fly from pillar to post amongst the various departments charged with specific responsibilities in the colonies. Nevertheless, the Rockingham ministry would achieve more solid progress on a comprehensive scheme of government for the province than any other administration up to 1774. Indeed, its recommendations would form the very basis of the legislation embodied in the Quebec Act. This breakthrough occurred not because the Rockinghams were genuinely more liberal or radical in thought than other governments of the period, but rather because they were better informed than both their predecessors and (to a degree) their successors; as a body of ministers, they acted on the intelligence available to them with the minimum of bureaucratic procrastination. In twelve months the government made great strides towards the complete revision of Halifax's ill-advised policies so earnestly canvassed by Murray.

The metamorphosis of the Rockinghams from novices to experts on Quebec policy proved a complex affair and owed much to their contacts outside as well as inside the government. Over the year, information, intelligence, and advice that formed the bedrock of policy initiatives came to the government from numerous official and unofficial sources. In one area in particular, however, they enjoyed a great advantage over their predecessors: access to the work about Quebec compiled by Grenville's administration. This was not a negligible matter. Just before they had entered office, for example, the Board of Trade had prepared a long report for the Privy Council on the fundamental problem of a religious settlement, a report from which all other policy would flow. In his first weeks in office, Dartmouth had the routine task of reviewing the report and board minutes on the problem and making what minor alterations he deemed necessary prior to its submission, with other proposals, to the Privy Council on 2 September.[8] Hillsborough's time at the board helped Dartmouth in more ways than one.

An equally important source of information, which was in many ways unique to the Rockingham administration, came from its mercantile allies in the City and country at large.[9] The merchants trading to North America had their own committee in London and played an influential role not only in Rockingham's agony over the repeal of the Stamp Act but also in his decisions on Quebec. In fact, several of the merchants, like Barlow Trecothick, who in 1764 had signed the London petition against Murray later published in the *Quebec Gazette*, were leading members of this committee and had definite views on how Britain's relationship with Quebec should develop. That they had the ear of ministers cannot be doubted. Another member of the committee of London merchants trading to North America, Brook Watson, acted as a go-between with the government in the settlement of the Canada Bills issue. It is indeed striking that the manner of organizing the petition against Murray's supposed damage to Anglo-Canadian trade in 1764 looks so much like a dress rehearsal for the petitioning movement against the Stamp Act. After Murray's early recall, Trecothick in particular must have considered the use of petitions a lethal weapon under Rockingham's government as he led the London merchants against the Stamp Act in 1766.

The last source of useful intelligence and advice available to the government came from the unclaimed and unsolicited reports sent to various ministers and boards over its year in office. These documents can be found in the public and private archives of the leading politicians in the Rockingham ministry. Whether or not they were all read and digested is a matter of conjecture, but they should not be ignored, for many offered incisive appraisals, often from first-hand experience, of the situation in Quebec. What is definitely lacking during these months is press comment on the Quebec issue, other than the normal trade news that appeared regularly. Until Francis Maseres, an able British lawyer of Huguenot extraction, published his pamphlet *Considerations on the Expediency of Procuring an Act of Parliament for the Settlement of the Province of Quebec* in the spring of 1766, it can only be assumed that the public had simply decided to give the ministry the benefit of the doubt as it set about devising a policy for the province.

How did Quebec policy emerge from the inner councils of the Rockingham ministry? There were three main stages: an initial burst of action and enthusiasm, followed by a period of reflection and distraction as the Stamp Act protests gathered momentum in the thirteen American colonies, and then a concerted attempt to implement a framework of government for the province in June 1766. The underlying thrust of policy decisions in each of these stages matured from a synthesis of the reports circulating among senior ministers, and can be traced from the initial weeks of the Rockingham ministry's dealings with the Quebec problem. Indeed, no sooner had ministers in the front line of policy-making, like Dartmouth, assumed their posts than they experienced a first taste of the extramural interests looking for a change of direction in the administration of the province.

H.T. Cramahé, Murray's personal envoy, was first into the fray, displaying a profound understanding of the mechanics behind the formulation of colonial policy. In early August 1765, he deliberately sought out those politicians at the core of the decision-making process on Quebec, first canvassing Dartmouth at the Board of Trade and then Mellish, secretary of the Treasury; he would have confronted Charles Yorke had he at that time accepted the seals as attorney-general and taken up his office. The first two calls, Cramahé reported to Murray on 10 August, offered cause for optimism.[10] Dartmouth "promised" to take Quebec's affairs into consideration as soon as the board met "and to give them all possible Dispatch." In a similar tone, Mellish assured Cramahé that "the Lords of the Board were sensible of the expediency of taking some resolution with regard to the revenues of Quebec." Cramahé was enough of a realist, however, to recognize that such reassurances could not be taken at face value, especially as Yorke, whom he was right to perceive as critical to any future judicial and religious settlement, had yet to be consulted. Cramahé therefore took the very sensible course of supporting his verbal representations with a written report on the state of Quebec, which he sent to Dartmouth on 24 August. It was done, he told Murray later, from the simple conviction that "when the present ministers began to do business, as they could not know much about the province, I thought it right to lay before them the present state of it."[11]

The document that Dartmouth received was a consummate piece of erudite prose on Quebec's difficulties at that time. In fact, it practically mapped out the very course the Rockingham ministry would follow over the next year in its dealings with the province. Cramahé spelt out the urgency of the situation in the report's first two pages, highlighting the three problems, "Ecclesiastical Affairs, Administration of Justice and Revenues" over which "the Canadians have been alarmed."[12] On the religious issue he displayed a keen understanding of the controversial decisions waiting to be made in order to satisfy the new subjects. Following a brief history of the church in New France, and a blunt reminder that the British government had taken no action over "Petitions presented in 1763 by the Clergy and laity on that subject," he recommended that the government calm the waters of the religious issue by appointing a bishop. In Cramahé's eyes, the ramifications of this action could only be beneficial. Logic determined it would please all the king's new subjects to have a resident spiritual leader, "subsisted out of their Revenues to perform the functions of his office decently without external pomp or shew." More important, however, it held a broader appeal for the decision-makers in that "This will be the means of having a Canadian clergy, a measure which sound policy seems to dictate, and in time the other dominions ceded to Great Britain may be furnished from hence with priests, which will be far more eligible than suffering them to creep in from France or other countries." Cramahé had certainly been clever in his approach to this issue. His practical commonsensical approach hit upon the fundamental concerns that would influence the future direction of Quebec policy. As he pointed out in his conclusion to the section on religion, the introduction of a Protestant ministry in the province would have to be undertaken "with a becoming decency." The rapid change of faith envisaged by Halifax and his declarations of intent would not achieve the end desired: in Cramahé's words, "If these people cannot be won over by gentle means, experience teaches, that compulsion or restrictions will only be apt to rivet them in their ancient opinions."

On the question of the administration of justice, Cramahé was equally forthright, believing that, in contrast to the religious issue, immediate remedial action could solve the difficulties that had arisen. First, it was imperative that the government's senior legal officers, and those acting for or against Canadians in the courts, be French-speaking and display some knowledge of the "original customs of the Province." This ill-disguised reference to the woeful Hey and Suckling was taken to heart in the following spring when Francis Maseres accepted the post of attorney-general in Quebec. Yet Cramahé wanted more than simple window-dressing. He also proposed that cases between two Canadians be heard in their own tongue and before juries made up of French-speaking subjects. Further, the person presiding over the case, even if from Britain, should speak French and be versed in the Canadians' law. A marginal note by Cramahé recognized that "this would tend to keep up the distinction between Canadian and British," but nevertheless he pressed the measures for, what to many modern Canadians has a familiar ring, the necessity "that all lawyers should well understand the French language." The empirical wisdom of these proposals was again stressed in the conclusion to this section. A practical manifestation of British understanding could not be neglected in the administration of justice because the results would be catastrophic. In ignorance, Cramahé wrote in his deadpan manner, "we shall never gain the affection of the people and ... they will seize the first opportunity that may offer, of returning under their old Masters." It could not have been put in a blunter fashion for the consumption of a politician. Cramahé's suggestions went right to the heart of the revision in attitudes taking place in the administration of justice. Only Cramahé's proposed clauses granting that a case between English- and French-speaking subjects should be tried before a split jury of six old and six new settlers were lacking from the settlement eventually proposed by the Rockingham ministry and later embodied in the Quebec Act itself.

The last section of Cramahé's paper, "As to the Revenues," appears more of a summary of the revenue situation and sundry related items. He surveyed the four main existing sources of income for the government: "The Farm of the Posts at Tadousac etc, The Quist Rents, The Lots et Ventes, The Duty on Rum and Other Spirits." Then followed a list of office-holders and public buildings, including those that would devolve on the crown after the expulsion of the Jesuits and certain female religious orders. A last brief passage covered relations with the Indians and contained a recommendation to build a citadel (fortress) for the defence of the city of Quebec and the surrounding country. Even in these basically descriptive passages, however, Cramahé made his point in style. First he showed how little serious thought had been given to changing the French system of tax-farming under the new regime – an amazing oversight in view of the prejudice and obsession eighteenth-century politicians expressed about exercising control over public revenues. Second, Cramahé's talk of an expensive citadel and of the officials now holding posts, to be supplemented with others in order to turn Quebec into a regularly staffed British colony, merely underlined his main point about the inadequacy of present revenues. The only flexibility that the governor possessed at that time was to increase public income through the old French duty on imported rum and wines. But, as Cramahé observed, consumption was limited so these duties could not be increased excessively or indefinitely to meet future needs. The implication was clear: the whole basis of future government and defence, even on primary matters like money for "silver medals, blankets, ammunition and other presents" for the allegiance of the Indian nations, required legislation.

It is doubtful that the Rockingham ministry really wished to hear such a message in the summer of 1765, as the cabinet dealt with the reaction to the Grenville ministry's attempts to raise revenue in defence of the North American colonies. Indeed, ministers were faced with a Hobson's choice over the matter. To take action on the revenue issue in the form of new taxes or duties would hardly be appropriate in light of the protests against the measures of 1763 to 1765. Not to move on the problem, on the other hand, would leave the government no other recourse but to continue block payments from the exchequer, under the various supply estimates, to support the Quebec establishment. Not suprisingly, in the light of the Rockinghamite retreat on the Stamp Act, ministers chose the latter, temporarily expensive but less troublesome, means of tackling Quebec's revenue problem. None of this detracts from Cramahé's achievement during the summer of 1765. In view of the early history of Quebec under British rule, it is impossible to overestimate the scope of Cramahé's submission to Dartmouth. In many respects he merely repeated what Murray had already stated. But the task was completed in only one precise and polished letter, to dramatic effect. The submission contained all the elements and most of the solutions to the problems of governing Quebec, and provided a perfect grounding for Dartmouth and his colleagues in the administrative complexities involved in governing the province.

Cramahé had been wise to move when he did, for nothing had changed when it came to lobbying on Quebec under the new government. Where Cramahé went, Fowler Walker, the agent for the British traders and interests in Quebec, was sure to follow. His appeal to ministers on the province's future reached Dartmouth's desk on 31 August 1765.[13] It was not the considered overview presented by Cramahé. Fowler Walker's purpose was simply to have the incumbent governor removed. The report took the form of a short letter from the agent, enclosing a long anonymous paper on the province by a Quebec resident – the latter most notable for the vindictiveness of its personal attacks on Murray's way of administering the province. Within these attacks, case histories were itemized *ad nauseam* to demonstrate how individuals, both English and French, had suffered at the hands of Murray's capricious decisions. Some episodes obviously suggested a great deal of shady behaviour by Murray, especially in the dispersal of land after the conquest. One common grievance in this tirade illustrated the powers available to the governor under a military regime. It concerned Murray's frequent "seizing the property of a merchant and taking it as he said for the King's Account at 150 per cent less than it was worth and afterwards causing the same to be sold *privately by his Agents* at an *enormous profit.*" Worse still for those merchants involved, no means of redress existed to counter the governor's arbitrary decisions – Murray remained judge and jury in these dealings, his contempt of the mercantile classes being given full rein and official sanction.

On such issues the case against Murray certainly held water. As the anonymous author of the paper pointed out, all the traders and merchants in Quebec were affected by the governor's "unfriendly" behaviour; the Canadians in particular, he added, "look upon all our boasted Libertys, they tell us, as nothing when governed by such a Man." Many of these strong points were weakened, however, by being submerged in the very lengthy *ad hominem* attacks not only on Murray but on every one of his appointments to the Quebec council and other civil posts. The impression gleaned from reading these interminable passages can only be that the writer was a man with a well-developed sense of paranoia, willing to grind his personal axes in public. The whole tone of the report found expression in the author's phrase: "I have no personal enmity or dislike to the present Governor of Canada as a man, but of him as Governor I have the highest detestation."

Fowler Walker was not blind to the glaring weaknesses inherent in his correspondent's report, and enclosed with it his own explanation. It proved nothing more than a confidence trick. Though Fowler Walker took care to explain his role as agent for the British merchants in "the unhappy province," he recapitulated the case he had been pressing against Murray since the early spring of 1765. He simply took it for granted that Dartmouth and his colleagues in the new ministry accepted Murray's guilt in the mismanagement of Quebec's government. The intent behind Fowler Walker's letter was to touch certain nerves in the ministry as a prelude to persuading cabinet of the wisdom of Murray's dismissal. The first point he raised certainly demonstrated his knowledge about the Rockingham ministry's political insecurities. In the best rhetorical fashion, Fowler Walker asked: surely Murray was only allowed to continue in office because Lord Bute "patronized and protected him"? The second point then showed his familiarity with the Rockinghams' constituent support. The truth of the "severe charges against Mr. Murray" by the merchants cannot be doubted, wrote Fowler Walker; the well-documented evidence made it impossible to prove otherwise. Thus, it was imperative that the government resolve the existing equation. The governor's actions damaged the economic ties between Britain and Quebec; if he was removed, so also would be the handicap to a prosperous transatlantic trade. The mixture of Bute, the Rockinghamite nemesis over the next two decades, with dire economic projections represented a brew strong enough to turn the stomach of all the new ministers.

In one week, therefore, Dartmouth confronted the two principal strategies among the range of possible solutions to the Quebec problem. Neither was solicited but both embodied the practical and ideological problems facing the new ministry. None of the lobbyists knew which way the government would turn, of course; but in the circumstances Dartmouth took the sensible course of urging a thorough research and deliberation on the topic, building on the work done by the bureaucrats to date and canvassing opinions from his contacts on more difficult points at issue. The government as a body did not seek to avoid the thornier religious or judicial problems facing it. In an initial burst of activity during August and September 1765, ministers undertook a wide-ranging review of Quebec's problems, which had already been given priority in the cabinet's first meetings. The initial impetus on the road to finding solutions came from Dartmouth, who had the advantage of taking office just as the old officers at the Board of Trade had completed surveys of each area of concern in Quebec's government. It must have struck Dartmouth straight away how the course followed by the administrators bore a striking resemblance to the terrain already mapped out by Cramahé and Fowler Walker. The hope for achieving a lasting settlement in the province revolved as ever, around the issues of religion, justice, revenue, and Murray.

The most important official report to hand in August 1765 concerned the religious issue, and originated in Murray's appeals to reverse Halifax's policies and in petitions from the French inhabitants for a spiritual leader and the fulfilment of promises that the British had made at the capitulation and in the clauses of the Peace of Paris. In fact, the revision of thought on this issue began in May 1765, in the last days of Grenville's ministry. In that month the Board of Trade spent two or three sessions discussing a document entitled "Heads of a Plan for Establishment of Ecclesiastical Affairs in the Province of Quebec."[14] The authorship of this paper is in doubt. It may have drawn on the work done by Shelburne at the Board of Trade in 1763, and also on notes on the problem submitted and "drawn up by me at Lord Halifax's desire," by the archbishop of York, Robert Hay-Drummond, in 1764.[15] That it is a composite of several views seems certain, for Shelburne read the paper in 1766 and did not like its general thrust, commenting: "the Plan proceeds upon the supposition that a conformity in religion is a necessary part of good Policy, and is I think in many respects both severe and defective."[16] This severity did underlie the final report approved by the Board of Trade on 30 May 1765 and passed to the Privy Council for their opinion and recommendation.[17] Much stricter regulations governing the practice of Catholicism than Shelburne had envisaged were put forward, with no mention of a bishop at all, simply a "Person, so licenced to superintend the affairs of the Romish Church."[18] Perhaps the author just could not bring himself to use the word *bishop*, the climate of anti-papist opinion being what it was. The more striking phrases of the paper certainly play up to such prejudices. In several passages there was an almost frenzied obsession with disallowing the Canadian clergy opportunity for "any outward Pomp or Parade ... public procession or other ceremonies." The hope was that with the establishment of a Protestant church and the Society for the Propagation of the Gospel, under the bishop of London's guidance, the French populace would be gradually weaned away from their church. In the eighteenth-century bureaucratic mind, it was obviously important to the process of converting Catholics that the visual image of the faith be obliterated before the spiritual transformation could begin. The one realistic argument in this paper was at last a recognition that Quebec could not be turned into a Protestant colony in the foreseeable future. The Privy Council discussed the document on 13 June 1765, along with the law officers' opinion that the English anti-Catholic legislation did not apply in Quebec. The result of this deliberation would prove quite a landmark in the history of the province, for their lordships of the council decided to proceed on the basis of toleration for Catholicism in its unique North American setting, only asking the law officers how this "may be properly and effectively carried into execution."[19] In the middle of this process of clarification the Grenville ministry fell, and the new government took office with the decision on how to proceed on the religious issue in the melting pot. This indecision was exacerbated by the fact that Charles Yorke, who would guide much of the Quebec policy under the Rockinghams, did not accept the attorney-general's post until 25 August. Still, the information was there to be reviewed by the new cabinet, and Cramahé's submission to Dartmouth had not left any doubt about the urgency and importance of settling the issue.

It was a similar tale with the revenue problem. On 14 June 1765 the Board of Trade had prepared a report on the means by which Murray had accrued revenue since the conquest for the support of the civil establishment.[20] It addressed the problem of the insufficiency and dubious legality of the governor's reapplication of old duties and impositions to support a new establishment, recommending that the Privy Council consider "whether a proper authority should not be given for collecting the same in the future, or such part of them as His Majesty should think proper."[21] This phrasing clearly raised several questions, as the Rockinghams would soon discover. The "proper" authority could, in theory, be an order by the king in council, an act of parliament granting the governor special powers to levy taxes, or an assembly in the province of Quebec promised in the Proclamation. The Rockinghams would consider all three possibilities settling on the second but unable to carry it into effect. Meanwhile the Privy Council appeared none too happy about being confronted with a decision on this point without any clear recommendations. On 21 June council discussed the revenue question but postponed further deliberation to an unspecified date.[22] Again, it was left to the new ministry to pick up the pieces. This the new council did on 22 August, referring the problem, in the tried and trusted manner, to the attorney- and solicitor-generals with an instruction "to prepare a draft of an instrument containing a proper authority from his Majesty for collecting the said duties."[23] The "instrument" or draft bill never became public knowledge, but it makes interesting reading in the context of the lobby by the Rockingham ministry's mercantile allies and their demand for an assembly in Quebec. There is no pretence here of ever considering the change of allowing a representative body to be called. The draft bill stated quite categorically that "the said Province of Quebec has not hitherto been, is not now, nor is likely to be for some time to be [sic] such as to admit for a Lower House of Assembly or House of Representatives being convened." The only sop to those critics who might perceive an attack on fundamental English liberties in this bill was the proposal that it be limited to fourteen years' duration.[24]

It can be seen from this just how much the realities of the situation in Quebec imposed a continuity in the revision of policy between the Grenville and Rockingham administrations. In addition, the government's legal officers would have an inordinate influence on the formulation of policy, though the direction it would follow was again predetermined by the decision to revise Halifax's approach in 1764. In the discussions on the administration of justice and the complaints against Murray, evidence of this is more readily apparent. On both these issues ministers seemed extremely well informed soon after coming into office. They had obviously been primed about Murray by the merchants, and had read the information on the contentious courts issue carefully. Indeed, there is every indication that the merchants had taken care to inform the newspapers of the problems on this front to help prod the ministry in the direction favoured by the group. In a rare exception to press ignorance on Canadian affairs at this time, the *Public Advertizer* published snippets of information on Quebec's legal problems in two August issues, of the 7th and 30th, albeit without editorial comment.

Two documents bear out the ministry's willingness to act immediately on these points. The first can be found in Granville's papers and is entitled "A Memorandum of things necessary for establishing Laws and government in the province of Quebec either by Act of Parliament Order of the King in Council, or by the proposed council at Quebec." It almost certainly dates from August 1765 because the proposals contained therein completely match the development documented in the public records. Ten recommendations were made about the policy to be followed in the province. The first made a general declaration "to get rid of the Proclamation of 1763"; the next two concerned the "instrument" by which revenue could be collected, and the last seven covered the reform of judicial procedures and administration.[25] It seems likely that it was drawn up for a cabinet or council meeting, embodying as it does the main ideas in another document on Quebec's problems emanating from the Board of Trade on 2 September 1765.[26] The thrust of both papers was to undermine Murray's ordinance of September 1764 and to take up Mansfield's hint that the hapless governor had not gone far enough with concessions to the Catholic Canadians. The particular points censured were the exclusion of Canadian lawyers from the King's Bench Court, the denial of French precedents in property cases, and the failure to provide for bail and writs of habeas corpus. The board made tentative recommendations at the end of the report for a new court structure and remedies to the main problems described above, but the inevitable conclusion reached was that Murray had done a disservice to all concerned and his ordinance could not be ratified. Needless to say, Charles Yorke was again asked to produce a formula for eradicating these administrative ills.

The ministry's initial energy over the Quebec issue was almost spent. Dartmouth and his board issued only one more report on Quebec during the summer. On 2 September they addressed the king with a "representation" about the constitutional problems of the province.[27] The document came in response to Murray's long-awaited report on the state of Quebec, originally requested in the wake of the attack on Thomas Walker the previous winter. Murray's submission was reviewed by the Board of Trade on 29 August and evoked the short retort or "Representation" of 2 September.[28] It highlighted two points for immediate consideration to remedy the constitutional difficulties in Quebec.

The first point raised produced the startling proposal "of calling a General Assembly consisting of the Governor, the Council and a House of Representatives."[29] The means to this end would be simple, according to the author. Quebec would be divided into three electoral districts, and, though only Protestants would be elected to the assembly, everyone would partake in the elections, "seeing that we know of no Law by which Roman Catholics, as such, are disqualified from being Electors." The logic in this proposition assumed that everyone would prefer an assembly of any description to the existing executive rule. "Above all," the report continued, an assembly would be able to provide "an equal and adequate taxation, a permanent and constitutional revenue." It is difficult to trace exactly how this opinion emerged, as it flew in the face of all official thinking at the time. Had the merchants, led by Fowler Walker, pulled off an impressive personal coup by persuading the novice Dartmouth that an assembly would eradicate mercantile agitation in the province? This is perhaps not so fanciful as it sounds. When Edmund Burke reflected on the achievements of the Rockingham administration in late 1766, it was this close working relationship between ministers and the trading men of the kingdom that he stressed: "That Administration was the first which proposed, and encouraged public Meetings, and free Consultations of Merchants from all Parts of the Kingdom; by which Means the truest Lights have been received; great Benefits have been already derived to Manufacture and Commerce; and the most extensive Prospects are open'd for further Improvement. Under them, the Interests of our Northern and Southern Colonies, before that Time jarring and dissonant, were understood, compared, adjusted and perfectly reconciled."[30] Obviously such claims had more to do with the Stamp Act crisis than Quebec. But the general thrust of the statement, and the common thread of personnel and method in the practice of lobbying, make the passage relevant to the whole North American trading empire and all the problems confronted there by the Rockinghams.

Whatever the motive for this proposal in the Representation, it never saw the full light of day. The Privy Council considered the document, along with others, on 3 October 1765, but postponed further consideration to another unspecified date.[31] This action buried the idea of an assembly along the lines proposed by Dartmouth and the Board of Trade. The concept of establishing a Protestant political ascendancy in Quebec was one philosophical nettle that the Rockingham ministry, despite the views of its allies, refused to grasp. The hard choice of continuing with executive rule was forced on the government by the realities of the situation in Quebec. Murray's warnings about the necessity of satisfying all the king's subjects in Canada still held true.

The one issue on which Dartmouth had his way in the Representation of 2 September was Murray's recall. However, he would not return in an odour of official condemnation. In the Board of Trade's view, the complaints against Murray had reached such a number and pitch that the government was left with no other choice but to request that the governor "return to this kingdom, in order to give your Majesty an Account of the state of the Colony."[32] In the circumstances Murray might have expected a worse fate. He had lost all his powerful ministerial allies with the demise of the Grenville administration, and his association with Bute, for whom the Rockinghams reserved an obsessive hatred, did not endear him to the new government or its supporters. Such natural political disadvantages coupled with the flood of criticism reaching London in 1765 could have spelt immediate dismissal. Yet the course of events did not reach this drastic stage. Murray's end as resident governor came with the government's realization that he had not only upset the English merchants in Quebec but also angered the French-speaking traders. A common complaint from the Canadian mercantile community was the lack of opportunity to share in the trading spoils of their new rulers, a situation exacerbated, in their opinion, by Murray's oppressive ordinances, especially his attempts to raise revenue to support the civil establishment. A letter from a French company in Quebec that found its way into Dartmouth's hands encapsulates the grievances felt at the new regime: "Their new masters ... instead of spreading riches they exact a heavy burden, which they cannot bear ... Trade dies out, the necessary, indeed indispensable, articles cannot be obtained and their own produce of which they make use cannot form the means of payment."[33]

Such intelligence certainly caused alarm in ministerial circles, where fear of the wider repercussions of Murray's behaviour ran free. The government knew that the Canadians were well informed of the governor's actions. In

February 1765 Murray had ordered that all his ordinances be published in the *Quebec Gazette*, circulated, and then read by the curés of every parish after church services.[34] If this measure had unwittingly helped to spread discontent throughout the province and the French mercantile community, where would it end? Apprehensive of letting Murray continue to supervise a worsening situation, therefore, ministers removed the governor from the firing line. It could not have been an easy decision, for in truth the Rockinghams had no clear idea of what to do in the short term. In many respects Murray had pointed the Rockinghams in the direction of policy decisions then being formulated in the government's inner councils. It was not a straightforward decision to dispense with Murray's legacy in Quebec and adopt policies favoured by the merchants. The governor's critics had not triumphed or ensured that he returned home in disgrace, as portrayed by Burt.[35] The Rockinghams were right to appreciate that there were two sides to every story. Many letters from Quebec, after the order to return had gone out, protested against Murray's removal. As one letter from "les Citoyens de la ville de Quebec" put it, reform not removal of the governor was the point at issue. They disavowed all published reports of Canadian discontent with Murray's supposed oppressive and arbitrary proceedings.[36] In these circumstances, bringing Murray home in the most protracted manner possible, and without outward show of disgrace or demotion, appeared a sensible compromise. It would be 28 June 1766 before the governor left the province, and his replacement, Guy Carleton, was simply a lieutenant-governor sent to take temporary command. The delayed recall allowed the Rockinghams invaluable time to continue the quest for an empirical policy so desperately needed in Quebec.

Now that the Rockinghams had paused for thought, and passed responsibility for policy to the government's legal officers, Quebec's problems tended to become submerged in the growing protest in the thirteen American colonies against the Stamp Act. Official records bear witness to how little was done with regard to the province over the next eight months. Nevertheless it would be misleading to imply that bureaucratic inaction meant that nothing at all was done to further the cause for a Quebec settlement. The information-gathering process continued through the fall and winter of 1765-66. The Rockinghams took a leaf out of Mansfield's book on the problem of formulating colonial policy by consulting what contemporaries then regarded as outside experts. Dartmouth, for example, corresponded with the leading Quaker physician and author Dr John Fothergill. In 1765 Fothergill wrote and published the influential tract *Considerations Relative To The North American Colonies*, which, among other things, advocated the repeal of the Stamp Act and a whole range of concessions to maintain the allegiance of the Americans. He had many friends and relatives in North America from whom he derived a sound knowledge of its political and economic affairs. It was this knowledge that Dartmouth tapped, expressing particular interest in the constitutional issues surrounding the revenue question in Quebec. Fothergill's response must have given Dartmouth pleasure. The good doctor saw no similarity between American and Canadian objections to the right of Britain to levy taxes on the people there. In Quebec's case, he said: "If no express agreement was made that they should enjoy the British privilege of having no moneys raised upon them but by the consent of their representatives, the British Parliament have a right as with [any] power to make what assessments upon them they think fit."[37] Murray's critics could, if the government so wished, be brushed aside with impunity.

Rockingham himself received similar advice from John Wentworth, agent for and future governor of New Hampshire, 1766–76. Wentworth was in London at this time to futher the interests of the family firm, and eventually became involved in the Stamp Act repeal movement. He, like Fothergill, saw Quebec's problems in a different light from those of the thirteen colonies. In a letter to Rockingham in the fall of 1765, after a long description of the economy and prospects for Anglo-Canadian trade, Wentworth advised against forcing the controversial revenue issue. It would resolve itself, in his opinion, once the economy had been set on a firm footing. "Greater benefit will accrue to this country from their trade," he wrote of North America, "than can be expected from their present ability considerably to increase or rather create revenue."[38] Further documents in Rockingham's papers show that he canvassed advice from all quarters, including the archbishop of York, on other important issues. These matters included religious questions and schemes for North American representation in the British parliament, in which Quebec was allotted two MPs in 1765.[39] Unfortunately, this plan for Canadian constituencies did not state how the MPs would be elected, only how they should behave. The whole consulting exercise, however, represented an efficient means of cross-checking the bureaucratic reports and recommendations over which many senior politicians harboured deep reservations. Rockingham, like Grenville, intended that ministers should continue to make the big colonial decisions.

On a more practical front, the sort of advice offered by Fothergill and the others must have appeared a welcome relief for the Rockinghams. It confirmed the policy initiatives they had already taken, while reassuring them of public approval for their approach to Quebec's problems – an important factor during the Rockingham ministry's embattled years with North American policy. Other, anonymous, reports on the state of Quebec dating from these months agreed with the general points put forward by the experts. One very impressive piece entitled *Hints of Regulations that might be useful in the province of Quebec* ran to six foolscap pages and thirty-three clauses on how to transform the province into a viable British colony.[40] It reviewed much of the work done by Murray in the province, and in like fashion cast doubt over any idea of a representative body for Quebec. Acts of parliament could take care of revenue in the short term, the author asserted; a prosperous trade and durable religious settlement were far more important to the future success of Quebec.[41] Another essay, *Some Thoughts Relative to Canada, as It appeared in 1765*, carried the same message of the futility in forcing sudden changes on the province. The bold first paragraph spelt out what the policy-makers should bear in mind about Quebec: "The people of this Province in general seem not at all dissatisfied with their new Masters, but having ever since their existence been governed by a Military power, are extremely adverse to our Forms of Civil Government, and very desirous (one and all) to be continued on their old footing."[42]

In November the government began to inch its way down the path to an overall policy for Quebec, using all this well-meant advice as best it could. Conway, the southern secretary, set the ministerial ball rolling in a letter to Rockingham on 10 October, reminding him of a cabinet meeting and "putting your Lordship in mind of Lord Dartmouth." Conway summarized Dartmouth's view of Quebec's situation as "Canada the same both as to Murray and the Government there and I think the Laws and the Bishop."[43] No significance should be attached to the order of these priorities, for the government did not set about these problems like items to be crossed off a shopping list. Ministers soon discovered, as Murray had repeatedly made clear, that each issue overlapped the next, the whole resting on the religious question. Indeed it was on the religious problem that the Rockinghams ventured where others had feared to tread, making their most telling contribution to securing Quebec's future loyalty under British rule.

The Rockingham government should be given credit for reading all the varying reports and recommendations on Quebec's problems, and then producing a synthesis that highlighted two important challenges confronting the policy-maker. First, the religious issue disturbed the Canadians more than any other grievance against the new order. Second, and in light of the first, if the government did not bring satisfaction to the king's Catholic subjects in spiritual affairs, their allegiance would always be in doubt. In recognition of these facts the Rockinghams began their remedial action at the top, intending the cure to gravitate downwards. In June 1766, the former grand vicar of Quebec, Jean Oliver Briand, arrived in Quebec city as bishop and official spiritual leader of the province's Catholic community.[44] It is difficult to overplay the importance the Canadians attached to this act. The report in the *London Magazine* for September 1766 sums up the scene of rejoicing in the city of Quebec: "On the 28th at eleven at night, arrived in this city from London ... Mr. Briand, bishop of Quebec, for the Roman Catholics. On the day following at five o'clock in the morning the bells of all the churches announced his arrival to the whole city, which gave general satisfaction to the Canadians. It was generally affecting to see them congratulate each other wherever they met ... It is likely that this favour conferred on the Canadians will effectually attach them to the British government." In granting official recognition to Briand as bishop, the Rockinghams had gone further than a simple act of good grace or "favour." The appointment represented the prolongation of Canadian Catholicism under the British crown. The clergy could be renewed and parish vacancies filled around the province, providing the spiritual succour lacking since Pontbriand's death in 1760. In short, the appointment symbolized the British government's intention to deal in good faith. This is not to say that the Rockinghams had abandoned the idea of Anglicanism prevailing in the future. Neatby has been right to stress that "at no time before 1791 was there official recognition of the rather ample powers, privileges, and property which the Roman Catholic Church actually enjoyed."[45] Nevertheless, the government had provided a solid basis for a day-to-day spiritual existence in Quebec free from persecution and calumny. After this step had been taken, a Protestant ascendancy in the province was out of the question.

In fact, Briand's appointment opened the door for a more tolerant attitude on the other problems in the government of the provinces. When Shelburne considered the calling of an assembly in 1766 he suggested the previously unthinkable idea of allowing Catholics to be elected representatives. In an extremely clever and novel view of the problem, he no longer saw religion as a bar to state service; political control would be indirectly exerted through language: "in case of calling a General Assembly it seems equitable that a Canadian should be eligible, but the sole use of the English Tongue in such an Assembly which must necessarily be insisted upon, will prevent the Election of any Canadians but such as are proper for that purpose and this will without violence introduce into Canada the study and practice of the English Tongue."[46] As most Welsh and Manx nationalists of today would testify, Shelburne knew his history and had hit on the most potent weapon available to assert English cultural and political sovereignty over the conquered territory. The whole exercise again suggests a softening of official attitudes to the practice of Catholicism in mid-eighteenth-century Britain. Political control, by whatever means, and suppression of outward "pomp and shew" by the Catholic church provided sufficient security for the government to feel safe against the threat of popery.

One of the most forceful expressions of this practical view came in Francis Maseres's pamphlet, *Considerations On The Expediency of Procuring An Act of Parliament for The Settlement of The Province of Quebec*, published in the spring of 1766 before he left to take up his post as attorney-general in the province. Maseres came from a Huguenot family expelled from France after the enforcement of the Edict of Nantes and possessed strong anti-Catholic sentiments. His three-year term of duty would not be a happy one, for Maseres found himself out of sympathy with Canadian religious devotion and cultural life. He did not possess the tolerance of his political masters, who fervently hoped for the conversion of the king's new subjects through pursuing a policy of death by a thousand cuts to those privileges enjoyed by the Catholic church in the temporal life of the province. In the immediate future, however, even Maseres found the case for toleration a strong one from "the reasonableness of the thing itself, they [Canadians] being almost universally of that religion."[47] The proposal did have a sting in the tail, however. Political expediency was fine in Maseres's view, but he wished the world to observe it in action. What he proposed was an act of parliament to declare Quebec a special case and clear up once and for all the confusion over the wording in the Peace of Paris permitting Catholic freedom of religion "as far as the laws of Great Britain permit." As Maseres saw it, the laws of Great Britain did not permit exercise of the Catholic religion, and legislation was required to remedy the situation. He had a strong constitutional point. By citing the clauses in 1 Elizabeth c.1 forbidding any "foreign prince, person, prelate ... power or jurisdiction, spiritual or temporal, within this realm, or within any other of your Majesty's dominions," Maseres maintained that the hands of the king and his council in this matter were tied. For the king to say now that Catholicism could be tolerated in Quebec would mean the use of the old Stuart mechanism of dispensing with the laws of the realm. So the argument, like many, many others in the eighteenth century, found its way back to 1688. To a good whig like Maseres there was no question of allowing prerogative power to dictate the course of policy. As he put it: "The Authority of Parliament seems to be a much safer foundation to establish this measure upon."[48]

Rockingham himself could not have expressed the whig creed more eloquently, but he was faced with constitutional problems that defied the application of theory drawn from the lessons of 1688. What residual prerogative powers remained to the mid-eighteenth-century monarchy were, and have been since, underestimated and obfuscated in a shroud of wiggish cant. Not only was the king free to act in times of constitutional crises, as in the corn embargo episode in 1766, but he was also positively encouraged to do so by whig politicians and he received tremendous popular support in the aftermath.[49] There was no question of taking the toleration policy in Quebec to parliament, therefore, once the Rockinghams had appointed Briand to his post. They had fulfilled the clause in the Treaty of Paris not by dispensing with existing laws but through a liberal interpretation of the constitutional powers residing in the executive branch of governmnet. As would be seen over the next four or five years, only the most zealous Protestant bigots offered criticism of the policy. In fact it would have been pure folly for the Rockinghams to confront parliament with a Catholic relief act for Quebec at the time of the protracted debate over the repeal of the Stamp Act. Such a toleration bill would require time in preparation and careful handling in the House, where much heat would be generated on the issue. The government had neither the time nor the political confidence at Westminster to undertake such a campaign. The Rockinghams needed a quick solution to the problem of a bishop and took the courageous step of allowing Briand, who had been in London since 1764, to proceed to France. In Surenes outside Paris, on 16 March 1766, he was consecrated as bishop for the province before leaving for Quebec City. No written record of discussions between Briand and the government exist, but it seems apparent that private commitments were made by both sides. The bishop's tactful behaviour in the province, operating between conquerors and conquered, showed his appreciation of the political difficulties faced by the policy-makers in Britain who handled this religious issue. The Rockinghams, in return, had gone out on a constitutional limb in fulfilling stipulations in the Treaty of Paris and the Articles of Capitulation. They paid the price everyone considered necessary for the future loyalty of the Canadians. The appointment of Briand marked a turning point in Anglo-Canadian relations, advancing the cause of toleration in both Quebec and the mother country in a way that would eventually lead to legislative relief.

The government's reponse to the religious question had inescapable effects on the remaining two problems confronting the Rockinghams: revenue and administration of justice. The Rockinghams' tolerant attitude to the appointment of a bishop, "approved of and sent to that province," as Shelburne put it, represented a bold step, but the initiative began and ended with Briand's arrival in Quebec.[50] Ministers did not want anything to do with a representative body containing Canadian Catholics or even a bastardized assembly along the lines proposed by Dartmouth in September 1765. In the wake of these decisions the government thus faced the problem Grenville's administration had skirted: how to secure the financial future of Quebec with no visible constitutional means of raising revenue. The initial reaction of the government was, as described above, to order a special "instrument" to be drawn up, granting Murray the necessary legislative powers to collect old duties under the new regime. This recommendation of 22 August 1765 had, by 22 November 1765, been abandoned.[51] In its place the Privy Council ordered that instructions under the sign manual be given to the resident receiver-general and his collectors empowering them to collect the revenues previously granted to the French crown. In essence this was a complete turn-around by Rockingham, and the adoption of a Grenville policy first put forward on 6 August 1764. The man responsible for producing this change of heart was the indispensable Charles Yorke. He recognized the legal basis supporting the Grenville administration's position and restated it in his report to the council on 2 November 1765: "it is most certain that all the Duties payable to the French King before the conquest and cession are now due, and payable to His Majesty, and as they are vested in the King, by right of Conquest, at common law, nothing seems to have been wanting since that time but the appointment of an officer duly authorized to receive and collect them."[52] The government merely utilized its power as conqueror, which many inside the bureaucracy, and some outside it, like Dr Fothergill, had long urged them to do. The prize of avoiding an embarrassing wrangle over an assembly made the effort worthwhile.

The course of this policy did not run entirely true, however. Ministers soon discovered that there was considerable residual confusion and obstruction in Quebec to the operation and collection of these old duties. Murray, in fact, pointed this out in his last report on the province to the government in the fall of 1765.[53] The governor had attempted to collect the old duties himself to furnish a revenue for the civil establishment, and also tried to widen the tax net by levying a duty on new spirits imported from Britain.[54] To the British merchants such policies had smacked of executive tyranny, for there was no assembly to sanction them. As a result, many court cases had arisen for non-payment, and the government in Quebec found it impossible to persuade a jury to bring in a guilty verdict against a British defendant. The situation did not improve under the more rigorous law officers sent out by Rockingham. In the fall of 1766 Maseres and Hey still complained of the inability to enforce the payment of these duties.[55] The Canadians were not really happy about the situation either. After the conquest, the province became sucked into the Atlantic trade network governed by the Navigation Laws. What French wine and brandy reached Quebec, therefore, had to go via London and be subject to duties payable there. This raised the price and curtailed supply. Worse still, from the Canadian point of view, British brandy was introduced into the province as a cheaper, more loyal, commodity for domestic consumption. By all contemporary accounts, the spirit was loathed by the French and British populace alike, who avoided it like the plague, and its introduction greatly increased smuggling. An American merchant, Mr Kelly, summed the situation up when examined before the commons on 27 March 1766. On being asked whether or not a lowering of the molasses duty would "prejudice the importation of British spirits to Canada," Kelly replied that he did not know, "but that the countries that he is acquainted with do not like the British spirits."[56] The Rockinghams did not exercise themselves over these problems, for they only became apparent after their dismissal in July 1766, but the legacy to succeeding governments could not be overlooked. A war of attrition in the courts of Quebec against the revenue measures led to an inadequate supply of funds, which, as Maseres recognized, could only be remedied by an act of parliament.[57]

The last issue to flow more directly from the tolerant attitude to religion concerned the administration of justice, and it was one upon which the administration came to grief. Yet the dramatic climax had a quite innocuous prologue. On 19 November 1765 the Privy Council ordered the government's legal officers to comment on the Board of Trade report submitted on 2 September,[58] which was so damning of Murray's ordinance of the previous year. The job was thoroughly done, with both Cramahé and Fowler Walker interviewed on the subject over the winter months.[59] The result remained consistent with other policy initiatives in Quebec: an ideological commitment to allowing Catholics more religious freedom was carried into the plan for a revision of Canadian court and judicial practice. The process passed through two stages now well known to historians.[60] The first culminated with an instruction to Murray on 24 February 1766 designed to provide first aid to a beleaguered jury system in the province. Murray was ordered to publish an ordinance "regulating the institution of juries and placing them upon a more equal and rational footing."[61] In short, juries in cases between two Canadians were to consist entirely of Canadians, those between two subjects from Britain entirely of English-speaking jurors, and those between a Canadian and a British subject of six old and six new subjects. In addition, futher clauses sought to remedy two obvious deficiencies in Murray's ordinance. Canadian lawyers would in future be "allowed to practice as Barristers, Advocates, Attornies and Proctors in all and any of the Courts within our said province," and Murray's fated ordinance of 17 September 1764 "shall be declared to be temporary only."[62] This last clause was a declaration of intent, putting Canadian minds at rest with a promise of more wide-sweeping reforms. There was indeed good intention behind this order in council and it did open the door for Canadian lawyers to make a living under the British crown. But it was not a solid lasting solution to the overall problem; it merely scratched the surface of Canadian discontent with the legal system.

It was in the second stage of this revision process that the real search for the broader solution to the legal problems of the province took place. Charles Yorke masterminded the decision-making after taking sole command of preparing an empirical plan during March and April 1766. Yorke followed the now well worn procedures of reviewing past reports, especially those submitted by Murray, and taking further evidence from outsiders like Fowler Walker.[63] Yorke then drew up a plan based on synthesis of this intelligence for the Privy Council, presenting it on 14 April 1766. The crucial point often missed by historians in their accounts of these events is that Yorke not only concerned himself with known defects of the existing judicial system in the province but was equally, if not more, interested in enacting his own vision of Quebec's future development through these judicial reforms. Thus the judgments of Humphrey and Morley Scott that the attorney-general did not "manifest a very shrewd understanding of the situation in the colony," and more latterly of Marshall, who commented that his report of 14 April "displayed little understanding of the current practice of Quebec law," miss the point somewhat.[64] In the first place, it would have been remarkable if Yorke had shown a deep understanding of Quebec law. He, like everyone else in London, had to rely on reports from the province drawn up by newcomers with nothing but a nodding acquaintance with Quebec's legal system. More important, however, Yorke's ideological purpose was to carry the tolerant attitude displayed on Quebec's other problems into the realm of justice. He certainly made errors of omission and assumption about the day-to-day practice of Canadian courts, but the philosophy behind his proposals cannot be mistaken. The earl of Hardwicke, Yorke's brother, explained the thesis behind the 14 April report to Rockingham two months later. "He has struck at, or *pretty nearly so* – the true medium," Hardwicke commented, "and I understand from him, that the Canadians like our free and *impartial* forms of Judicature."[65]

Why did Yorke canvass what in eighteenth-century terms appeared such a strong liberal view of the province's judiciary? The best clue to an answer comes in an opening paragraph that Yorke wrote to support his 14 April proposals. Justification for the reforms was divided in two: an intent to remedy past indiscretions on the government's part, emanating from misinterpretations of the Proclamations embodied in Murray's ordinance; and a more revealing general declaration that Canadians "may see that it is our Royal intention not to govern them with the rough hand of Conqueror, but in the true spirit of a lawful sovereign by making such provisions for the due and impartial administration of justice."[66] If the Privy Council read this statement closely they might have noticed that it had a familiar ring to it, for it echoed, almost to the letter, Mansfield's rebuke to Grenville of 24 December 1764 about Murray's ordinance.[67] Indeed, Yorke's proposals could be seen as a sincere effort to fulfil the great lawyer's wishes on Quebec's legal future. Yorke, like many of his contemporaries in law and politics, respected Mansfield's judicial opinions to a point bordering on reverence. Mansfield's criticism of Murray had implied that the whole thrust of British policy on the administration of justice gave no consideration to Canadian laws and customs under the new regime. Yet no one could accuse Yorke of such insensitivity. He completely overhauled sections of the Board of Trade's report of 2 September 1765 dealing with the judiciary, and went much further than even Mansfield might have contemplated in concessions on the exercise of English law in Quebec. Two commonly cited examples are worthy of note. All cases relating to real property, irrespective of the time they originated, would be determined by the custom of the province. In reality this meant French law. The other striking proposal was the recommendation that a number of Catholic Canadian magistrates should be appointed. No precedent or law could be drawn on to support such an action. Its justification rested on the practicality of the measure and that need to introduce "free" and "impartial" justice so earnestly desired by the attorney-general.

What to an eighteenth-century British politician and modern British historian appears as honest endeavour towards a noble goal looked, and has looked ever since, decidedly different to the Canadians. Concessions in one area of justice did not paper over flaws in another as far as the French-speaking community was concerned. Criminal law remained English, as, essentially, did actions covering trade, commerce, and debt. As Hay has so perceptively pointed out in his essay, this stipulation sent shock waves through the sections of Canadian society involved in such litigation.[68] Many of the procedures of the Coutume de Paris reflected the social stratification in French society and these would now be undermined. Even the jury system, for example, regarded as the font of English liberty in London, harboured terrors for the Canadian noblesse. In trials it could give rise to the position where seigneurs would be judged by their social inferiors – an unthinkable concept under the old regime. In certain aspects, Yorke's proposals also sowed the seeds for the marginalization of the French legal profession under early British rule. The lucrative practices had been left open for English-speaking lawyers, steeped in English law. Flaws or not, these distinctions in legal practice, later embodied in the Quebec Act of 1774, were laid before the Privy Council on 13 May 1766 for approval.

The reaction of the council on this day proved favourable, though Yorke and others "in the law line" were absent from the 13 May meeting.[69] Those present passed the proposals to the Board of Trade with a view to framing an instruction for the governor in Quebec to put the reforms into effect. The Privy Council considered the board's version of the intended judicial policy on 13 June 1766 and found it wanting, referring the report back for more detailed instructions on the enacting clauses.[70] Yorke himself again took over the drafting at this point. He wrote a prologue to a revised series of recommendations, emphasizing the urgency of correcting the miseries suffered by the Canadians. In addition he proposed that Murray's provincial ordinances regarding the legal system be annulled as soon as the new policy and instruction received council approval.[71] These measures reflected a creditable consistency on Yorke's role in the whole affair, and he prepared to receive his victory garland at a council meeting on 24 June. It all went sadly awry. The chancellor, Northington, torpedoed the proposals in their entirety. Worse still, over the next two weeks failure to proceed on the Quebec business became the rock upon which the ministry foundered: Northington refused to attend cabinet, which in turn provided George III with an excuse to dismiss his ministers.

Langford has established beyond all doubt that Northington concerted his sulky and petulant behaviour over Quebec policy with the king.[72] This should not be taken to mean that Northington had no knowledge or interest, as he claimed in cabinet, in Quebec's problems. On the contrary, he understood the fundamental issues very well. His objection to Yorke's proposals was that put forward by Maseres: only parliament could make policy for Quebec after the initial post-conquest settlement. It was a position that Northington had maintained under Grenville, and in point of legal precedent it looked considerably more authoritative than the Rockinghams' haste to act by order in council. Furthermore, Northington's obduracy on this matter went beyond generalities. The duke of Richmond's dramatic account of a cabinet meeting on 27 June, where ministers made a second attempt to bring the chancellor round to their way of thinking on Quebec, reveals the detailed objections posited by Northington to Yorke's proposals and his distaste for the direction of government policy since 1763:

It being however agreed to read the instructions, the Chancellor objected to several parts. First to the appointing Canadians being Roman Catholics to act as justices of the Peace or as Judges, he doubted whether the crown could give that power to Roman Catholics and whether the Penal laws did not extend to Canada. Secondly he objected to appeals from the Superior Courts of Judicature to the Governor and Council. He said they should be to the King in Council in England .. His Lordship also said that he thought the old Canadian laws were to subsist till by the authority of Parliament they were altered. To this it was objected to him that the King had issued a Proclamation in which he promised all his new subjects the benefits and advantages of the English law. To which His Lordship replied, I know that, and a very silly proclamation it was.[73]

This outburst showed, as Hardwicke observed later, that Northington would "neither Lead nor Drive."[74] The argument had reached stalemate. Ministers believed that they were simply amending the stipulations of the post-war settlement, while Northington held that they wanted a change in policy, and this meant parliamentary action.

Despite such obstruction and disgruntlement on the chancellor's part, the government still pushed on with the reforms, unaware of the darker side of Northington's behaviour. In Richmond's words, "it was absurd to neglect the business of the Country and not do what was right because one great Lawyer objected."[75] In different circumstances, supported by the king, the government probably could have pulled off the policy by order in council. Two further cabinet meetings on 3 and 4 July discussed Quebec's legal provisions, but what filled the air was empty rhetoric. The king had deserted the Rockinghamite ship of government, and on 10 July 1766 it sank without trace. Yorke's Quebec proposals were shelved for the next eight years. This abrupt end to a government poised to undertake vital reforms on Quebec's legal structure created an unexpected hiatus in the province's development under early British rule. The direction and decision on policy remained intact but unenacted for almost a decade. For the Rockinghams it was a grievous disappointment. When Burke reflected on the ministry's achievements in late 1766 he could not claim the true measure of the courageous steps taken in Quebec, just that "a Liquidation of the *Canada* Bills, to the Satisfaction of the Proprietors" had been obtained.[76] The fact that Rockinghamite policies were cruelly baulked at the last hurdle did not, however, lessen their indelible mark on Quebec. In the long term the Rockingham's brave effort at liberalizing attitudes to the roles of Catholics in all levels of society would bear some fruit.

In the summer of 1766, however, the picture looked less than rosy. Without reforms, the future for Canadians under British rule would be near that of colonial serfs. They would exist in spiritual isolation, bereft of traditional legal forms and condemned to an economic life of hewing wood and drawing water. This prospect was a far cry from the promised rule "in the true spirit of a lawful soverign" so readily made in the spring of 1766. How quickly the picture had changed!

CHAPTER FIVE

The Lost Years 1766–70

The failure of the Rockinghamite initiative on Quebec ushered in an enigmatic period in Canada's history. To all outward appearances a policy vacuum ensued, broken only by the sudden introduction of the Quebec Act to parliament in 1774. This inertia was summed up aptly in the phrasing of two historians when they commented: "with the formation of the Chatham administration a curtain fell on Canadian affairs."[1] To some degree the accuracy of this statement cannot be challenged. No concerted policy did emerge from the government during the years 1766–74. But the residual impression from such views – that the British simply twiddled their thumbs over Quebec in this period, only being prompted into action in 1774 by the threat of cession from the thirteen American colonies – should be dismissed. This resilient idea has led some historians to paint a completely false picture of these years. A very lively debate, and protracted effort to solve Quebec's administrative problems, did take place in London. Moreover, the politicians and bureaucrats were joined in this empirical discussion by pamphleteers and journalists with an interest in any settlement for the province. An examination of this debate will help raise the curtain concealing Quebec's real part in colonial policy-making in these years. The reason why no policy emerged for the province before 1774 lies not so much with activities in Quebec itself, of which a good deal is known,[2] but with a domestic political tradition unable to cope easily with the alien problems arising from the conquest. Added to this were serious practical difficulties of continuity in an age of political instability. All in all, it was a recipe unlikely to produce a well-leavened settlement.

Yet to outside observers in the summer of 1766 there seemed good reason to hope that the new ministry would do something about Quebec's government. Did not the leading lights in the new government have the knowledge, sympathy, and expertise to meet the demands of the situation in the province? The titular head of the ministry Lord Chatham, previously William Pitt, was known simply, but evocatively, as the "friend of America" – the man who had moved mountains to make the victories in the Seven Years' War possible. Although this reputation was based more on fiction than fact, as recent work has shown, it appeared inconceivable that Chatham would not govern in the best interests of an empire so dear to his heart.[3] Shelburne looked similarly well placed, as southern secretary, to put into practice the radical ideas he had briefly unveiled at the Board of Trade in 1763. To underline his intent once in office, he took pains to reclaim all the powers of his office that had drifted away to Dartmouth's officials under Rockingham's administration. Shelburne intended to be the power over colonial policy in deed as well as word. Further reasons for optimism could be drawn, if necessary, from Charles Townshend's appointment to the Exchequer and Conway's continuance in senior office, this time as northern secretary.[4] Both held cabinet posts and had a long acquaintance with North American problems.

At first it looked as though measures would match the men. In the immediate priorities set out by ministers, Quebec was, as it had been in the first days of Rockingham's administration, high on the agenda for attention and then action. Two documents in Shelburne's papers illustrate the sense of purpose in this matter. The first, most certainly drawn up in August, was on a general schema of problems to be tackled in the North American empire.[5] The second, drawn later, referred to specific questions regarding the new acquisitions. Three areas came under scrutiny: the development of trade, defence expenditures, and government in these territories. The former two categories raised questions common to the whole of North America after the Seven Years' War, and much excellent work has been done in the field to explain the evolution of British policy.[6] But the third looked trickier. Of the new acquisitions, Quebec represented the largest headache, and in two short passages Shelburne identified the fundamental issues that the cabinet would have to come to terms with in finding a settlement: "1. What privileges have been preserved by *capitulation* to the ancient subjects? 2. Whether it be expedient to retain the *ancient* form of government or to what degree depart from it?"[7] Charles Townshend expressed complete agreement with Shelburne about tackling the Quebec problem at an early stage. On 4 September he told the duke of Grafton, the new first lord of the Treasury, that "with respect to the affairs of Canada, I did imagine that the servants of the crown intended to have *a Cabinet* upon the *general* state of that province and that, having *there* settled a plan, the necessary orders for the execution of it would have come before council."[8] This echoing of Mansfield's strong idea about where colonial policy should be decided characterized the resolve of the ministry to do something about the province. It had the will; all that was required now was an agenda for action.

This agenda proved an elusive goal. Hopes for immediate action on Quebec were baulked by a seemingly intractable mixture of practical and philosophical problems. Of the former there is an appearance of farce to twentieth-century eyes. Despite the cabinet's commitment to act in the summer of 1766, it is obvious that no one had the slightest idea how to proceed. In short, the government fell victim to instability at the top level of government. All the work done on Quebec by Charles Yorke left office with the Rockinghams. None of the new ministers could discover what action Yorke had intended or find a written record of his proposals. Not even Francis Maseres, whom the Rockinghams had appointed attorney-general to the province, knew of Yorke's plans. He told Fowler Walker the following year, "I can't find out who the quondam minister was who had taken a step toward regulating this province, nor what that step was."[9] Northington, who might have been in a position to help, refused to proffer advice to his new colleagues on a subject that had caused him so much irritation. He retired to the country in a huff during the summer, only returning to London in the winter for parliament's opening session. Thus, though Shelburne, Conway, Townshend, and the others in the new cabinet had some knowledge of Quebec, they hardly possessed enough to concoct an overall policy for the settlement of the province.

To exacerbate this practical difficulty there was a philosophical consideration that very clearly determined the course of policy-making over the next few years. Up to the dismissal of the Rockingham administration in July 1766 it had been assumed that action on Quebec would always be taken through council. Over the summer of that year this assumption dissolved into a commitment to resolve the administration of the province through parliamentary legislation. This change of heart on procedure altered the whole thrust of the government's thought and purpose with regard to Quebec. To prepare parliamentary legislation required a collective effort on the part of ministers, in which information would have to be gathered and relayed to various departments for comment and approval. There could be no "quondam minister" in this scheme of things. After ministers had familiarized themselves with the subject of Quebec, their plans would have to be laid before parliament. The time scale for this process could not bear comparison with action in council. It could take, as is now known, at least eight years.

Why did the government change its mind about proceeding by order in council, conceding, in essence, Northington's case against the Rockinghams in June and July 1766? The most obvious reason was the sound practical one that all previous efforts at acting through council had failed. With the failure of the Rockinghamite initiative there could now be no back-door settlement. A more profound cause for this change in ministerial thinking, however, was the constitutional consensus, evident amongst office-holders in the new government, favouring a parliamentary solution to the Quebec problem. In brief, Chatham's government was composed of more strict whigs than its predecessor. Northington was just one of many who felt uneasy about allowing Quebec policy to be determined by king in Council, a procedure which implicitly sanctioned use of prerogative power at odds with their perception of the constitutional settlement of 1689. Thus no matter how badly Northington wanted the Rockinghams out of office, his views on the technical aspects of the Quebec case cannot be ignored or treated simply as a political ploy. The right of conquest certainly allowed the British to establish a new governmental structure in Quebec, but any subsequent changes had to be implemented through parliamentary legislation.

From 1766 on this message was relayed time and again to London from officials in Quebec, like Maseres and Carleton, and reinforced by opinion within the government's own ranks. It was this principle that Charles Townshend attempted to impress on Grafton in his letter of 4 September, where he advised that action on "the *whole* situation of Canada" was a matter "hardly fit for the knowledge of open council."[10] In a similar vein, a report by Barrington, the secretary at war, saw the problem of Quebec's governance soluble only through legislation. The paper concluded: "It is now very difficult to settle matters well tho' easy at first The first wrong settlement has made a right one exceptionable and dangerous to the Privy Council Therefore leave the whole to Parliament."[11] It is ironic that the Rockinghams, who boasted an unblemished whig heritage from the middle of the seventeenth century, should find themselves on this constitutional spot, and their behaviour would eventually cast a shadow over their attitude to opposing the Quebec Act in 1774. Not only had they supported the vigorous exercise of executive power residing in the council over Quebec but they had also nominated a bishop for the province and canvassed a policy of toleration for the Catholic population that a great number of their domestic political allies found repugnant. In fact, the Rockinghams never quite came to terms with the agony over principle highlighted by the Quebec settlement.

From the government's point of view, the task of proceeding on Quebec policy looked less complicated with constitutional theory. In the person of Shelburne, the government could not have had a more diligent minister for the job of providing information on Quebec to the new cabinet after Rockingham's departure. The southern secretary assumed the power and responsibility for conducting all North American policy, and set about a methodical process of gathering intelligence on the province and its problems. Shelburne's office controlled the whole procedure. A glance through the papers of the Privy Council or the Board of Trade journals for 1766 and 1767 reveals few business entries on Quebec, giving the impression that little was done about the province and advice ceased to flow from the advisory board.[12] This is a mistaken assumption. A great deal of work was done on Quebec, but under Shelburne's firm guidance. He merely followed the line of thinking about executive control already propounded by Mansfield and others, which in turn reflected a lack of faith in the Board of Trade's advisory role. Such prejudice is not difficult to understand, as from Shelburne's point of view the Board had to that point displayed a singular lack of brilliance in resolving Quebec's problems.

Right or wrong, Shelburne cut the board out of the policy process in 1766. He had his own style of administration, and anyone who has worked on Shelburne's papers can see right away that he was a bureaucratic magpie. He initiated research on Quebec's history both before and after the conquest, collecting and hoarding all official documents and proclamations concerning the province to date. Indeed, the plethora of internal government documents on this topic in Shelburne's papers represents, in many ways, a better documentation of this period in Canada's history than the more recognized holdings in the Colonial Office papers of the Public Record Office. The problem that Shelburne must have encountered was not a lack of information but a surfeit. The physical effort of working through the mass of papers at his disposal helps explain in itself why progress towards a Quebec settlement proved so tardy. Shelburne's thoroughness of preparation covered the usual contacts with other departments and officials on both sides of the Atlantic, but also ran, in the matter of judicial affairs, to a personal emissary, Maurice Morgann, sent to the province in 1767. Shelburne hoped to take account of all personal vendettas and bias in the reports reaching London, so that when his recommended actions came forward they would embody a composite view of all shades of opinion on Quebec's future. Yet there was a slip 'twixt cup and lip. Shelburne soon found that gathering intelligence on Quebec would be the sum total of his efforts on this front. In the two years or so that he held the post of southern secretary, nothing like a draft bill on the government of the province ever emerged. His quest for information revealed many difficult administrative problems, which, in turn, ruined any hope of a lasting settlement.

The reasons for this failure were not of Shelburne's own making. The vacillations in ministerial dealings with Quebec over the previous three years produced an uncertain and divided political climate in the province. It is well documented how the Quebec council splintered after Murray's departure. Two factions developed initially: one devoted to the old governor's cause, the other well disposed to Carleton, the new lieutenant-governor. Of the former, Paulus Irving, Murray's deputy, and Adam Mabane, the old governor's surgeon friend, were the leading lights. Many of their reasons for dissatisfaction under the new regime were imagined rather than real. An immediate slight was perceived, for example, when Carleton called a council meeting after his arrival, omitting most of Murray's friends, who were unavailable or unable to attend. It was at worst a piece of poor judgment on Carleton's part, and yet the old governor's party, as they became known, attempted to make a constitutional issue out of the episode. Mabane organized a petition, seeking assurances that Carleton would never repeat this act of exclusionism.[13]

This episode got relations off to a bad start and naturally pushed Carleton towards the latter group in council, led by Maseres, Hey, and H.J. Cramahé, now damned as a turncoat by Mabane and the others previously connected to Murray. Unlike their rivals, these council members and their associates addressed Carleton in effusive terms, envisaging an end to Murray's approach to Quebec's governance and the start of a new order favourable to the Protestant/mercantile groups.[14] As Maseres told Rockingham in a letter on 20 November 1766: "I take the liberty of informing your Lordship that your appointment of General Carleton to the command of this province has been of infinite advantage to it, in allaying the animosities that had hitherto subsisted here, and introducing a spirit of tranquillity and harmony amongst the inhabitants."[15] As before, the disputes in Quebec were carried back to London on the Atlantic packets, and it is difficult not to sympathize with those administrators in Britain who ignored these reports. What could possibly be made of the contradictions between one report, like that of Maseres, who saw Carleton as a knight in shining armour, and another, like Mabane's in October 1766, which observed of the same man: "Stuffiness and Dignity, an affectation of wisdom by a constant reserve and silence are the only parts of his character that have yet appeared at Quebec.?[16] Shelburne and his advisors soon recognized that a power struggle had developed as one faction saw its patron depart and its opponents seized a chance to make political capital at their expense. Both sides misjudged Carleton, and the government wisely stood aloof as the new lieutenant-governor ploughed his own policy furrow. Much to everyone's surprise, there would be more continuity with the approach to policy post-1764 than ever seemed possible after Murray's withdrawal.

This is not to say that residual administrative disputes did not exist in the province. Long-standing arguments ranged from petty jealousies, such as the fact that George III granted Carleton the civil and military powers so dearly craved by Murray, to more important matters central to the survival of the province.[17] Unauthorized trade with the Indian nations in the interior, for example, had reached the point where no one really knew whether the trade had been thrown open by a declaration in the *Quebec Gazette* of 1 January 1765, or restricted to licensees of the firm Dunn and Grey. The dispute soon polarized opinion into the two established rival camps, and on Murray's departure the matter was brought to a head when Thomas Mills, the receiver-general, issued a prohibitory order that required all traders not under licence to Dunn and Grey "immediately to retire."[18] Mills, Dunn, and Grey were not connected to the old governor's party and Carleton was faced with counter-petitions as soon as he arrived. He reacted wisely, nullifying Mills's proclamation and writing for new instructions to London about the trade. It was a vital point, for it threw light on another concern facing Carleton – the boundary dispute with New York. Indeed, it was this problem that prompted the new lieutenant-governor's first report to England.[19] In the circumstances Carleton made a fine analysis not only of this dispute but of all the others left over from Murray's regime. He recognized straightaway that the territorial argument with New York interlocked with the post-war land and settlement grants and the maintenance of peace with the native peoples, which in turn depended upon well-regulated trade in the interior. The whole edifice, however, rested upon unified command in Quebec and all the inhabitants pulling in the same direction. As Carleton put in his report to London: "I stated to Major Mills (the Receiver General) the many evils that must accrue from that open Opposition and disagreement of the King's servants in this province."

This unity proved easier to describe than to put into effect. The internal disputes within the province were not wholly focused on profit and loss or seedy patronage struggles. Ideological rifts over such matters as the right to have an assembly or how to collect revenue survived all the changes of personnel amongst the king's servants, and had yet to be addresed. In fact it could be argued that Carleton faced an even more trying situation than Murray on this front. The application of the Stamp Act in Quebec from 1 November 1765 until its repeal in April 1766, in particular, had brought fundamental constitutional issues into the public eye and accentuated divisons within the province's mercantile community. Much more work needs to be done on this episode, for the principles involved have relevance not only to British Canada's early history but also to wider imperial themes. The standard presentation of the Stamp Act in Quebec is short and sweet: it was enforced with minuscule opposition, unlike the situation in thirteen American colonies, which had imbibed radical and democratic notions of government. This picture requires revision. True, there seems to have been no groundswell of popular protest against the Stamp Act, but neither did it pass unquestioned.

On 21 June 1764, the *Quebec Gazette*, the government's own creation, actually gave a fair indication of the scope of the debate and protest on the act. In the case of those clauses of the legislation pertinent only to the newly conquered territories, the paper was especially revealing. An editorial on 27 June 1765 reported that the Stamp Act would come into force on "1st of November next," with the additional information: "It is no ways milder than the resolves, except that the extraordinary duties on things in any other than the English language, do not take place within Quebec or Grenada for 5 years."[20] This subsection to the Stamp Act for Quebec and Grenada has been steadfastly ignored by historians, but it could have changed the province's political and cultural future considerably. Had the Stamp Act not been repealed in 1766, the French-speaking population of Quebec would, in 1770, have been faced with a punitive surtax for simply reading documents and papers in their own language. This policy looked like the sort of tool for the anglicization of Quebec that Halifax would approve of, and he could have borne the responsibility for the clause. It did not break new ground, for the stipulation was long embedded in the stamp legislation affecting the mother country. Yet it is interesting that it slipped by Grenville's watchful eye, for it ran counter to the spirit of all other policy for the province in 1765. Was it simply an administrative oversight? The only solace for the Canadians was the grant of a five-year period of grace before the extra duties came into force. Unfortunately, little else is known about the clause, rendered null and void the following year by the repeal. The *Quebec Gazette* paid no more attention to the story because other copy made more interesting reading. From the 25 July–1 August 1765 issue, the paper began printing news from Boston about violent resistance to the Stamp Act. On 10 October 1765 it spiced this kind of news with the revelation that, due to the new duties, the cost of the *Gazette* "would rise by half a dollar to two dollars payable in advance." Then came the greatest shock of all: there were no issues of the paper from no. 72 on 31 October 1765 until no. 73 on 29 May 1766, the period of the Stamp Act's enforcement. The 29 May 1766 issue was a special edition. It carried the banner headline either side of the headpiece, "La résurrection," and led with a defiant editorial that read: "Having passed a long and irksome Winter with the most sensible pleasure we find ourselves emerged from an involuntary inactivity, and once more at liberty by means of the Press, to congratulate our former customers, and the Public in general, on their being freed from the impositions of the grievious Stamp Act; an Act more dreadful than the icy chains of our inhospitable winter." Such sentiments can be seen as little more than empty rhetoric after the event. Yet the Stamp Act debate, revolving as it did around the question of taxation and representation, certainly highlighted the fundamental constitutional issue facing the politicians directing the government of Quebec. How sensitive they were to the public debate is hard to tell, but the *Gazette* was shut down after it began publishing reports of protest and resistance elsewhere. Though more needs to be known about the mechanics of contacts between Quebec and the northern colonies of America, Neatby had a point when she wrote, "Quebec merchants had submitted to the Stamp Act but some were certainly infected with the radical views of Massachusettes."[21] It seems unlikely that merchants in New York, for example, in regular contact with Quebec trades did not discuss the Stamp Act and find common ground, or that some of the discontent with the legislation in Quebec, which was denied an assembly, let alone a say in policy, should not find its way back to London.

Indeed, Murray recognized that such developments were under way, and tried to downplay their significance in his last report to London. "Tho' stimulated to dispute the Stamp Act by some of the licentious traders from New York," he commented, "they cheerfully obeyed it in hopes that their good behaviour would recommend them to the favour and protection of their sovereign."[22] It was understandable that Murray should worry about such contacts. He had already suffered from one campaign against his leadership, directed through the established channels of communication linking mercantile interests in London and Quebec. The infection of discontent could be spread very quickly through these agencies. Furthermore, not only were there *ad hoc* committees of British merchants trading to Quebec, like those who had already petitioned the government for an assembly, but in 1766 there was also an official Canada Committee for those involved in the settlement of the Canada Bills.[23] The government recognized the Canada Committee as a consultative body in the negotiations with France over the bills, and its membership met regularly at the same London taverns and coffee houses, of which the New York and Will's near Lincoln's Inn were the most popular.[24] The bond between this group and the *ad hoc* bodies was the ubiquitous lobbyist on behalf of the discontented Quebec merchants, Fowler Walker – the close friend of the new attorney-general to Quebec, Maseres, and the man who had thoroughly briefed Carleton before his departure to North America. Thus the web of plot and counterplot in Quebec politics, of which the Stamp Act formed a part, stretched across the Atlantic, defying the administrators in London to untangle its strands.

It fell to Shelburne and his advisers over the winter of 1766–67 to interpret the different signals emanating from Quebec. To a casual observer of the time it must have appeared that change was afoot. A fresh ministry, a new lieutenant-governor, and a bouyant mercantile community on both sides of the Atlantic implied a different approach to Quebec's problems. And, to a degree, there was a shift of emphasis away from confrontation, to listening and consultation. Carleton sought to ameliorate the differences of opinion over the future government of the province rather than meet them head on. He sympathized with some of those who had felt the rougher edges of Muray's rule, like the regular clergy whom Murray had inadvertently ordered "not to admit any new covenants" when he meant the Jesuits alone.[25] Carleton also found fault with the old governor's handling of the finances of the province, "where he found no public money, but many debts and demands." He also broke with the tradition of accepting the "fees and perquisites" due to the governor of the province by right of conquest, declaring in a public-spirited tone of self-denial "the numerous fees and perquisites are really bothersome in the present impoverished situation of Canada." Yet as Murray's opponents in London and Quebec soon discovered, Carleton had no axe to grind with the general: he was his own man. Carleton simply rejected Murray's style and the matters of detail. It rapidly became clear that Carleton's policy recommendations embodied continuity with the old regime. Though the new lieutenant-governor displayed more patience in his dealings with Quebec's vociferous merchants, he never thought of courting their aims and aspirations.

These developments came as a shock to Quebec's English-speaking minority, though, on reflection, they need not have done so. There were several early indications of Carleton's intent. The continuation in the council of H.T. Cramahé as an adviser to the new lieutenant-governor provided the most positive link between the old and new regimes. The acceptance of the two judicial ordinances issued in July 1766 by Irving, as a stepping stone to involving the new subjects in the administration of Quebec's judicial system, was another.[26] Most important of all, however, Carleton made no secret of the fact that he agreed with the main trend of official thinking on Quebec's future. It was a view he shared with Murray, and Barrington summarized it perfectly in his memorandum on the subject when he commented: "The two great points in respect to Canada was to make the Colony affectionate to us and to make the people happy."[27] Carleton soon realized that the route to this goal did not lie with a narrow Protestant clique, controlling both the law and local economy. The tenor of his reports during 1766 and 1767 hardly differed at all from those of Murray before his departure. The significant difference between the two periods of British rule lay in the fact that everyone now accepted the necessity of parliamentary legislation to secure the province's future. Even Francis Maseres, who hated Murray in equal measure to the Catholic church, saw the benefits of proceeding with toleration by statute. He wrote to London on 30 September 1766:

I am more convinced that nothing can put this Province in proper order and regulate the fundamentals of the constitution such as the state of religion, the degree of encouragement to be given to the Protestant, the degree of toleration to the Catholic Religion, the taxes to be paid by the merchants and other inhabitants, the continuation of some of the French laws or modification of them, the introduction of some of the English, the matters of proceeding in courts of judicature, and perhaps some other important particulars, but the Authority of Parliament. An Assembly here is at present absolutely impracticable.[28]

The commitment to a future of benign executive rule could not have been better stated. This last sentence of Maseres's report cut the English-speaking merchants and their allies in Quebec adrift from the ruling élite, forcing the legislators to consider the selfsame problems confronted by Murray. The ultimate destiny of the province now lay firmly in the hands of the politicians in London. The point was driven home with the exoneration of Murray before the Privy Council on 2 April 1767.[29] After his return to London in the winter of 1766, Murray had taken great pains to acquaint both politicians and the press with a personal history of his experiences in Canada. The case put in the *London Chronicle*, for example, expounded the view that Murray had fallen foul of a rancorous group of British merchants rather than ministers in London or the population of Quebec.[30] This version of the general's rule offered a direct challenge to his enemies in London, represented as ever by Fowler Walker and the committee of London merchants trading to Quebec. It could not be answered, and Murray conquered again. Fowler Walker and his allies secured a recall but a conviction completely eluded them. The inescapable practical realities of Quebec's unique problems under British rule vindicated Murray's career in Canada.

There was therefore much room for optimism about a resolution to Quebec's future problems in the spring of 1767. At long last the moving force in London, Shelburne, and his Canadian counterpart, Carleton, saw eye to eye about the nature of a policy to settle the future government of the province. A consensus on this point did not, however, imply immediate action on legislation, and the reasons for this inertia appear quite straightforward. Shelburne had simply not finished the job of gathering information on the province. Worse still, in those areas where a considerable amount of intelligence had been acquired, action proved impossible. On the problem of policing the interior, for example, no consistent line could be followed by the Southern Department because of revisions and vacillations in general cabinet policy. The British government's original idea had been to enforce the Proclamation of 1763 with military posts on the interior boundary line, dividing the white settlers from the native peoples on a north-south axis.[31] It soon became an impractical vision. The actual boundary line took no account of colonists already established in the interior, the military posts had no financial support once the Stamp Act had been repealed, and it proved quite unrealistic to expect the Indian natives to accept a sudden rationalization of established trading patterns with the white settlers and merchants. The failure, as Marshall has explained so well elsewhere, was due in part to contradictory orders emanating from London, but it also sprang from the fact that interior policy was seen by the British as a continental affair and the Canadians refused from the beginning to recognize or participate in any such empirical plan.[32]

Some of this resistance from Quebec in the immediate post-1763 world was certainly based on personal jealousies. Envy and rivalry rebounded in triangular fashion between William Johnson, superintendent of Indian Affairs for the north, General Gage, commander-in-chief in New York, who was the paymaster of the Department of Indian Affairs, and General Murray in Quebec – a man highly sensitive to any encroachment on his territorial power. Yet there was another side to the coin: real fears that interior policy conceived in London would be at odds with Canadian practice. Dealing in the province's main industry, furs, revolved around a three-cornered structure of traders, merchants, and voyageurs which ensured that supplies from the interior reached their European markets. It was planned in the early 1760s to throw this structure over in favour of trading posts, licences, and inspectors – a policy fashioned to meet the needs of the American fur trade around Albany. The Canadians wanted no truck with its notoriously corrupt middlemen and inspectors. Indeed, this was probably the only instance where Murray and the Quebec merchants found themselves in agreement. They resisted the employment of this framework and triumphed. Quebec never operated either the interior policy or the Indian trade regulations in the way envisaged in 1763. In fact, it would be true to say that the Americans themselves never really observed the full letter of the law in this field, and the whole interior policy was thrown over in 1768.[33] The North Americans were delighted at this turn of events, but the ghosts of the intent behind the 1763 decisions would come to haunt the policy-makers in 1774.

Such practical difficulties can explain the policy impasse even after Shelburne and Carleton began to see eye to eye in 1767. But it is not the whole story. General administrative difficulties were, in many respects, peripheral to the essential point at issue. The resolution of the interior problem, for example, did not depend on the establishment of a civil government; one could be achieved without the other. In other words, in 1767 Shelburne and Carleton had still to address the issue of how to integrate a Catholic population into a constitutional structure founded upon Anglican exclusivity. Wrestling with this conundrum in the first half of 1767 has led historians to believe that nothing was done on Quebec until an opposition campaign at Westminster in June forced the government to declare its hand on the province's affairs. It is difficult to support such a position after looking at the papers of Shelburne and his advisers. If they are to be accused of lacking initiative, it is not with regard to Quebec's religious problems. Far from it, they went over and over the problem *ad nauseam*. Even the archbishop of York's report on this subject of 1764 was resurrected, and the prelate himself asked to rewrite it for further considerations in April 1767. This new draft was then submitted to James Marriot, the advocate-general, for his comments and opinion. In the event, they proved quite unhelpful, for Marriot clung to the common prejudice that education, religious control, and specific political and economic inducements would turn the French population into good loyal Protestants over a generation.[34] Shelburne had abandoned such ideas as unrealistic in 1762 and never took Marriot's opinion seriously. Those advisers who most closely reflected the earl's views on religion in Quebec received the most serious attention, as might be expected, and especially Lauchlin MacCleane in 1767.

It was MacCleane, one of Shelburne's confidants and general factotum in his clique, who prepared the most persuasive and penetrating reports on Quebec in these months. He did not start his theorizing from the premise of conversion, but concentrated on the means of adapting English laws and tradition to the actualities in the province.[35] The main areas of concern were now very familiar: legal structures, a religious settlement, and representation. On the question of legal structures, MacCleane echoed Yorke's desire for a more equitable balance between French civil law practices and English criminal law than was embodied in Murray's ordinance of September 1764. On the latter two problems, however, MacCleane moved the philosophical debate forward considerably. He at last talked of the religious and civil questions in terms of practicalities. In MacCleane's view, the logical progression from an acceptance of the necessity of Canadian involvement in Quebec's future under British rule was a twofold adjustment. First, the Privy Council would have to revise certain clauses in the letters patent issued to Murray and Carleton, especially the contentious legal and religious administrative forms that the government had obliged their officials to apply. Second, new oaths for the Canadians under British rule would have to be prescribed, retaining the essential phrases of loyalty to the new crown without offending Catholic consciences. This dual solution to such intractable problems appeared simplicity itself, and MacCleane even provided Shelburne with an outline for the new oaths:

I have examined the Act of the 1st of William and Mary for the abrogating the old oaths of allegiance and supremacy and appointing other oaths. The Canadian subjects will take these oaths; they only desire to be excused from the Test and signing the declaration against Transubstantiation. Although the act of King William says that these oaths are to be taken by all [and] Persons who hold offices, yet it may be argued that the Act extended only to Great Britain and not to the colonies much less to Dominions not then conquered. [If] the Canadians however take these oaths there is no force in the objection, and any arguments drawn from this Act of King William must fall of course.[36]

A reading of this short document shows that MacCleane had done his legal homework well. These proposals reflected a continuity in official thinking about Catholicism in the empire from the earlier part of the century to the most recent pronouncement by Fletcher Norton and De Grey on 10 June 1765. Viewed from a broader perspective, however, this rough draft represents something of a watershed in the history of the Hanoverian period, for here is the first real attempt at providing a practical solution to the toleration of Catholicism in civic affairs. Shelburne's retreat from a Protestant ascendancy towards a more tolerant view of Canadian involvement in Quebec life had now been complemented with a feasible enabling mechanism.

Yet there was a catch to this commitment, which Shelburne and Mac-Cleane soon discovered when they sat down to thrash out the details in a plan of action. It was quite all right in theory to draw up estimates of the numbers of Catholic Canadians permitted to sit in a proposed assembly and "allow the new acquired subjects some share in the Administration."[37] But it was quite another thing to enact such proposals. Even if Shelburne and MacCleane could aggregate the number to satisfy all shades of opinion, an act of parliament was still required to put the whole into effect. This was the one problem neither Shelburne nor his advisers seemed willing to address at the time. Why was this? It is frequently cited that culpability lay with a lack of interest and laziness on Shelburne's part, but this is clearly not so. Indeed, there were more profound reasons why Shelburne never introduced legislation on this subject, and they have been ignored. What lay at the core of the legislative inaction was the elementary fact that a bill advocating Catholic toleration in Quebec would touch the rawest of political nerves in England. This is not to imply that a like measure would be destined to fail; events in 1774 would prove otherwise. There was, as recent research has shown, a growing sympathy both in the parliamentary classes and in what historians like to call "polite circles" with the concept of toleration.[38] Nevertheless, in 1767 Shelburne was in the political front line, without a ministerial captain leading the troops, and he had to consider taking on not only an immense residual popular antipathy to Catholic toleration but also the prejudices of the king – which on this subject ran very deep. Convincing the king that Quebec was a special case in religious matters proved to be the great achievement of North's ministry in 1774. Though it is not known how this was done, the measure of the success can be judged by comparing this issue to George III's attitude to Irish emancipation and Pitt in 1801. The delicacy of this subject cannot be overstated, and it certainly came to the fore in June of 1767 when the parliamentary opposition attempted to gain some mileage from the government's inaction on Quebec.

Much has been written on the thrust of the opposition campaign in May and June 1767, in which the lack of a policy for Quebec provided a third of the ammunition in a concerted attack on the Chatham ministry's imperial policies. The other two, far more publicized, thirds concerned the behaviour of the Massachusetts legislature in granting pardons to Stamp Act rioters and the failure of New York to comply with stipulations of the American Mutiny Act.[39] As it happened, the Quebec issue quickly became submerged beneath a spirited debate in the Lords on Massachusetts and New York on 20 May, fuelled by the rare sight of the king's brother, the duke of York, opposing the court and forcing a very close division.[40] When the issues came before the Lords again on 27 May, the spotlight shifted from Quebec onto those matters offering the best chance of embarrassing the government. In the context of a history of opposition politics, therefore, the tendency has been to treat Quebec policy as peripheral, a makeweight in the primary debate on New York and Massachusetts. This neglect is definitely regrettable, for it ignores some important lessons to be learned from the debate – not least the success of the opposition case in Quebec.

This does not mean that the campaign on Quebec policy was wholly rooted in a profound concern for the province's future. On the contrary, when Richmond began planning his attack on the government's inaction in early May two factors were uppermost in his mind. First, revenge on Northington had to be exacted for his bloody-mindedness the year before, and second, the Rockingham party's fortunes depended on active and effective opposition to government policy, exploiting whatever issues existed at the time to embarrass the government. On the latter, Richmond was not particular about principle and enlisted the duke of Newcastle's support to orchestrate the attack in the Upper House. The old duke welcomed the involvement and challenge of helping to organize strategy. He utilized all his political contacts, writing missives to spiritual and temporal lords with whom he had the least acquaintance, impressing upon them the worthiness of the cause Richmond espoused. What is clear throughout this hectic exercise is that Newcastle did not have a clue about the worthiness of the Quebec cause. As he admitted to the archbishop of Canterbury on 17 May 1767, the details of the case from the year before were unknown to him because of his absence from council, but the merits of the case in general were so self-evident he could do no other than oppose the government. "It is," he wrote, "a most trying thing, that a colony now ceded to the Crown of England, should be without any government whatever."[41] Such platitudes hardly boded well for the cause, and there is no doubt that Newcastle was not the only Rockinghamite in the dark. If the preparation for this campaign proved anything, it was that party politics were alive and well in the spring of 1767.

To be utterly dismissive of Quebec's place in opposition politicking of May and June 1767, however, misrepresents the episode. The way strategy was enacted and the government's response that was elicited reveal significant insights into the contemporary perception of Quebec's problems that should not be overlooked. The choice of the Lords for the campaign on Quebec was certainly pertinent and sensible, for it contained the majority of personnel with expertise on the subject. Furthermore, headway was made in debates on the subject of 20 and 27 May, and then 2 June. Richmond's pique and Newcastle's ignorance apart, motions came forth, papers were laid before the Lords, and a resolution was passed by the Upper House on 2 June, stating: "That it appears to this Committee, that the Province of *Quebec*, for a considerable time past has wanted, and does now stand in need of further regulations and provisions, relating to its Civil government and religious establishment."[42] The government had no objections to the words in such a resolution, because it excused the ministry from a specific commitment on a topic on which it had yet to conceive a united policy front. Yet a closer look at the resolution and the narrow division that preceded it suggests that the matter was in fact decided more or less as the opposition had planned it in May.[43] An examination of the resolutions discussed by the Rockinghams before the first motions for papers on the subject on 20 May reveals little that was specific either. All that the Rockinghams, and their allies the Bedfords, wished for was some "proceeding on the matters," and this is what they obtained on 2 June.[44]

The interesting question here, then, is why the Rockinghams were so general in approach. In part the reasons must have been practical: to appeal to the widest possible audience and cement an alliance with the Bedfords, whose views on this subject remained unknown prior to May and June 1767.[45]

Yet practicalities explain only a small part of the story. The Rockinghams, faced with a prickly ideological problem, chose to circumvent it. How could Richmond have been more specific without publicly supporting the unsupportable idea of Catholic toleration? Only by addressing this issue would a real "proceeding" on Quebec be possible, as Richmond knew. He also recognized, however, that the Rockinghams' mercantile supporters in the City and around the country would have been greatly offended at such a declaration. As a result, Richmond boxed clever. His motion on 20 May was only specific on the point of saying that the government should have done something with regard to the Board of Trade's draft instructions to the Quebec governor of 24 June 1766. Of course, this was the very report with which Yorke would have changed the province's legal system, and which, in turn, prompted Northington's wrecking tactics. No one doubted at the time that Richmond intended to kill two birds with one stone by his motion.

What could the government do in response, other than concede ground? Shelburne was certainly not prepared to declare publicly that he had been wrestling with the Catholic toleration question and favoured a liberal solution. Nor had Richmond any intention of forcing such a concession from the government, for fear of internal criticism from Rockinghamite supporters. Thus the general statement of purpose that emerged on 2 June seemed to satisfy everyone. Indeed, the wisdom of compromise on this subject was brought home to those lords present immediately after the Quebec resolution when Lord Radnor "proposed that the bishops should give in the numbers of Papists in their several dioceses, which was ordered, and much evaded by the Catholics."[46] True, Radnor's proposal applied to Britain, not the colonies, and so little is known about the episode that it is impossible to say what prompted the move. Nevertheless, coincidence seems too simple an explanation for this day's proceedings. Perhaps Radnor did seize an opportunity to nip concessions to Quebec Catholics in the bud. Two responses to his action certainly mirror the sort of painful debate that Shelburne and his advisers experienced grasping the nettle of toleration. To George III, Radnor's action warranted unreserved praise. "I wish to know who have most distinguished themselves in support," the king told Grafton, acting premier, "Lord Radnor's zeal on this occasion is very meritorious and I shall certainly when I see him thank him."[47] This was one side of the argument; on the other was the diarist and MP Horace Walpole. In Walpole's opinion, the problem was much overrated, and his summary of the debate embodies that germ of tolerance which eventually allowed the parliamentary classes to accept the Quebec legislation of 1774. Of Catholicism in Britain in 1767 he commented:

In fact, there was no singular increase of that sect. Many Jesuits had fled hither on the demolition of their order; but it was not a moment to make Popery formidable. It was wearing out in England by the loss of their chief patrons, the Catholic Peers, whose number was considerably diminished. The Duchess of Norfolk, a zealous, though not a religious woman, of a very confused understanding, and who believed herself more artful than she was, contributed, almost singly, to conversions, by bribes and liberality to the poor. But Rome was reduced to be defensive; and unless, as I apprehend, the Methodists are secret Papists, and no doubt they copy, build on, and extend their rites toward that model, Popery will not revive here, when it is falling to decay in its favourite regions. [48]

It is difficult not to believe that the politicians wanted this subject kept under wraps, whether it concerned the empire or not. A look at the experience of the Rockinghams from 1766-69, for instance, leads to the conclusion that they escaped trouble over Quebec by the skin of their teeth. While in office, they had been outwardly responsive to the public and parliamentary demands for establishing a permanent settlement in the province in the best English tradition of Protestant representation. The recall of Murray and the appointment of people like Hey and Maseres bore witness to this fact. And the whole thrust of Rockinghamite policy was underscored, it seemed, by the publication of Maseres's tract, *Considerations on the Expediency of Procuring an Act of Parliament for the Settlement of the Province of Quebec*, in 1766. The pamphlet was clearly perceived as a public version of Rockinghamite thinking on Quebec's future. Unfortunately for the Rockinghams, a credibility gap opened soon after when their theoretical stance on the province was compared to the reality of Rockinghamite policy while in office. This was the administration, after all, that had appointed a bishop to the head of the Catholic church in Quebec, canvassed legal reforms that accepted French custom, and put off *ad infinitum* the establishment of an assembly. This gap between theory and practice explains not only why the Rockinghams kept the campaign of 1767 so low key but also why they remained so quiet up to and on through the passage of the Quebec Act. By focusing on a general commitment to act on the province's problems, they could at least claim consistency. The nuts and bolts of a policy that openly embraced Catholic toleration ran the risk of alienating Rockinghamite support, and they refused to gamble with such high stakes.

Even more remarkable, however, is the fact that it took until 1769 before the public tumbled to the distinction between myth and reality in Quebec policy. It was a group of Dissenters and Unitarians, led by Thomas Hollis, who spearheaded the public and press campaign against the idea of concessions to Catholics, no matter where their location. They found an especially sympathetic editor, Thomas Mortimer, in charge of the *Political Register*, and this journal became a vehicle for several diatribes against the government's handling of Canadian problems. One of their chief bones of contention was the Rockingham ministry's double-talk over Murray's recall and Briand's appointment. This group believed that the governor's fall from grace resulted from his failure to push ahead with an assembly and the introduction of the

Protestant faith, but they eventually realized that Briand's appointment sanctioned Catholicism under the Crown. Maseres's pamphlet obviously assuaged some misgivings on this score, but not all. In May 1769 a long piece in the *Political Register* exploded Rockinghamite pretensions on this issue.[49] In the bluntest manner, which must have made the Rockinghams wince, this critic pointed to the truth of the matter when he wrote: "In some late publications, great pains have been taken to defend the Rockingham administration[50] and it is certain the general tenor of conduct during that administration was highly beneficial to the commercial interests of the nation, nor were the rights and privileges of the people invaded ... but as if this great King was doomed never to know a perfect administration, it must be remembered that during that period the religious establishment of the Roman Catholics in Canada took place." Yet this piece was not simply a polemic – effective though it stood as that – for it also struck some general blows at administrative tardiness in producing a settlement, blows that struck at the heart of ministerial fears and prejudices about Quebec. The wider ramifications of the religious questions fell under particular scrutiny. As the author pointed out, using for his text a sermon preached by the bishop of Llandaff, John Ewer, at St Mary le Bow on 20 February 1767, if Quebec could have "*bishops*" and "*seminaries*," what will be the response of "the people of Ireland of the Romish persuasion?" This represented a fair question in the circumstances of mid-eighteenth-century Anglo-Irish relations, and one that merits further investigation to discover how action in one part of the empire influenced policy in another. An equally penetrating observation concerned the author's assertion that permitting Canadians to retain their religious affiliation would undoubtedly encourage divided loyalties. This point turned the argument of benign sovereignty on its head by offering a new twist to the position developed by the little Englanders in the early 1760s. In the author's view, the French population would always be a fifth column within the empire, "and revolt with first fair opportunity in time of war to their former sovereigns." From the parliamentary perspective the only weakness in the case put forward in this tract concerned legality, for the writer erroneously maintained that "the laws in force against popery extend to all his dominions." But this technical error could hardly be refuted by politicians seeking justification for their actions in a lively public debate. Indeed, it is unlikely any such course of action was considered, because there was a footnote to the sentence on the laws against popery which raised a question that could never be answered to everyone's satisfaction. As the writer put it, the laws against papists must apply to all parts of the empire, for "if their efficacy is destroyed in one part, it is injustice to urge them with rigour in another; but surely no real lover of his country would wish to see them evaded in any one instance in any part of the British empire, for on the due execution of them depends the preservation of our present system of government." Herein lay the enduring kernel of the philosophical assumptions about Catholicism that polite opinion had overcome, though such people had not yet had the courage to make their more tolerant view public.

This theoretical approach to the threat posed at home by imperial expansion and supervision became commonplace in the discussion not only of Quebec but America and India as well. On the whole, it did not prove a very salutory debate. It is hard to believe that the general reader took the charges of malignant popery creeping over Britain and its empire very seriously. Like Walpole, most informed observers accepted the evidence of their own experience, which suggested that Catholicism was on the wane. Nevertheless, the sting in the articles published by the *Political Register*, and the column space given to other zealots, like "Pliny Junior" in the *Public Advertizer*, should not be underestimated.[51] Their efforts formed part of a wider racial and anti-Catholic campaign,[52] that in the right circumstances could be fanned into violent and bloody flames, as the events of 1780 showed all too well. Their bigoted cant revealed as much about strains and divisions within the British body politic as it did about their perception of Canada's role in the empire. But it was fortunate for all governments in the 1760s that the lid was kept on the Quebec business and no consistent reporting of parliamentary debates took place, for anxieties and tensions about Catholic toleration might have reached the centre of the political stage at an earlier date. As it was, the articles of the type discussed above petered out in the fall of 1770 with parliamentary action over Grenada.[53] All the participants, however, had offered the first serious challenge to the optimistic preconceptions about assimilating Quebec into the empire so prevalent after the conquest.

Optimism was certainly in short supply in Shelburne's department in the summer of 1767. The usual explanation for this is the obvious one of dismay at the recent parliamentary activity. The opposition campaign on Quebec in the Lords prompted Shelburne and his advisers to act on a question that they would have preferred to leave untouched. Once he was active, it is then believed, Shelburne became converted to the idea of settling Quebec's problems through parliamentary legislation, especially the administration of justice. This presentation of the events in 1767 requires revision. If Shelburne and his officials seemed depressed at the prospect of action on Quebec, who could blame them? In practice they were being asked to go over ground now very familiar to them. Shelburne knew from his investigations over the past nine months that the province required regulation; he did not need a resolution in the Lords to tell him so. Nor was Shelburne a sudden convert to the idea of parliamentary legislation on one problem or another affecting Quebec. Indeed, it seems apparent, on looking at the material he gathered and the discussions recorded in 1766–67, that Shelburne had plans for what is known today as an omnibus bill. Such a measure would include clauses regulating religion, justice, and representation. It would also address the lack of a means to raise revenue, and even the boundary dispute with New York which took on such importance to the settlement of 1774.[54]

In these circumstances the actions that Shelburne took after the debates in the Lords should be cast in a different light: he did not simply succumb to parliamentary pressure. Rather than putting Shelburne and his department on the spot, the events of June 1767 actually assisted his policy goals. On 20 June he was able to write to Carleton informing him of the unremarkable fact that, "As the right administration of government in Quebec is a matter of the greatest importance to that province, the improvement of its civil constitution is under the most serious and deliberate consideration of His Majesty's Servants."[55] Just over two months later the Privy Council met to discuss what was required to secure legislative settlement of Quebec's administration. The ministers who assembled on 28 August made up the effective cabinet, and there could be no doubting that Quebec's future still lay with decisions taken at the very top.[56] The one great achievement of this day was the decision to reject the draft instructions from the Board of Trade on reforming Quebec's legal structure originally submitted in June 1766, as being "so general, and so unsupported by any specific or particular proof of any grievances."[57] In their place another information-gathering exercise was initiated. Shelburne must have smiled a wry smile of relief at this turn of events. He had never taken the instructions of 1766 seriously, and, with their rejection, the idea of an empirical solution lived on. Shelburne issued the requisite orders to Carleton to begin collecting data on the judicial processes and its problems in December 1767. But he also took the important step of choosing Maurice Morgann to co-ordinate the investigative effort between governments in Quebec and London. Shelburne must have envisaged Morgann's role as a trouble-shooter, one empowered to cut through the immense amount of contradictory documentary advice flowing from the province. Morgann would see the reality of the situation first hand, communicate with Carleton, and return to England to finalize details of a parliamentary bill.

The plan backfired. Although Shelburne had conceived a bold, sensible strategy, it never came to fruition. A series of events quite beyond his control unravelled the plot over the next year. The reverses began in January 1768 with the creation of a new post to rationalize imperial administration. It took the form of a colonial secretaryship, and the earl of Hillsborough became its first occupant. On the surface this development had great potential; giving cabinet rank and power to a minister whose sole function was to supervise colonial affairs seemed long overdue. In practice it did not work out quite like this. Shelburne did not relinquish any of his official powers over North American policy to Hillsborough or to what he considered a junior department. Thus, until Shelburne resigned in 1768, he and Hillsborough went their separate departmental ways on colonial policy in general. This situation was bad enough, but it worsened considerably when it became obvious that Shelburne and Hillsborough had differing views on the future of Quebec. On taking up his post Hillsborough recognized the need for a settlement in the province, and yet his early discussions at the board indicated that it would not be along the lines favoured by Shelburne. Hillsborough's knowledge of Quebec's problems had been gained while serving with Halifax at the Board of Trade in the early 1760s and his ideas had not progressed in any perceptible way by 1768. From his first missive to Carleton in March 1768, Hillsborough talked of enforcing the Proclamation, encouraging the Church of England to convert the Canadians, and tolerating some French legal procedures in a way that one scholar of his career termed "clearly absurd."[58] To canvass proceeding in this manner simply revealed Hillsborough's lack of understanding of the state of Canadian law, religion, and society. Instability and lack of continuity again came to haunt Quebec policy-making.

It might be thought that, once Shelburne left the government in October 1768, Hillsborough's job of concocting a legislative package would have been much easier. But there were two major obstacles to overcome. First was Hillsborough's ideological naïveté with respect to religious questions in the province. Hillsborough appeared impervious to the work of Shelburne and others on this issue. The instructions to Carleton issued in 1768, and prepared by Hillsborough's board, for example, made no concessions on oaths or tests to be taken before holding office. They were, in fact, little more than a rehash of Murray's instructions.[59] In addition, even had Hillsborough wished to proceed with a parliamentary settlement he could not have done much, for the Board of Trade was still bound by the Privy Council decision of August 1768 to gather information prior to legislation. Hillsborough accepted this situation for a while, but in July 1769 he attempted to gain approval for a revised version of the old draft instructions of June 1766 as a basis for some permanent arrangement for the administration of Quebec.[60] The draft was prepared in response to an order from the council in September of the previous year. Yet this piece of bureaucratic theatre had been repeated so many times before that, not surprisingly, the Privy Council rejected Hillsborough's draft on 20 November 1769, refusing to act until Maurice Morgann returned from the province with his own report.[61] This really represented an affront to Hillsborough, and yet the lords of the council could be forgiven for believing, like Shelburne, that perhaps Morgann alone offered the best chance of a consistent report and plan of action. The impulse for rejecting Hillsborough's July 1769 report had been the fact that Carleton and his law officers in Quebec fell out over the type of report on the future of the legal system they wished to be sent to London. So, in essence, three documents on this subject reached Britain in November 1769: Carleton's own version of the report on legal structures, Carleton's version with a dissenting appendix by Hey, and Maseres's damning report of Carleton's effort. The story of their preparation has been told many times, but the impact they had in London is usually neglected.[62] What else could Hillsborough and his colleagues in council have been but confused? It is no wonder that they clutched at the straw of Morgann's return, and, better still, in ministerial eyes, allowed Carleton to return home on leave in 1770 to tell the story first hand. As the governor put it in a letter to Hillsborough of 15 March 1769: "I really believe I could more effectively promote and advance [the king's interest in Canada] by a residence of a few months in London, than of so many years in this country."[63] No one disagreed with the idea that two experienced heads might be better than one.

It is not surprising amidst these circumstances that a policy impasse occurred. Ministerial changes, Hillsborough's attempts to turn the clock back on the problem, and the quandary over which reports should be given credence all conspired to make sure that nothing could be done. There is one aspect of the story, however, that has remained untold, and it is a crucial one. When the Privy Council ordered Hillsborough to prepare a report on Quebec in September 1768 it had done so in response to two letters submitted for consideration in the spring and early fall of that year. One emanated from the Canada Committee at the New York Coffee House, the other, more interestingly, from "Sundry Merchants Trading to and deeply interested in the Province of Quebec" of the same address.[64] The issue they confronted was that of an assembly. Nothing new in that, so it seemed – only their excellent timing: the Treasury had just been considering Carleton's reports pointing out the necessity of raising revenue in the province, and with Hillsborough's appointment the climate again looked favourable for petitioning on the assembly issue.[65] Here, the merchants must have thought, was a colonial secretary straight out of the old whig mould, guaranteed to lend a sympathetic ear to pleas for a representative body anywhere within the empire. The striking feature of these pleadings, however, was their acceptance of Catholic Canadian involvement in the future constitutional arrangements for the province. These petitioners were "humbly recommending that a full Legislature may be speedily granted to the Province of Quebec, and that a Number of His majesty's Roman Catholic subjects there may be admitted into the Council and House of Representatives."[66] This plea represented a remarkable breakthrough for Shelburne's vision of the future for Quebec and came right out of the blue. The wording of these letters could not have contrasted more sharply with the bellicose language of Protestant ascendancy of four or five years earlier. How ironic that it coincided with Shelburne's departure from office!

A seemingly insignificant concession by the merchants in London trading to Canada thus held some unexpected promise of a settlement in the near future. It bore witness to the fact that going public on Catholic toleration, albeit heavily qualified, would not now be the political folly everyone feared in 1767. If the government had convinced those mercantile classes most closely involved in securing Quebec's economic prosperity that only toleration provided hope for a lasting empirical settlement, then parliamentary support for legislation along these lines must surely follow. If the debates on the repeal of the Stamp Act in 1766 had proven anything to informed observers, it was that commercial opinion could have an impact on imperial trade questions and, in the long run, general policy. The problems of representation, raising revenue, and administering justice in Quebec had always hinged on the involvement of Catholic Canadians in these processes. Now, the dichotomy between the spiritual issues and policy-making for the province had been bridged by important groups both inside and outside parliamentary circles. The foundation for a settlement of Quebec's future had at last been laid.

CHAPTER SIX

The Quiet Revolution 1770–73

"That country has been exceedingly ill used. It has been neglected both in its civil and military departments, may I say, shamefully neglected. Has any arrangement, has any measure been taken, to please those new subjects, that you should have touched with delicacy? Have you tendered it to them, with a wise and prudent hand? Have you enabled them to relish the blessings you meant to bestow?"[1]

These poignant rhetorical questions about Canada were put by Isaac Barré to the House of Commons on 7 December 1770. It is doubtful that Barré, a retired soldier who had seen service with Wolfe at Quebec, expected a reply, or even that anyone present could have given him one. The speech highlighted a common concern about the lack of public information, and to a degree official reticence, about the state of policy for Quebec. It proved an awkward moment for the government, but no one suggested a remedy for the situation there and then. Hopes for progress on this issue had been vested in the return of Maurice Morgann and of the governor-in-chief himself, Carleton. The former returned in 1770 but had little new to recommend, and in the reality of the changed political climate in London, Morgann's role as catalyst in this manner had been long superseded by Carleton.[2] The governor was expected home in the winter of 1770, and to that point it appeared to observers like Barré that nothing had been done, was being done, or could be done. This appearance of public inaction did not tell the whole story, however. In 1770 a quiet revolution in British thinking and policy-making on Quebec began, which by 1773 had paved the way for parliamentary legislation. This movement had nothing to do with events in the thirteen American colonies but was founded upon continuities in personnel, like Carleton and H.T. Cramahé, and ideologies, particularly the commitment to Catholic toleration. These figures and strains of thought linked the articles of capitulation to the Quebec Act.

It must be emphasized that Carleton prepared for his return to England meticulously. He left the government of the province in the hands of Cramahé, a man perfectly in accord with Carleton's own views about the future settlement of Quebec's religious, civil, and judicial problems. If their approach had to be summed up in the light of other opinions current at the time, in particular those of Hey and Maseres, "turning the clock back" might suffice. The belief embodied in Carleton's mission to London was that damage to Canadian society and its institutions since the conquest had to be repaired to ensure the security of a permanent settlement and the loyalty of the king's new subjects. Carleton's detractors did not espouse different goals; they just canvassed different means of achieving the same ends. At the root of these differing approaches lay the ever-present religious issue. It would not and could not go away, because it infused all the unresolved problems. To those on one side, like Hey, Maseres, and Hillsborough, involved in the nuts and bolts of policy-making, the dream of a Prostestant colony with its concomitant English institutions could not be given up entirely. Measures of short-term expediency could be passed, as in religious affairs, and even concessions in legal practice might be granted to facilitate the application of English legal norms. Yet, in the end, whether it were over one, two, or even three generations, Quebec could, and should, in their view, be transformed and Anglicized. Moreover, they believed that change could be wrought immediately by building upon the advances already made through Murray's judicial ordinance of September 1764 and by the establishment of the Church of England in Quebec. In short, the Canadians had to adapt to the British way, not vice versa. If read between the lines, this was the case put forward by Hey and Maseres in their dissentients to Carleton's report on the administration of justice in Quebec of 1769. To Carleton, on the other side of the fence, all such thinking was impracticable and unjust. The governor had had a large enough dose of the bigotry of the English-speaking merchants in Quebec to convince him that any policy they favoured would be poison to the future of the province under British rule. Carleton had abandoned any notion of Anglicizing Quebec soon after his arrival. But what sort of constitution and society did he wish to establish in the province? Not surprisingly, it seemed to be the one with which he was most familiar in Britain – a gentrified élite holding sway over national (or, in this case, provincial) and local offices and their functionaries. In pursuing this creation Carleton thought that a simple turning of the clock back to 1760 would do the trick, but he erred in his reconstruction work. The one section of Canadian society that he believed would prove the bedrock of the gentrification of Quebec – the seigneury – was just not up to the task. This class had never performed a similar function in local society under French rule; the men for this job, as Ouellet and several other scholars have pointed out, were the captains of militia.[3] No matter; in 1770 this was the powerful vision of Quebec's future that Carleton possessed, and which he intended to sell to the politicians in London in his arrival.

Carleton set the revision process in motion before he left Quebec with two reforms that represented a firm declaration of intent. The first concerned the administration of justice, and was passed in an ordinance by the Quebec council in February 1770.[4] It arose from disquiet with the behaviour of JPs in Montreal and its environs which was later highlighted in an investigation by Maseres into complaints by the local populace. As a result, the civil jurisdiction given to magistrates in the ordinance of September 1764 was withdrawn, leaving JPs with only their criminal and police jurisdiction. To compensate, the Court of Common Pleas was expanded and ordered to sit more frequently to handle small civil cases. This reform aimed directly at restoring practice under the old regime and eliminating abuses that had been a by-product of introducing English custom to an alien culture. Isaac Barré expressed similar opinions about what should be done on this front in a speech to the Commons on 8 May 1770. As he put it: "The fact is shortly this. You have given the laws of this country to the Canadians. They do not understand, they cannot relish the law. You have changed the capital point that they have hitherto been accustomed to. Besides this the poor peasant of the country had every week a court of justice to go to, a regular appeal. You have now introduced into the rich colonies all the litigious spirit, the delay, the expense, all the worst doctrine of Westminster Hall."[5] This must have been the only time that Lord Mansfield and Barré ever agreed on a political issue, for these words truly echoed Mansfield's diatribe to George Grenville in December 1764 about keeping Bleak House out of Quebec and allowing "the conquered their own laws and usages."[6] Carleton had obviously struck a resonant chord here that augured well for the future.

The second parting shot from the governor in July 1770 concerned the church. It had long worried those sympathetic to the existence of Catholicism in Quebec under British rule that no stipulation had been made for continuing the episcopacy. Briand's surreptitious appointment represented a unique event which could not really be repeated. The only way to avoid having the Canadian episcopacy dependent upon clergy trained and ordained in Europe was to appoint a coadjutor in Quebec. This measure Carleton inclined to after 1767 because it offered security for his vision of the religious settlement in the province. He had suggested it to Hillsborough in 1768 as a sensible policy to follow, but the earl's Protestant prejudices forbade his sanction of the appointment.[7] On the eve of his departure, Carleton boldly and unilaterally declared the Canadian priest L.P.M. Desglis coadjutor for the province. The necessary bulls for the consecration were obtained by Briand through friendly Quebec clergymen now settled in Paris. In this classic compromise, Carleton sidestepped accusations that Rome had interfered directly in British affairs.

In hindsight these two reforms look quite separate, but no one at the time believed them to be so. There was opposition in Quebec to both measures, and some filtered through to London. It is not difficult to see why. Carleton had begun his mission of delineating the image of Quebec's future in terms that all his contemporaries understood. Preservation of religious and legal practices from the old regime spelt the end of the intended Protestant mercantile ascendancy. There were protests at this in the province once the realization dawned. The English-speaking merchants in Montreal condemned the judicial restructuring as a threat to the liberty of the king's subjects. [8] Their anger may also have prompted the petition for an assembly sent to the king from Quebec in 1770, which stated quite categorically, in the language of 1763, "That there is now a sufficient number of Your Majesty's Protestant Subjects residing in and possessed of real property in this Province, and who are otherwise qualified to be Members of a General Assembly." [9] Carleton had expected this response, however, and played a clever covering game. In mid-eighteenth-century English politics it was an unwritten law that every petition or polemic should be met with a rejoinder, and sure enough Carleton had one up his sleeve. At the same time that the "General Assembly" was being canvassed, the king received another petition from his new subjects in Quebec endorsing the governor's efforts to preserve French law and custom. They pleaded a recognition "de quelle importance il étoit pour leurs interrêts d'être Jugeés et Gouvernées suivant les Loix, Coutumes et Ordonnances, sous Lequels Ils sont nés." [10] One of the signatories to this petition, F.J. Cugnet, is worth noting, for he provides a direct link to Carleton. Cugnet was the secretary to the Quebec council and the man Carleton ordered to prepare a survey of all ordinances passed under the old regime. There were fifty or so in number and Cugnet presented the document to Carleton in late 1769. The governor, in turn, brought the information to London with him, and during his campaign to persuade the government to follow his recommendations on legislation for the province in 1772, he strengthened his case by publishing Cugnet's manuscript in London. [11]

Despite his meticulous preparatory work before departing, Carleton could have been under no illusions about what difficulties faced him in London. There was the unknown quantity of Lord North, now leading the government, whose views on Quebec were a mystery. Beyond North, there was still Lord Hillsbourgh, the colonial secretary, who was known to be antipathetic to Carleton's view of the future for Quebec. How did the governor approach his task, therefore? In many respects Carleton's method over the two and a half years after he reached England proved to be like a twentieth-century sales pitch, and it could hardly have been a more effective campaign. A clear pattern existed in Carleton's dealings with the politicians in London, in which he sold the idea of conserving Canadian custom and practice wherever possible. He began with the broader picture of security in North America in the event of a French war of *revanche*. After 1768 it is evident from reading not only Carleton's dispatches, now in the colonial office records, but also other correspondence that flowed across the Atlantic from Canada that the idea of imposing a large permanent military presence in Quebec had been abandoned as impractical and undesirable. Even "numerous garrisons," one Canadian correspondent of Lord Egmont wrote in 1770, "may by some unforeseen accident one time or other be wrested out of the hands of the English."[12] The predominant focus from 1768 on with regard to defence was on the security of the town of Quebec itself, and, more particularly, on the construction of a citadel. Carleton had recognized the necessity of developing these defence works in the town from the beginning of his term of duty, and he was certainly not alone in this. One typical description of Quebec by a fellow British officer began thus: "This famous city is situated on a commanding point of land formed by the influx of the River St. Charles into that of St. Lawrence, the highest part of the upper town called Cap Diamond commands all round and with a good citadel which it undoubtedly ought to have, would be immensely strong."[13] The soldier then concluded with a comment that the Kirke brothers, who had first conceived and executed a plan to take the city of Quebec in the 1620s, would have been proud of: "It always has and always must be esteemed the key of Canada, which now seems a natural part of your American Empire and ever should have been thought so, nor should we upon any account ever part with it." Committed though the British were to this ideal, it would in fact be the 1820s before Quebec was a fully fortified town, and the fear then was of the United States of America waging war, not France!

Promoting the idea of a citadel as vital to Quebec's future security, however, was the easy part of Carleton's task in London. The hard part began with trying to explain how, in the absence of a large army of occupation and interior posts, Canadians' loyalty to their new rulers could be guaranteed. Surely, Carleton was asked many times, the French were not going to cease their efforts at undermining British authority in the area? Isaac Barré saw the dichotomy quite clearly in 1770, and berated the government, present and past, for missing an opportunity to involve the Canadians in defence of their own countryside. "You might have raised a small body of troops in that country," he told MPs, "which you might have scattered about among a large body of natives, which would have effectively ruined the French interest in all the back settlements."[14] This was not a flippant suggestion; it had precedents in Britain only a few years earlier. The return to respectability for many Scottish Jacobite families after the failure of the 1745 rebellion had come in the Seven Years' War when they offered their military services to the Hanoverian crown around the globe. What better way could they have underwritten their loyalty to the new regime?[15] Murray had been sympathetic to such a plan for the Canadians, and Carleton does not appear to have opposed it, but it could not be done under existing laws, and herein lay Carleton's trump card. As the governor perceived it, and later expressed the idea to ministers, defence and security of Quebec could not be considered in a vacuum. Once the option of garrisons and permanent military occupation had been rejected, the question of loyalty and Canadian service in British forces could not rest on a citadel and patchwork contingency measures. It had to be founded on the legitimation of British rule through legislation of the sort now being considered by the government. Who could refute this unerring logic?

Carleton peeled off the next layer of this onion in 1771 by canvassing the practical economic reasons for an equitable legislative solution. There were two sides to this coin for Quebec, as can be seen in both public and private statements on the issue. A great deal of optimism about Quebec's future in the empire, for example, can be found in the press. It ran from the moment of conquest through to the passage of the Quebec Act. Reports such as that appearing in the *Public Advertizer* in July 1770, which told of "upwards of 100 families gone up to settle themselves on Beaver Island, situated in the middle of lake Ontario, abounding with the finest furs in all of Canada," appear frivolous enough at first sight, and yet they performed a serious function. They were of the utmost importance to those in Britain investing in an expanding trade to Canada, while offering a shop window for others with the potential to do so. It has been shown that the appetite for news of this nature was almost insatiable in mid-eighteenth-century Britain, and was found in all sections of the population. Investors could just as well have been small shopkeepers in London as the more familiar wealthy merchants in control of large trading warehouses.[16] Such reports lacked the glamour of the long treatise on religious affairs, but in the long term they proved vital to the dissemination of commercial information in Canada. Further research in this field of Britain's past will reveal a more profound countrywide influence on the early entrepreneurial thrust into Quebec.[17]

The government itself also recognized Quebec's economic importance when, in April 1771, it passed an act granting bounties on certain Canadian naval stores and wine imported into Britain.[18] Everyone connected with the administration was thinking along similar lines when it came to the importance of Quebec's resources to the economic empire run from London. Such thought is revealed in government documents that ranged from those at the Board of Trade overwhelmed with petitions for grants of land in Quebec, to the soldier, Robert Innis, writing home to a Scottish politician, James Grant, that "the exportation of corn now becomes a considerable branch of trade here, and will become a vent for their superfluous grain."[19] Carleton knew, however, that the other side of this picture was not so rosy. Quebec's hopeful economic future could only be secured by creating an environment for the king's new subjects in which they could prosper and develop. Without this provision the great spectre of depopulation and emigration might become a reality, and any hope of economic viability for the province would perish.

This argument, in turn, emanated from the belief, of course, that there was no hope of outpopulating the French-speaking Catholic population with Anglo-Saxon Protestants in the foreseeable future. On 1 October 1773, Cramahé explained this philosophy to Dartmouth, the colonial secretary who had replaced Hillsborough in 1772, in the most succinct manner: "fourteen years experience have proved that the increase of the province must depend upon its own population, few or none of our discharged soldiery, the only aid in that way which it has received since the conquest, apply themselves to the cultivation of land, they are mostly artificers, retailers of spiritous liquors, or servants."[20] There had been contention in the early 1760s on this population issue, but by 1771 Carleton had obviously played his part in creating a consensus among his own servants in Quebec and political circles in London that no longer accepted the likelihood of rapid Protestant settlement and population growth. Indeed, the tide of opinion was flowing in the opposite direction. When the solicitor-general, Alexander Wedderburn, came to prepare his report on Quebec in 1772, preventing emigration to Quebec from Britain was one of his major concerns – a philosophical position that endorsed Carleton's arguments to the full. The question that all this postulating on population and prosperity raised, in the last analysis, was how it could be achieved. And within this interrogatory could be found the core of the outer layers.

To Carleton the answer to Quebec's future security and economic viability lay in the past. It was up to the British to enact a legislative restoration of all that Canadians held dear in their society, especially the Catholic church and legal practices based on the Coutume de Paris. The wheel had now turned full circle. In the view of Carleton and his advisers, who must have discussed the matter many times before his departure, the locus of all revolving problems in the province, from defence to the economy, was religion. The need for an equitable religious settlement had always been evident in the advice sent to London, and even approved in the 1770 petition sent to the king on the administration of justice and signed by Cugnet. There, immediately after the passage recommending the usage of laws under which the Canadians "sont nés" cited above, can be found the boldest statements on the matter of religion and loyalty of the new subjects:

La Religion, Sire, que nous professons, et dans la profession de Laquelle Il vous a plû nous assurer que nous ne Serions jamais troublées, quoique differente de celle de vos autres Sujets, Seroit-elle un motif (du moins dans Votre Province de Quebec) pour Exclure une si considérable peuplade d'Enfants Soumis et fidels à La participation aux bontés du meilleur des Roys, du plus tendre des peres. Non Sire, Le préjugé ne perça jamais Jusqu'à Votre Thrône; vous aimés également et Sans distinction tous vos fidels sujets, vos Canadiens auront toujours pour Votre auguste personne Le plus parfait armour, La plus grande Soûmission; c'est à ces titres, Sire, qu'ils attendent de

Votre Majesté La même bienveillance, La meme protection que vous accordés a tous vos Sujets.[21]

This statement certainly met the problem of religion and allegiance head on, positing an essential truism that became enshrined in the Quebec Act. Nevertheless, it was never a foregone conclusion that the idea of toleration as security for loyalty would be accepted. There were one or two fictions in this petition that could have been rejected out of hand. No eighteenth-century Catholic Irishman, for example, would have signed a petition containing the clause "Le préjugé ne perça jamais Jusqu'à Votre Thrône." In the event, however, the petitioners did catch the mood of an administration in London determined to avoid past errors. When William Knox wrote his apologia for the Quebec Act in 1774, the first twenty or so pages hammered home the absolute desire amongst the politicians not to create another Irish imbroglio.[22] In discussions up to 1773, when the first orders went out to prepare the Quebec Act legislation, the religious question in the province was an ever-present refrain. It never tired of repetition. As H.T. Cramahé told Dartmouth, the sum of Quebec's future under British rule had two integral parts: "To gain the affection of Canadian subjects they should be granted all possible freedom and indulgence in their religion."[23]

Official acceptance of this equation was a slow process, but recognition began in earnest at a cabinet meeting on 7 June 1771. There is a fascinating record of this gathering: in many ways what is left out of the report is more worthy of note than what is included. The decisions taken were quite precise with regard to legislative action on Quebec, and the report acknowledged Carleton's personal lobby in no uncertain terms. In the words of the first section of the account: "The Reports of the Board of Trade, Governor Carleton, Chief Justice Hey and other papers relative to the Province of Quebec being considered, it is resolved to recommend to His Majesty on the opinion of the Committee that the said Papers be referred by the Privy Council to the King's advocate the Attorney and Solicitor General taking to their assistance Governor Carleton and such others as they should think fit to consider of and draw up a general code of civil and criminal law for the said Province."[24] It can be seen from this that the only specific policy issue in the balance was the legal settlement in Quebec. That this point remained contentious is significant, for it implies that the manner of proceeding on other problems had been resolved in ministerial circles. An examination of the decisions taken in the period 1770 to 1773 suggests that this indeed was the case. On all the important issues the groundwork for clauses in the future Quebec Act had already been done.

In the first place, everyone now accepted the need for parliamentary legislation to establish a civil constitution in Quebec; a delayed triumph, in many ways, for the much-maligned Northington, who had canvassed this policy back in 1766. Second, some form of religious toleration would have to be enshrined in the Quebec legislation. The appointment of Briand in 1766, supported by the introduction of a coadjutor in 1770, had sealed the fate of this issue. Even some of the English merchants trading to Quebec had come to terms with this concept in 1769, and such concessions not only helped reduce popular antipathy to the measure but also encouraged ministers to go through with the policy.[25] Third, the thorny problem of the boundary dispute with New York, which in turn was linked to interior policy in general, had been directed towards a solution favouring Quebec. Progress to this position was unerringly simple. After the withdrawal of the interior posts in 1768, it was feared that the lands west of New York, Pennsylvania, and Virginia would become lawless frontiers, peopled by the less savoury Indian traders and land speculators of the kind who had never recognized the Proclamation line of 1763. Two options appeared in 1769 to resolve the dilemma: either joint supervision of the territory by the three colonies and Quebec, or its annexation to one of the colonies. New York favoured the first in July 1769 and put forward a strong case for a new interior jurisdiction that would eradicate the boundary dispute and lawless wilderness in one fell swoop. Quebec demurred at this proposition in 1769, favouring annexation of all the interior west of the Great Lakes and Ohio River to the province. It based the claim on an extremely strong economic and geographical argument, highlighting its traditional ties through the fur trade with these territories. In short, the new Canadian government would take over from where the French used to operate.[26]

These contrasting views put the ball firmly in the British government's court by 1771, and an inkling of which direction ministers favoured can be found in the fourth matter on which a consensus had evolved by the time of the cabinet meeting on 7 June. The point at issue was government in Quebec without an assembly. The record shows that "All the Lords agreed except Hillsborough who is entirely of opinion to agree with the report of the Board of Trade (10 July 1769) for immediately convening a full legislature in the said province for the settling their laws, revenues, etc."[27] The colonial secretary was nothing if not consistent in his whig ideology, and yet to be fair to Hillsborough his resistance on the issue of an assembly may well have sprung from the dispute on interior policy. What stopped the idea of joint supervision favoured by New York ever getting off the ground was the fact that Quebec had no constitutional means of levying taxes to bear its share of supporting such a scheme. On the other hand, none of the others (New York, Pennsylvania, or Virginia) had sufficient funds on its own to govern the annexation of such a vast territory. The logic of the situation thus led to a Quebec takeover of the interior, with a direct monetary grant from parliament for its governance. The idea of an assembly also perished long before the Quebec Act was cobbled together. The official distaste for an ascendancy body was mirrored in lay opinion over and over again. As one Scottish officer, Lieutenant Marr, told Dartmouth in March 1773, a legislature consisting solely of Protestants could have but one undesirable consequence: "a general Disgust among the whole Canadians."[28]

Having built the momentum for legislation and on 14 June asked for further reports, the cabinet was again left waiting for advice from its law officers.[29] This was now a familiar scene and it raised the question whether progress could ever be made following this routine. In essence the cabinet only asked "the King's advocate, the Attorney and Solicitor General ... to consider of and draw up a general code of civil and criminal law" for the province.[30] But no Quebec problem could be treated in this categorical manner, as the legal officers soon discovered. And, as happened earlier, as soon as this fact dawned on two of those responsible for preparing the reports their analytical powers diminished accordingly. The three reports were not produced in any particular order. Alexander Wedderburn's appeared in December 1772 and those of James Marriott, the advocate-general, and Edward Thurlow, attorney-general, were completed in 1773. These latter two efforts are worth examining first, for they betray a complete lack of recognition of the realities in Quebec since the conquest. Where they were short on knowledge, they tried to compensate with prognostication and uninformed opinion. The salient characteristic of their statements was the way they reflected the old ideological divisions opened up when Halifax was southern secretary. Their efforts were thus quite useless as a guide for action by the administration.

Of the two, Marriott's report was by far the wittiest, but in a sense the most disappointing. Here was an advocate with some detailed knowledge of Quebec's religious problems. Along with De Grey and Willes in 1767, Marriott had prepared a document on the "Ecclesiastical Settlement" in Quebec, which was later submitted to the Privy Council for its consideration.[31] The council found it difficult to act on their information for the report was just that – an account of what existed in the province to the law officers' knowledge. No recommendations came forward because, as they put it in one passage referring to Catholic orders, "there is not sufficient information before the Law Officers for them to judge of the legality." The document represented an exercise in evasion; in view of this, could the government expect any better from Marriott in 1773? Apparently they could not. Marriott's report had many characteristics that suggested his heart was not in the task. First and foremost were the factual mistakes, which the historians Shortt and Doughty cryptically point out in their edition of his work.[32] Indeed, there are some remarkably crass errors, such as the passage where Marriott has Murray calling an assembly "for all the parishes but Quebec." Second, there are the assumptions on which Marriott based his thesis about Quebec society. On the first page of his report, for example, P.F.X. Charlevoix made an unexpected appearance after some fourteen years' absence from official documents. The message that Charlevoix carried had not changed at all. The shortcomings of Canada, seen through Marriott's eyes and distilled in turn from Charlevoix, were rooted in its people, whose "natural intolerance, ignorance and poverty" hindered all efforts by France to turn the colony into a going concern, and would do so again if Britain did not take steps to circumvent these inherent failings.

What steps these should be was answered in the next section of the report. In these passages Marriott abandoned Charlevoix for the more contemporary authorities Maseres and Hey. The belief that the Anglicization of Quebec must take place was then expanded. Marriott actually went further than his sources by still favouring an assembly. He was not specific on timing or who should be elected, simply stating: "I conceive that no laws *in the detail* can be well formed for any country but by a legislative body upon the spot." In the legal sphere, Marriott conceded more ground to the French-speaking population than on any other issue. As he put it in one passage, "the Canadians *must be restored in integrum* to all their ancient laws and usages." But as he said elsewhere in this section, this situation could not be frozen in time: "as men move forward, the laws must move with them." Restoring old ways had its limits, and Marriott did not doubt that the onward and upward progress of Canadian society lay in English ways. English legal practices, in cases such as property and criminal law, ought to be injected into the existing system, and hopefully the abuses in both might be eradicated in time. So, in short, Marriott did not canvass a simple turning the clock back. Within his proposals there existed obvious inbuilt revisions to one old legal system (or maybe even two).

To conclude, Marriott's idiosyncratic views were no better illustrated than in the passages on religion. He could not hide his Protestant prejudices, and contrived a unique scheme for the regulation of the spiritual life of the province which tolerated the Catholics' practice of their religion but not the doctrine, organization, or government of the Roman church. It is difficult to believe that ministers understood this novel suggestion, for it never cropped up again in debate or discussions on Quebec. It appears that Marriott was trying to order a philosophical compromise between clauses in the fourth article of the Peace of Paris that talked of professing Catholicism as far as the laws of Britain allowed. Marriott had two arguments against the prevailing wisdom on this topic. First, he did not accept the 1765 decision which ruled that British laws against Catholics did not apply to the colonies. Second, he did not consider the laws in Britain against Catholics worth much. In his words, "if the penalites of the laws are not felt by the professors of the Romish religion in England, it is by connivance from humanity and policy." This was a moot point that exercised many of Marriott's contemporaries, but with regard to Quebec the advocate-general had a specific remedy. An act of parliament would be passed that permitted the Quebec Catholic population the right to worship but precious little else. There would be no processions, preaching, or conversions, or any outward show at all. Such a policy of toleration envisaged an end to Catholicism in the province by attrition. To the cabinet, it was in the end too clever a play for its own good, for it failed to take account of the state's actions to date in appointing clergy who would ensure the survival of the church in Quebec. Marriott was not apologetic about his policy, however. In a searing concluding statement that challenged the rising deism of politicians like Shelburne and Carleton, Marriott wrote:

is it fit to tolerate all the doctrines of the Romish church, or the ecclesiastical establishments, and powers for the support of the doctrines? To this I answer no: and for this plain reason, because the Romish religion itself (of which the conduct of France in many instances in history, with respect to conquered places, affords sufficient example) *will neither tolerate nor be tolerated*. In some of the articles of its system, on the presumption of its being the dominant system among the several states of Europe professing Christianity, it will give no quarter and therefore it cannot take it without the destruction of the giver.

Thus were European prejudices transported into a vision of a Protestant Quebec with England's institutions and most of its law. The whole could be achieved by four acts of parliament, effecting two legal reforms, security of revenue, and a religious settlement. The ideology can easily be traced in a continuum from Halifax through Hillsborough to Hey and Maseres, and was eventually damned for this. As Alexander Wedderburn, the solicitor-general, commented to a colleague, relying on Maseres for advice and guidance would be fatal: "He is a very good man but both in religion and politics he has a good deal of the Huguenot spirit in him, and the capital error in his plan is the great detail of regulations."[33]

The second of the two reports completed in 1773 by the attorney-general, Thurlow, should perhaps have been more profound.[34] Thurlow would eventually be lord chancellor and presume to some greater role in the dispensation of English judicial practice. It would, however, be a kindness to say that his report was a jumble of half-baked opinions. Thurlow attempted to do in five pages what Marriott had failed to do in fifty: grapple with the practicalities of governing an alien people and their culture. In his brief effort Thurlow made the obvious mistake of trying to consider a plan for the civil and criminal law in Quebec without reference to other issues. For the first two-thirds of the report, therefore, Thurlow went from pillar to post endeavouring to discover which bits of old French usage should be married to English common and criminal law. His own bewilderment at this exercise could not be concealed, and is amply expressed in the passage where he addressed conflicting opinions on the state of the law in Quebec:

I have rather presumed to trouble your Majesty with a copy of their expressions than any abstract of their opinion; because though I subscribe absolutely to the truth and good sense of their [Yorke's and De Grey's] positions, I freely confess myself at a loss to comprehend the distinction whereby they find the criminal law of England introduced and the civil laws of Canada continued, by instruments which seem to establish all the laws of England both civil and criminal at the same time, in the same sentence, and by the same form of words, if they are understood to establish any, or to relate to Quebec.

This is certainly a remarkable last sentence, for if the legal work done over the previous eight years on these issues did not apply to Quebec, a lot of people had been wasting their time drafting and redrafting reports.

Thurlow appeared to miss the point that any settlement of legal problems involved other constitutional issues. Or did he? Towards the end of this short document, he makes reference to the religious problem in a way that suggests he understood that there were other considerations at hand: "Religion also, so far as it affects the state and becomes an object of establishment or toleration, seems to be a matter of policy and state; and yet it is sufficiently obvious what a multitude of laws must follow upon any given establishment or toleration, more or less according to the degrees in which the religion is incorporated with the state." Indeed it was "sufficiently obvious" to all those who thought deeply about this problem that the religious problem would have to be settled first before progress could be made elsewhere. Yet Thurlow shied away from this responsibility. The passage cited above was followed by a disclaimer so strong that the cabinet must have wondered why Thurlow ever bothered to write the report in the first place. "Being totally uninformed of your Majesty's royal pleasure touching these important articles, I feel it extremely difficult to state any certain scheme of civil and criminal laws, or any which must not receive deep and material alterations for that which your Majesty shall be pleased to determine on those heads." This said nothing. Maybe Thurlow could be defended on the grounds that he had never been to Quebec and preserved only a passing acquaintance with the documentation on the problems there. Nevertheless others, with a similar lack of experience of the province, did a better job.

This was nowhere more apparent than in the case of the solicitor-general, Wedderburn. His report truly endeavoured to produce the required end set by the cabinet on 7 June 1771. Indeed, the ideas expressed in this document proved to be the very basis of the Quebec Act itself, and a little more besides. Given Wedderburn's career, it is perhaps not too surpising that he seized the initiative. He was a brilliant lawyer who eventually became lord chancellor in 1795. In the early part of his career in Scotland, Wedderburn had moved in the intellectual circles of Edinburgh that included such figures as David Hume, Adam Smith, and William Robertson. He was a respected parliamentary debater and thinker on imperial affairs who contributed to the debate on India's place in the empire at this time as well as that of Quebec. He was described by one contemporary as an "inventive genius" in policy-making, and there is no doubt that a fine legal and constitutional knowledge allied to a sharp brain equipped Wedderburn perfectly for tackling the Quebec issue.[35] Three versions of Wedderburn's report are well known to historians, being reproduced by Shortt and Doughty via another scholar, Christie, in their collection of constitutional documents.[36] The first report, catalogued for 6 December 1772, is the longest, running to six pages of summary that Shortt and Doughty gleaned from archive material in Canada. There is nothing essentially wrong with this précis, which is an honest reflection of Wedderburn's work on Quebec, but it should be appreciated that it represents a most severe editing process. One draft of Wedderburn's original report, now amongst Burke's papers in Ottawa, amounts to nineteen foolscap folios of detailed analysis.[37] In this exercise Wedderburn not only formulated a practicable code of law for the province but also encapsulated the aims and aspirations behind the pending legislation for Quebec, and, it could be argued, future colonial conquests too.

Indeed, the preamble to Wedderburn's report is most noteworthy for its discussion of the rights of conquest by one nation over another. In eighteenth-century historiography, great emphasis has always been given to Mansfield's verdict in the case of *Campbell and Hall*, November 1774, this judgment being seen as the definitive statement on the issue. The weight of Mansfield's decision cannot be doubted, but the basis of the argument lies in Wedderburn's statement on Quebec two years earlier:

Canada is a conquered country. The capitulations secured the temporary enjoyment of certain rights, and the treaty of peace contained no reservation in favour of the inhabitants, except a very vague one as to the exercise of religion. Can it therefore be said that, by right of conquest, the conqueror may impose such laws as he pleases? This proposition has been maintained by some lawyers who have not distinguished between force and right. It is certainly in the power of a conqueror to dispose of those he has subdued, at discretion, and when the captivity of the vanquished was the consequence of victory the proposition might be true; but in more civilized times, when the object of war is dominion, when subjects and not slaves are the fruits of victory, no other right can be founded on conquest but that of regulating the political and civil government of the country, leaving to the individuals the enjoyment of their property, and all privileges not inconsistent with the security of conquest.

This does not imply that such views did not originate with Mansfield. He knew Wedderburn well and had expressed more or less these sentiments to George Grenville in 1764, who, in turn, was a mutual friend and colleague. The interesting point here is that perhaps British experience in Quebec should be treated as the real foundation for the judgment in *Campbell and Hall*, with Grenada simply acting as the catalyst.

After discussing the rights of conquest, Wedderburn moved on to responsibilities arising therefrom, or what he called the "political constitution." The first consideration in normal circumstances, he wrote, would have been the establishment of an assembly. Wedderburn had no truck with this idea, however, for it simply could not work. The reasons, as he saw it, were obvious and had been so since the conquest. In short, who would elect the body, and who would then sit in the assembly? Even if these hurdles could be overcome, it was clear that new subjects mixed with old in a legislature so soon after the war would be "an inexhaustible source of dissension." It thus followed that what had to be put in its place was what already existed in practice, a governor and council ostensibly appointed by the king with legislative powers over local affairs. Revenue for Quebec would be the exception, with the British parliament enacting legislation levying duties on spiritous liquors in the province along the lines suggested in Carleton's report to the Treasury of 10 December 1767.[38]

The next part of "the political constitution" to be secured was the religious settlement of Quebec. Wedderburn was very much aware that this facet of policy would be central to the province's loyalty under British rule. He, like Marriott, considered the problem of allowing Catholic worship as far as the laws of England permitted, and even agreed that the laws enacted in the mother country were "seldom exerted." Unlike Marriott, however, Wedderburn saw no future in a war of attrition against the Catholic church in Quebec. He interpreted the clauses of the Peace of Paris affecting worship as meaning toleration and survival of Catholicism in the province. In a most profound statement, which again reflected changing attitudes in British political circles, Wedderburn stated bluntly:

The safety of the state can be the only just motive for imposing any restraint upon men on account of their religious tenets. The principle is just but it has seldom been justly applied; for experience demonstrates that the public safety has been often endangered by those restraints, and there is no instance of any state that has been overturned by toleration. True policy dictates then that inhabitants of Canada should be permitted freely to profess the worship of their religion; and it follows of course, that the ministers of that worship should be protected and a maintenance secured for them.

This turned the view of the Catholic threat to the state from 1688 onwards upside down. Rather than decrease the danger, Wedderburn argued, penal statutes had exacerbated the problem. It took a brave man to espouse such a theory, but it was echoed elsewhere, especially in the work of William Knox on Quebec. When Wedderburn spoke of "experience" demonstrating the errors of past policy, it could only have been Ireland he had in mind, just as Knox had in the first section of his pamphlet recounting the sad litany of popish persecution in that country under British rule.[39] Yet Wedderburn did have precise limits to the degree of toleration when it came to the direct influence of Rome in Quebec's religious future. All orders owing allegiance elsewhere were to be expelled, the Jesuits being the first to go. There would also be strict political control of ecclesiastical appointments at all levels, and the payment of tithes was to be closely supervised not only to exclude non-Catholics from payment but also to regulate stipends for the clergy. The whole plan was ingenious, and had all the appearance of trying to establish the Catholic church of England in Canada.

The last section of Wedderburn's report was concerned with that code of civil and criminal law originally requested by the cabinet. There were no radical departures from the groundwork done by Yorke in 1766. Indeed the 1766 proposals, those of Wedderburn, and the five clauses in the Quebec Act covering legal matters are linked by a common thread that sought to marry the old and the new in order to satisfy every prejudice, but particularly that of the Canadians, "because that class is the most numerous," as Wedderburn put it. The now familiar argument revolved around the goal of introducing English criminal law, "superior as it is to all others," and preserving French custom wherever possible in civil cases, though not in all tenure disputes. Wedderburn wished, in particular, to overcome the evil of infrequent sittings of the inferior courts, hoping "that the administration of justice is conducted with as much integrity, dispatch and cheapness under the new as it could under the old." The last suggestion, with which Canadians became very familiar over the next century, was the right of appeal to a committee of the Privy Council in London on cases "concerning the rights of the clergy, the profits of benefices, and the presentation to them." Oddly enough, this forerunner of the Judicial Committee of the Privy Council proved to be one of the few ideas Wedderburn expressed that was not embodied in the Quebec Act of 1774.

The whole report represented a personal coup for Wedderburn. Historians really need look no further than this document for the immediate source and impetus behind the Quebec legislation. There is little wonder that the cabinet focused on Wedderburn's proposals out of the three submitted in the spring of 1773. The power of the man's intellect on this issue simply soared above that of Thurlow and Marriott. In his work Wedderburn had distilled thirteen years of research and writing on the province into this document. He identified and developed into a concise analytical framework omnipresent strains of thought about Quebec, evident since Shelburn's tenure at the Board of Trade in the early 1760s and surviving still with the incumbent governor, Carleton. Indeed, while figures like Carleton provided the public encouragement for the Quebec Act, and have since been praised for being instrumental in its passage, the labours of the craftsmen such as Wedderburn now require acknowledgment and recognition. It is a commonplace even today to consider "the storm which at this very time was blowing up in America" a prime motivating force behind the tolerant spirit and timing of the Quebec legislation of 1774.[40] What can be done to dispose of this myth once and for all? Fifty years ago both Coupland

and Burt said that they could find no evidence to justify such an assertion, with Lanctôt repeating the message in the 1960s, and nothing has yet come to light to contradict them.[41] The only way to support a link between the Quebec issue and unrest to the south is by pointing to coincidence. Yet even this method is flawed. It ignores the fact that all these recommendations for the Quebec Act were in place by the summer of 1773, culminating a quiet revolution in ministerial thinking about Quebec in which the doubters were converted to Wedderburn's way. The whole process, in fact, took place during one of the calmest and most prosperous periods in Anglo-American relations during the whole pre-revolutionary decade. Surely it is time to knock this old whig view on the head until some concrete evidence emerges showing that a conspiracy against liberty in North America took place. There was a storm of protest gathering against the Quebec legislation itself, fed by the English-speaking merchants in the province and their sympathizers in London. They vainly bombarded the government with pleas for a Protestant assembly, after prompting from Maseres and Fowler Walker, once they got wind of the government's plans in the spring of 1773.[42] It all came to naught; they were petitioning against decisions already taken.

A more rewarding line of inquiry about the timing of the Quebec Act might well lie in the political stability achieved by the North ministry since it came into being in 1770. No other government responsible for the Quebec settlement since 1760 had established itself in the confidence of both king and parliament or had the unity of purpose to proceed with such a difficult, and potentially damaging, policy. Indeed, though so little detail is known about these years, it could be argued that they are the most crucial to the history of the province under British rule. The simple fact cannot be ignored that North achieved what had eluded all premiers: convincing king and cabinet of the necessity of a tolerant policy towards Quebec.

The premier took the direct route to a legislative settlement. Once the reports had come in from the law officers in the spring of 1773 and been reviewed by the cabinet, North, as Maseres reported after conversing with him in July, "seemed fully determined to do something towards the settlement of that province in the next session of parliament."[43] The relevant papers were in fact sent from the lord chancellor's office on 4 August 1773, and remained with North until orders went out in November to begin preparation of a parliamentary bill.[44] John Pownall and William Knox, undersecretaries in Dartmouth's office, were then given responsibility for writing up a preliminary draft for the cabinet. Pownall did not relish the task. In a fit of pique he told Knox that "after so many years neglect of the business of Quebec from the first establishment of it, everything now is to be done in a hurry. Lord North has begged that he may have from us a précis of the affairs of Quebec from the first establishment of it, so far as regards the claims and complaints of the new subjects and what has passed thereupon etc. You know how little able I am to sit down to such a work, and you know that nobody but you and I can do it."[45] Write it they did, however, and, with Dartmouth's support, their efforts eventually came before parliament as the Quebec legislation. But it could hardly be called a hurried plan. The Quebec legislation had been in gestation for seven years, and it was now up to North to deliver the brain-child of his law officers' labours onto the statute book.

An Elastic Spirit in Our Constitution: Differing British Views on the Passage of the Quebec Act in 1774

The reaction of historians to the passage of the Quebec Act in 1774 has been as chequered as the genesis of the legislation itself. A myriad of analyses, interpretations, and judgments have characterized the writing on this event since the eighteenth-century. Contemporary debate on the act has been reflected in scholarship right up to the present day. Opinions cover the gamut of late-eighteenth-century feeling towards the legislation, from those in the American school who spelt out the act as the death-knell of liberty to those in England who wished to present the act as a piece of sublime imperial statesmanship and ending more latterly with scholars in Quebec favouring the decapitation theory when assessing the impact of the legislation.[1] In short, treatment of the act has been a reference point for some other historical purpose, whether to explain the flickering light of a democratic spirit in America or the growth of separatist movements in twentieth-century Quebec. The course of such scholarship has not always run true, but, overall, the results have been rewarding – not least in the emphasis placed on a piece of legislative activity by the British parliament that was both unique and crucial to the history of the old Atlantic empire. One facet of this oblique approach to the act that requires revision, however, is the English context to its passage. This theme has been touched upon in studies dealing specifically with Canadian history and the outbreak of the revolutionary war, but its broader significance has not really been appreciated.[2] It is not intended that this narrative will be repeated or reworked in the pages that follow. Instead, it is hoped that some of the mythology surrounding the government's motives during the passage of the act will be dispelled, allowing examination of how the challenge of Quebec obliged the British to think deeply about fundamental constitutional questions affecting their own lives. For if the struggle to formulate policy on Quebec had shown anything since 1760, it was that the domestic and imperial debate could not be separated.[3]

It is impossible to pinpoint a consensus amongst the ruling élites over the

Quebec legislation, for, as could be seen in the debates from 1770 to 1773, none really existed. However, there was a genuine spirit of toleration and concilia-tion motivating those responsible for the legislation, a spirit reflecting a change in the political assumptions that were the legacy of the events of 1688. This shifting view was beautifully encapsulated in the confidence in the English constitution expressed by one member of the ruling classes at the time. To Sir John Eardley Wilmot, sometime chief justice of Common Pleas in the mid-eighteenth century, there was no challenge to which the English constitution could not adapt itself. When reflecting on this point in 1771, he told his son: "whatever transient storms may arise here, there is an elastic spirit in our Constitution which will preserve it; and though many other climates are pleasanter, yet no part of the earth is, or ever was, blest with a Constitu-tion so admirably fitted and adapted to securing the religious and civil rights of mankind."[4] Of course, this "elastic spirit" in the constitution would be stretched beyond breaking point over the next decade, but in terms of the im-mediate policy for Quebec in 1774, Wilmot's premise proved highly ap-propriate, and would do so again even after the loss of America. Indeed, this confidence lay at the heart of the government's case for supporting some uni-que clauses in the Quebec Act. When Lord North and other government spokesmen defended the legislation during May and June 1774, this underly-ing faith in the adaptability of British institutions and traditions carried the day. The retreat from the principles of religious exclusionism and political ascendancy that would not only secure Quebec's future under British rule but eventually recast the structure of society and politics at home found no clearer illustration than in the public and parliamentary debate on the Quebec Act.

The process began at a most unpropitious moment in relations between Britain and her American empire. After North's government had committed itself to doing something about Quebec's governance in the fall of 1773, news of events in Boston harbour intervened to dash any hopes of a quiet parliamentary session in the spring of 1774. Before the Tea Party it is known that the government intended to bring forward the Quebec legislation early in the new session. In the wake of the American crisis, and demands for a quick response, however, the timetable for the Quebec business obviously had to be rewritten. The affairs of the province were simply pushed down the ministerial list of priorities. This is an important point because it is so ger-mane to controversies that have arisen over the sequential state of British policy in 1774, especially over the Quebec Bill. No new evidence has come to light to suggest that North meant to abandon the legislation for the province because of events in Boston, but he did have to postpone it until the tail end of the session. This postponement, however, became the subject of specula-tion, with many contemporary observers expressing the opinion that North intended a subterfuge. It was said that the premier had a hidden agenda in this controversial legislation, which he wished to slip through parliament in a period when few people remained at Westminster and criticism would be muted. John Dunning expressed this very fear in a Commons debate on 26 May, declaring that the legislation "carries in its breast something that squints and looks dangerous to the other inhabitants of that country, our own colonies."[5] There appeared to be weight in such opinions, because the facts seemed to support the argument. The legislation was passed late in the session with what seemed low attendances in a House containing MPs clearly ignorant of the issues involved. In addition, North also refused to lay all the relevant papers before the Commons when requested to do so by his critics. This defiance was then compounded in the eyes of the government's detractors by the displays of ministerial secrecy in debate. On one important debate over the religious clauses in the Quebec Act on 7 June, for example, the public were ejected from the Commons' gallery in order, it seemed, to restrict information about the question. Even the fact that the legislation originated in the Lords on 2 May has been interpreted as sinister evidence of secretiveness and a failure on the part of ministers and their supporters to deal fairly with the issues.

What can be said to refute such a strong case? The answer must be a great deal. Because of the recent invaluable publication of all the parliamentary debates on the Quebec legislation, it is practicable to revise some of the mythology surrounding this episode and reveal the proper context of the act. To deal with general issues first, attention must be paid to the question of timing. To accuse North of irregularity on this point presumes doubt about the first lord's sincerity in the fall of 1773. But no reason has ever been offered for questioning North's commitment to act on Quebec in 1774, and it is difficult to believe one will arise, for it was certainly not his style to promise something and not deliver.[6] The whole argument about wilful timing of the Quebec legislation assumes that action on this front was tangential, that the government was pushed into it because of the American crisis. Suddenly all the assurances of the summer and fall of 1773 about Quebec's governance meant nothing. Thus was the fallacy of the act as a coercive measure against America developed, with hybrids of that view constantly emerging before anyone who cared to look at the secondary literature on the topic. Even in Lord Donoughue's balanced account of the Quebec Act's passage through parliament, there appears the unsupportable, but characteristic, aside that "the incipient colonial rebellion probably precipitated the timing of the Quebec Bill."[7]

Related but more specific points about timing also require revision. Much has been made in studies of this period about the Quebec Act's introduction late in the parliamentary session, with low attendances and limited debate.[8] Yet much of this line of argument is erroneous in the full context of imperial issues in British politics at this time. There had actually been several precedents in recent years for discussing such matters well into June because of an ever-busy parliamentary schedule in the spring. Perhaps the best example was the East India Company business of 1767, on which debate ended on 25 June. The legislation passed in that month has certainly not received the attention that historians have reserved for the Quebec Act, and yet evidence from divisions that took place at Westminster in that session offers a sharp corrective to scholars keen to condemn North over timing.[9] In the Commons on 26 May 1767 a vote to reject government interference in East India Company affairs was lost by 151 votes to 84 – anomalous numbers indeed if the equation between late session and low attendance is to be accepted as a hard and fast rule. The debates in the Upper House were more impressive, however. On 17 and 25 June 1767, divisions in the government's favour numbered 73 to 52 and 59 to 44 respectively. These attendances far outshine those in 1774 where, for instance, the Commons vote to pass the Quebec Act on 13 June numbered 56 votes to 20, and that in the Lords on 17 June produced a division of 26 votes to 7.[10] Thus the question is raised: why have historians commented so authoritatively on the timing of the Quebec legislation and ignored parallel examples? The explanation lies in the fact that timing and low attendances are red herrings, fit only to be discounted by scholars interested in these events.

It is clear throughout this period that subject matter was the determining factor in attendance at Westminster, whether early or late in the session.[11] North himself recognized that lateness in the session could be a sensitive point and apologized for the circumstances that had forced him to introduce the Quebec legislation when he did. Nevertheless, it was not then the controversial issue it has since become for some historians. There were odd complaints over the four weeks or so that the bill was before parliament about lateness in the session and committee meetings, but they should not be taken too seriously. In actual parliamentary debating time the Quebec Bill received more attention than similar imperial legislation of the period. Indeed, several of those attending the sittings in June complained of interminable debate, not lack of it.[12] If MPs had wished to attend the discussions on Quebec, they could and would have done so. The low attendance should not be taken as implying a widespread lack of interest on the part of those at Westminster confronting Quebec's problems. Rather, it indicates that many of the politicians seeking an immediate response to the legislation as a whole faced a philosophical dilemma. They simply voted with their feet when the Quebec business came up.

Indeed, this dilemma was the key to low attendances and seeming lack of interest, for it made it impossible for the Rockinghams, by far the largest group in opposition, to present a united front on the issue. Certain members of the Rockingham party sat through committees on the bill and sniped at clauses they found offensive, but there was no concerted attack as there had been in 1767 when Richmond and Newcastle led the troops into battle. The reason for the fracturing of the Rockinghamite opposition can be found in comparing the thrust of their policies while in office during 1765–66 with that behind the Quebec Bill produced by North in 1774. The two policy directions represented a continuity of thought and approach on how to manage the fate of an alien culture under the imperial system without jeopardizing the loyalty of the king's new subjects. This legacy forced the opposition onto the defensive, and the situation was complicated by the fact that the act evoked responses that cut across political and ideological ties. Isaac Barré, for example, who would lead many of the assaults on the legislation in the Commons, was a close friend of Shelburne; yet on this issue they found themselves on opposite sides of the fence. Shelburne, though in opposition in 1774, offered no critical leadership in the Lords against the legislation. Nor was he expected to, for he had played his own part in the construction of North's bill for Quebec. The same split is more evident amongst the Rockinghams, whose leadership in the Lords appears to have decided from the beginning to keep the business low key. There are a few rambling notes in Rockingham's hand amongst his manuscripts that presumably formed the basis of a few technical questions in the clauses regarding the new oath to be administered in the province, but precious little else. [13] The party members like Burke and Lord John Cavendish chipped away at the bill on their own cognizance, not because of any outward encouragement to do so by the leadership. Thus what tended to happen in debates on the legislation was that a splintered core of constitutional and religious hard-liners skirmished with North without any coherent plan of action or defined strategy. To seasoned parliamentary campaigners, this futile way of proceeding could only have fortified other doubts about the legitimacy of opposition on a bill of this special nature. Those that stayed the course in opposition are certainly worthy of note, however, for their arguments do reveal all the tensions and uncertainties about formulating imperial policy at odds with accepted political assumptions and traditions.

That the Quebec legislation appeared first in the Lords on 2 May has often been presented as evidence in itself of a surreptitious tactical move. It has been seen as an attempt to sneak an awkward bill through with least fuss and publicity at the end of a difficult parliamentary session. Again, the evidence for this view is circumstantial, though to many radicals at the time the precedents for this sort of action were ominous. The Septennial Act of 1716 and, more recently, the actions against John Wilkes had been opened in the Lords, and both were seen in radical eyes as clear examples of executive tyranny. Whatever North's motives, however, certain other factors need to be considered before it is taken for granted that some foul play was afoot on 2 May. First, most of those with expertise on Quebec on the government side (and, for that matter, on the opposition benches) sat in the Lords, including most of the politicians who had already been involved in this issue in the past like Dartmouth, Shelburne, Richmond, and Hillsborough. Acknowledgment of this fact came not only in 1774 but also, as seen above, in 1767. Indeed, it was the Rockinghamite opposition that had launched the campaign on Quebec in the Lords in 1767, and had thought about doing so again in 1769–70. Why this convention developed remains a mystery, but the second significant fact in the relationship between Quebec and the House of Lords is the resolution of June 1767 which left the whole business in the air with the words "Quebec, for a considerable time past has wanted, and does now stand in need of further regulations and provisions, relating to its Civil Government and Religious Establishment."[14] In reopening the Quebec business in 1774 in the Lords, where it had been left untouched since 1767, parliament may simply have been observing constitutional proprieties of precedence. When the Commons came to discuss the Quebec Bill after it passed the Lords on 17 May, some MPs did express concern at the role of the Upper House in this legislation process. Yet they were concerned not with the general constitutional point of the legislation originating there, but with the fact that revenue clauses relating to the collection of tithes identified in the act offended the sacred principle that all money bills be initiated by the House of Commons.[15]

The speed with which the Quebec Bill passed the Lords suggested little trouble at its inception, but this impression needs correcting. A great deal of debate and drafting took place after Dartmouth had issued the order to prepare the legislation. The ministry knew what it desired to achieve with the act, but experienced difficulty in phrasing those ends. It is clear from the papers of the colonial secretary that the cabinet met several times on the issue to thrash out its priorities. One of the final gatherings, probably in April, then came to an agreement on ten points to be embodied in the legislation.[16] All the issues highlighted were now familiar to ministers, running from the desire to be rid of the Proclamation of 1763 to establishing legal structures, providing, in turn, a civil administration and revenue to support them, and concluding with the all-important religious question. It is also evident, however, that disagreements took place when it came to translating priorities into clauses. Wedderburn drew up the first draft of the act and submitted it to Dartmouth for comment. In late February 1774 he received an unexpected request from Dartmouth to rewrite certain sections on the judicial arrangements and the powers of the king to appoint and dismiss future members of the Quebec council. Wedderburn agreed to this demand rather grudgingly, and a second draft appeared on 2 March. This document, like the others, underwent further examination focusing on the new boundaries and jurisdiction to be given the Quebec government. Even at this late stage it is worthy of note that even those without office, but with knowledge of Quebec, played a role in these discussions. Lord Hillsborough, for example, who had resigned in 1772, was paid the compliment of having cabinet papers circulated to his residence. In May Hillsborough expressed two objections to the drafts: one relating to the rights of property tenure, which the government struck out of the act after other objections, and the other concerning the interior boundary. This subject had been resolved in its broad terms long before 1774. The intention was to bring the interior under Quebec's jurisdiction, but Hillsborough believed that extending the boundary around the Great Lakes in the north and the Ohio Valley in the south-west would not only encourage Catholic settlement in the interior but also ruin the Indian trade and future prospects of peace with those natives. Dartmouth believed that the opposite would be the case: emigration would be hindered and trade regularized because of the establishment of the normal agencies of law, order, and government in the interior. The two men certainly had no respect for each other's opinion. When the matter came up in the Lords on 6 May Hillsborough commented that the bill "must have been the work of a child in politics," which prompted the rejoinder from Dartmouth that here was "the objection of an old dotard."[17] Indeed, Dartmouth must have wondered why he ever bothered to canvass Hillsborough's opinion in the first place!

The third and final draft that appeared after these discussions might have gone forward to parliament had Dartmouth not had the good sense to submit it to Lord Mansfield for his comments. The thoroughness of Mansfield's approach prompted him to spot two areas of concern that would have rendered the act unworkable in its present form.[18] First, the clause confirming French custom in civil law cases, but with the option of trial by jury, would have to be clarified, for Mansfield saw only confusion ahead. He cited the example of old and new subjects in Quebec becoming involved in litigation over property in which the former demanded trial by jury and the latter rejected it. Though Mansfield himself made no recommendation, he was in no doubt that the government had to choose one way or the other. "I conceive," he told Dartmouth, "that clause must be wholly struck out or more particularly explained." The second area of concern, which neither Dartmouth nor Wedderburn had worried about, related to religious clauses of the bill. It was all well and good, as Mansfield said, to tolerate the Catholic religion in theory, but no practical provision for support of the clergy existed in the draft submitted to him. As the clauses on the Roman church stood, the priesthood would have to depend on voluntary contributions from their parishioners to survive. This did not represent the sort of toleration Mansfield believed that the government had in mind, and he made specific recommendations to rectify this deficiency. In Mansfield's terms, the government would have to tolerate a practical, as well as a spiritual, manifestation of Catholicism, with strict provisos regarding the ultimate authority of the crown:

does your Lordship apprehend any mischief or great inconvenience would arise from acknowledging their right to a decent and moderate maintenance under the sanction of a British Act of Parliament.

To say nothing of the discontent it would occasion will your lordship think it quite consistent with the terms of the Treaty – under which the property of the Clergy as well as Laity seems to have been reserved to the owners – and the right to a decent support by Tithes seems to be as much as the Property of the Clergy, as the seigneurial lands of the seigneurs, or any lay Property whatsoever of a Layman.

Power and authority neither belongs to them by treaty nor is it consistent with a Protestant Government to suffer them to be retained – but subsistence seems to be their right ...

This entirely practical solution to an extremely sensitive spiritual problem found its way into the Quebec Act and did guarantee the survival of the Catholic clergy under the British crown. Moreover, in the government's eyes, it did so without openly compromising George III's ecclesiastical supremacy. It proved fortunate for the government that Mansfield was able to stiffen the backbone of the draft bill, for the issues of juries, boundaries, and tithes were just those that came under closest scrutiny when the Commons took up the bill in late May.

The smooth passage granted the Quebec legislation in the Lords would not be repeated in the Lower House. Debates – some spirited, others languid – accompanied the Quebec Act on to the statute book. What made the comparison to the Lords more interesting still was the fact that a parallel and at times co-ordinated public campaign against the act developed too.[19] It would be misleading to say that North did not expect this sort of reception for the legislation, he was far too experienced to ignore this possibility. The government's stategy was thought out to meet this challenge: the law officers presented the act with measured tolerance, thus avoiding the necessity of blatant recourse to tactical adjournments and divisions. North's strength and reputation over his dozen years or so as premier rested upon a magnanimous approach to the cut and thrust of political debate. He was a witty, fair-minded man not prone to mean-spirited or egotistical behaviour in the House. In short, he occupied the vast middle ground of parliamentary opinion on Quebec, and all these assets came to the fore in May and June 1774.[20] This is not to underestimate the fact that the ministry had some big guns on its side when it came to explaining and defending the legislation. Apart from North's considerable talents, there were the legal expertise and debating skills of Wedderburn and Thurlow and Carleton's testimony at the bar, which MPs heard first hand. There was no guarantee that the government would have an easy ride in the debates in the act; some internal differences over detail still existed. But what the government stategy did achieve was to neutralize the uncommitted MPs in the House. At this time about thirty-five MPs with direct knowledge of Quebec's affairs, either through office-holding, trade, or military service there, sat in the Commons. Of these, only nine are known to have taken an active part in the opposition to the Quebec legislation.[21] The typical reaction of those members without an obvious connection to the province or to the main opposition groups led by Rockingham and Chatham was to give the legislation a chance. The interventions of MPs such as William Pulteney (Cromartyshire) and George Prescott (Milborne Port) were always prompted by the desire to keep the debate going and let North have his say, and not to condemn the legislation for narrow prejudicial reasons.[22] As another MP attending the committees put it, after hearing Carleton extol the virtues of a tolerant approach to religion and law in the province: "He is the most valuable witness I ever heard in my life."[23]

In addition to these practical limitations on the opposition to the act, there were more serious theoretical and ideological problems preventing the opposition from showing a united front. There was simply no overcoming the fact that MPs who disliked the Quebec Act did so for various selective reasons. Except among a small number of hawks, no blanket hostility to the legislation existed. Some MPs disliked the clauses on juries, for example, while harbouring no ill will towards the religious settlement, and vice versa. This trend was evident from the very beginning of the committee sittings on 31 May 1774, though it could not be said that it was a case of divide and rule on the government's part. Indeed, North's timetable for discussion of clauses in the bill in a simple categorical fashion did not preclude a united opposition front at all. On the 31st there were two motions to hear petitions against the bill from Pennsylvania and the London merchants trading to Quebec, then two more requesting that witnesses appear and that Carleton's report be laid before the House.[24] All these moves appeared to give real focus and impetus to the opposition case as the legislation moved through the next stages of hearing witnesses and debating the bill clause by clause. First would be the boundary on 6 June, then religion on 7 June, and finally the legal structures on 8 and 10 June.

The prospects of garnering public support for the opposition campaign also looked promising, once North's intent had been taken seriously. Sections of the popular press and then the City of London had moved into gear to oppose the legislation outright by early June. Newspapers like the *Middlesex Journal*, the *Public Advertizer*, and the *London Evening Post* did not hesitate to take the extreme view. In fact, the *Public Advertizer* was one of the first organs to print a hostile critique of the bill on 19 May. It encapsulated the meat of the argument against the legislation that would become so familiar to readers over the next four or five months, and stands out as one of the better pieces to appear:

The intentions of administration with regard to America are now apparent. The bill brought in called the Quebec bill, is to enlarge that province so as to take in half America, to establish it in the Roman Catholic religion, the French law, and to make the King with the governor and council the legislature of the province. Thus, at one stroke, they meditate the subversion of the church, the law, and the constitution of England. The King of England is to be put in the place of the King of France, and have a taste of what is deemed so delicious, arbitrary power. Lord Mansfield will have at length the pleasure of triumphing over what he hates, the trial by jury. The first west wind may blow this arbitrary system over to this country, when once it is established in that. Yet are we so absurd as to countenance the scheme, and aid in digging the pit for America into which we ourselves must fall.

Herein were the themes that would dominate the protests against the Quebec legislation. Most had been raised before: the establishment of the Catholic religion contrary to the revolutionary principles of 1688; no elected assembly; and French law allowed to exist side by side with English law. To make the message more immediate, these possibilities were offered as a threat to English liberty. If the government was able to get away with it in the colonies, who would stop it in Britain?

The City of London took the same path. At a meeting of the Common Council on 3 June, a petition against the passage of the bill was formulated for presentation to the Commons. The areas of concern matched those in the press, though the wording proved less dramatic. The petition bemoaned the lack of trial by jury in civil cases in Quebec, "whereby the freedom of person and security of the property of his Majesty's subjects are rendered precarious." It then condemned toleration of Roman Catholic worship "without any provision being made for the free exercise of the Protestant religion which may prove greatly injurious and oppressive to his Majesty's Protestant subjects." In a last side-swipe at the government's overturning of yet another sacred principle of 1688, the petition concluded with an attack on the idea of an appointed council instead of an elected assembly, "which is totally inconsistent with the liberty and principles of the English."[25]

Thus the prospects for opposition to the Quebec Act seemed healthy. North's conciliatory attitude on 31 May, for example, when he had responded favourably to Pennsylvania's request to adjust the boundary, combined with the loud and lively press campaign against the legislation, appeared to play right into the hands of the government's opponents. Yet by early June the opposition had all gone awry, and left the government triumphant on an issue that seemed fraught with danger at every turn. Since knowledge of the press campaign and parliamentary debates has recently become available, it is now much easier to understand this process. This material makes it clear that opposition was fractured and fragmented. In the Commons, MPs opposed to the act made simple tactical errors during debates and frequently revealed a lack of knowledge about the problem, which the government exploited.[26] Yet more important was the inability of those in opposition to come to terms with the fundamental issue of tolerating Catholicism in Quebec, and this, in turn, led to an erratic parliamentary campaign sometimes at odds with the opposition's sympathizers in the press.

To deal with the tactical mistakes and difficulties first, a great deal in the opposition case rested on publicizing grievances against the act arising both from the American displeasure with the interior boundary and from fears for the constitutional rights of the new English settlers in the province. The two petitions heard on 31 May fired the initial shots in this direciton, and the battle continued in the examination of witnesses on 2 June. Carleton carried the burden of being the government's expert and spokesman at the Bar of the House more or less single-handed, and suffered several hours of arduous interrogation. He performed brilliantly, defending his record and the general tenor of the Quebec legislation with enviable poise. In contrast, the interrogators on the opposition benches displayed a singular lack of ability. Their ignorance of the issues at stake in Quebec and of its society and institutions was manifest. But more evident was a phenomenal prejudice and bigotry about British institutions. Many opposition speakers greeted with incredulity Carleton's assertions that the Canadians did not desire an elected assembly or trials by jury in civil cases. The assumption was that the governor had become tainted with the despotic Catholic society under his charge and that sensible Protestant witnesses would right the balance.

The opposition also assumed that when Maseres and Hey were called as witnesses, they would give a full airing to their differences of opinion with Carleton and reveal the governor's misguided ways. Maseres certainly did not hold back, and became involved in a lengthy cross-examination about Carleton's evidence, which was given on different occasions in early June. Unfortunately, Maseres became carried away during his examination, and Wedderburn, patiently observing this scene, prepared to move in for the kill. Maseres systematically contradicted all Carleton's statements, asserting that Canada wanted an assembly in the long run, along with trials by jury and habeas corpus. He even went as far as saying that many of the new subjects were ripe for conversion to the Protestant faith. When Maseres mentioned the act, however, he went too far by claiming that it gave George III powers to issue *lettres de cachet* as had been the case under the old regime. This statement was too much for Wedderburn, and he asked the bluntest of questions, which elicited a surprising retort:

Mr. Solicitor General. What form of government have the Canadians expressed themselves most desirous of?
Mr. Maseres. They have no clear notions of government, having never been used to any such speculations. They will be content with any you give them, provided it be well administered.[27]

This, as Wedderburn sensibly pointed out, was exactly what the government hoped to do with the Quebec Act. Worse still for Maseres, the solicitor-general then tempted the witness into showing how the legislation enabled the king to issue *lettres de cachet*. Maseres could not, for he did understand the basis of the power under French law and in what ways it applied to Quebec after the conquest. Wedderburn obviously took great pleasure in explaining the matter to Maseres, and concluded with the withering statement: "I dare say Mr. Maseres must now see this matter in the same light that I do, and be convinced that no *lettres de cachet* can legally be used in Canada by virtue of this Act."[28] At the end of the debate William Hey underwent examination at the Bar, which proved a non-committal affair. The chief justice would not go as far in his mild criticisms of Carleton's report three years earlier, and avoided being drawn on specifics in the bill altogether. It was a good day for North.

These proceedings made the opposition slightly desperate when the examination of witnesses continued on 3 June. In fact, by day's end, when this stage of the bill's progress was complete, further disasters had occurred. Carleton and Hey reappeared before the House and repeated their performances of the previous day: Carleton confident and dominant with Hey retiring and hesitant.[29] This forced the opposition's hand, and several speakers called for further witnesses. The two that appeared were Marriott, a man known to be hostile to the spirit of the act, and, from Quebec, Michel Lotbinière, whom Carleton dubbed a "blackguard." The situation went from bad to worse for the opposition. Marriott refused to answer any questions directly and turned in a comic performance, parrying all hostile queries with the rejoinder that precedent would not allow him to divulge in the House information from a report that he had written for the king's eyes only. Lotbinière was produced afterwards in the hopes of proving that Canadians who favoured an assembly rather than an appointed council did exist. He certainly testified to this fact but rather undermined the case by adding that all Canadians should be allowed a full role in establishing this body. If this had been allowed, what else could it have been but a body completely composed in its electoral rolls and representatives of Catholic subjects? This was not what the opposition had in mind at all, and witness Lotbinière never saw the light of a Commons day again. So confused were opposition speakers like Thomas Townshend Jr about finding a reliable expert to support their cause that many argued for calling the old governor, Murray, to the Bar. How they had conceived the belief that the general would not support the act is unknown, but North's refusal to heed the request and force a division was an unintentional favour to his critics.

At the conclusion of the day's proceedings, opposition speakers, not surprisingly, attempted to shift the emphasis off the spoken onto the written word. Their attempt took the form of a motion to have all the most important reports and papers relating to the province laid before the committee. Where the oral evidence had failed to aid the opposition cause, maybe hard evidence of dissension within the government's own ranks via the reports would achieve the end desired. North denied the request outright. He saw the motion as a destructive delaying tactic designed to embarrass the government. North can be forgiven for being bloody-minded on this motion and circumspect in response to charges of introducing secrecy to the process of seeing the bill through the House. If all the contradictory reports gathered since 1763 had been laid before the House, the Quebec Act would have sunk without trace after the second reading. It sounded trite when North maintained that no time existed for producing and examining the reports, but it was the truth of the matter. The papers on Quebec had, over time, been examined to death, and it was a lack of action, not of deliberation, that had consistently baulked a legislative settlement.

A last tactical point on which those opposed to the Quebec Act also suffered a reverse concerned publicity for their cause. It appears quite evident from the account of the debates that spectators filled the Speaker's Gallery throughout the committees on the act. Several of these observers were definitely taking notes of what was said so that accounts of the debates could be written up later for the popular press. Such action represented a technical breach of Commons standing orders, and the editors and publishers of these debates could have been brought to the Bar of the House and forced to apologize for contempt on pain of imprisonment in the Tower. The government refrained from taking this retributive step and reports of the Quebec Act debates flourished, especially in the radical press, which aligned itself with those opposing the legislation. The ministry's attitude remained ambivalent towards these developments. It allowed reporting from the Speaker's Gallery to go on while no one objected, but if someone protested to the public presence during a sensitive debate a clearance took place. These ejections from the gallery took place several times during debates on the coercive Acts in April and May, and there were at least three clearances during the passage of the Quebec Act. On 7 June, the day that religious clauses in the act came up for discussion, for example, the gallery was cleared, much to the annoyance of opposition speakers like Burke.[30] In their eyes the clearance was simply a ruse to keep the matter under debate secret and avoid public embarrassment over awkward clauses granting toleration to Catholics. North did not deny the accusation in its narrow sense, but the action had a broader motive that all MPs could sympathize with: it avoided misrepresentation.

Late-twentieth-century politicians complain long and hard about being misquoted in the press, and yet it is not a modern phenomenon. One of the salient features in the way Thomas and Simmons have laid out the reports of debates on the Quebec Act is the often glaring difference between the full accounts of Henry Cavendish, who sat in the House, and the type of summary published in papers like the *Middlesex Journal*. From the latter, it is hard not to believe that Burke and Fox were the most ardent Protestant bigots, which could not have been further from the truth. In pre-Hansard days of parliamentary reporting, MPs had more than sufficient grounds to complain about scandalous treatment in the press. It made no difference whether members sat on the government or opposition benches. In 1771 Wedderburn had complained thus about a newspaper report of one of his parliamentary speeches: "Why to be sure, there are in that report a few things which I did say, but many things which I am glad I did not say, and some things which I wish I could have said."[31] Nothing had changed three years later. Thomas Townshend Jr, who led many of the attacks on the Quebec legislation in May and June 1774, said in the House in February that same year: "I have sometimes borrowed a paper to hear what I said myself, sometimes very much surprised at it." Thus there was little mileage in complaints of the opposition about clearances. In fact, after 7 June, there were few tactical manoeuvres left for opposition speakers to employ. Their last effort on 8 June was to move that the bill be "periodical," that is, limited to a certain number of years, and then be reviewed.[32] The idea may have come up because that session had just seen Grenville's Election Act of 1770, another "periodical" bill, made permanent. Nevertheless, the suggestion received no support at all, and was, in essence, a confession of defeat. It was the best that the opposition could have hoped for in the absence of rejection or modification.

Even if the opposition could have surmounted these procedural difficulties, more serious obstacles stood in the way of any attempt to undermine the Quebec legislation. This is perhaps best explained through a comparison between the government's presentation of the legislation and the ground chosen by the opposition from which to attack. For the government, trouble never really threatened at Westminster. Between 1770 and 1774, it undertook a long and painful search for a consensus on the type of legislation required to secure Quebec's future under British rule. There was never unanimity of official opinion as such, but by the time Dartmouth brought the Quebec Act to the Lords on 2 May 1774, both the government's troops and an unsympathetic monarch had been brought into line. No gaps in the ranks existed to be exploited in debate or the press. Carleton's vision of the future for Quebec, which in its turn built upon a continuity of thought evident in the work of others like Shelburne, Murray, and Cramahé, held fast. In a nutshell, tolerance and tactical concessions for the greater imperial good created a unity of purpose that made it much easier for North to take the lead, confident that there would be no ambush from the rear. Furthermore, at the purely practical level, Carleton's impressive performance as a witness enabled North to deal effectively with those critics concerned with timing and procedure. The whole strategy, in fact, was carried off to near perfection.

For the opposition, the experience of these weeks could not have offered more of a contrast. In the first place no consensus on how to oppose the bill in *toto* appeared. Dissatisfaction with the legislation spread not only between clauses but among the parties in the House of Commons. On examining the speakers over the three weeks of debates, it is clear that three types of member took part in opposing the bill. First were those attached to the largest opposition party at Westminster, led by the marquess of Rockingham. Among their number could be found good speakers like Burke, Lord John Cavendish, George Byng, and George Dempster, and yet they were by no means representative of the whole party. As the small divisions and differing positions expressed in debate would show, only a minimal concerted effort at opposing the legislation was made. The next group opposed to the Quebec Bill consisted of followers or admirers of Lord Chatham, the former William Pitt. It included Isaac Barré, John Dunning, and Thomas Townshend Jr, and though not the largest group opposed to the Quebec legislation it was certainly the most vociferous. The last group was made up of what might be called renegades: MPs who had their own axes to grind against the government no matter what the issue. Amongst them stood Charles James Fox, a recent casualty of North's administration, and Governor George Johnstone, a former governor of West Florida 1763–67 who took a completely independent line on imperial matters despite his election on the interest of one of the government's keenest supporters, Sir James Lowther.

What did these groups have in common? As it happened, very little at all, and they found it impossible to unite. For the Rockinghams the position was particularly difficult. Here was a party obsessed with justifying its conduct while in office from 1765 to 1766, in order to sanctify its consistency in opposition since that date. In view of what policies the Rockinghams had produced for Quebec in 1766, they were left with little room for manoeuvre. How could the members of this party attack clauses of the bill dealing with legal structures and the survival of the Catholic faith which, in essence, they themselves had been responsible for while in government? For the Chathamites, no such ideological constraints existed. There was ample opportunity for taking a strict whig, or "patriot," view of the constitutional settlement proposed for Quebec. Moreover, this approach would be in perfect accord with the line Chatham had followed on similar occasions affecting both domestic and colonial questions; in particular the Peace of Paris, the Stamp Act, and the rights of electors, 1769–70. For the last group, predictions and generalizations have no meaning. In many respects they were representative of a dying eighteenth-century ideal – members of parliament who judged each issue on its own merit rather than opposing government policy for opposition's sake.

Whether they liked it or not, these three groups were thrown together in the campaign against the Quebec Act. It was a campaign that, in practice, fell into two distinct phases. In the first there was agreement and progress among the opposition in confronting certain of the less controversial stages and clauses in the passage of the bill. This was not too surprising, for the petitions presented on 31 May and examination of witnesses on 2 and 3 June allowed MPs to indulge in a free-wheeling debate. Personal dislike of one clause or another became submerged in the general question-and-answer discussions. When the debate became focused on the first section of the Quebec Act relating to the boundary clause on 6 June, however, the cracks in opposition opinion began to surface.[33] A definition of exactly what would constitute Quebec proved an awkward problem, and the government found itself not entirely convinced of where the interior boundary should be. Two lines of argument emerged at odds with the government case. The first, from Governor Johnstone, questioned the whole notion of getting rid of the Proclamation line and expanding British jurisdiction from Quebec City into the hinterland. Like Hillsborough before him, Johnstone believed that such a policy would be the ruin of the Indian trade and would deflect settlement from a necessary north-south axis. All this, he added, would be to the advantage of the French, who were still active in the backwoods area. Also like Hillsborough, the governor received little sympathy for his views. But sympathy went to another objector, Edmund Burke, who spoke in his capacity as New York agent. He believed that the boundary had been drawn in the wrong place, and offered to amend the mistake in co-operation with Wedderburn. North accepted the offer and the two retired from the chamber to redraw the interior boundary in a fashion that proved acceptable to all those present.

The interesting aspect of the debate was that everyone agreed that the boundary represented an important issue and should be fixed in its proper place with care. Yet Burke was the only speaker to see the broader implications of American fears about the boundary line. As was his wont, Burke also expressed these anxieties in very dramatic terms. For those in disputed areas skirting on the boundary to be drawn two possibilities appeared, Burke told MPs: on one side of the line would be freedom, on the other despotism: "The Crown has a power at a stroke to turn them into slavery." Oddly enough, no one else in the debate that day developed the theme, though Governor Johnstone did echo it later. The more radical newspapers, on the other hand, were not so slow off the mark. The *Public Advertiser*, for example, selected the passage from Burke's speech as a sensational example of the government's nefarious dealings with the colonies and the more recent conquered territories in North America. The report concluded by putting the following words into Burke's mouth: "I have drawn a line of compromise. But for Heaven's sake let some line be fixed, then Englishmen on that immense continent may know where it is that he [*sic*] can be free. It is a point which cannot be left to commissioners. Shall commissioners be appointed at the pleasure of the Crown to determine on the rights, the privileges and the freedom of thousands of their fellow subjects"[34] Such excerpts fitted well into the popular campaign brewing against the Quebec Act in the summer of 1774. The articles appeared to provide more evidence in forging that mythological link which portrayed the Quebec Act as yet one more of the repressive Coercive Acts. The connection escaped most MPs and informed observers at the time, but proved highly marketable in the popular press, and has done so since in scholarly texts.

These small chinks in opposition opinion on the Quebec Act were blown wide open on 7 June, however, when the clauses covering the religious settlement in the province came before the Commons. During the previous debates on the bill much shadow-boxing on this issue had taken place. But nothing, as Clark hammered home in his recent study of Hanoverian England, was likelier to touch a raw political nerve than a debate on faith.[35] So it proved in the discussion of the religious clauses in the act. Any veneer of rationality and respect for the other's position suddenly disappeared when the problem had to be addressed. Differences of opinion, as always on the issue of religion, ran across party lines and swallowed up what little unity of purpose existed on the opposition benches. Very little room for trimming was possible on this subject. Members either accepted toleration for Catholicism in Quebec as a guarantee of its future loyalty under British rule or wished to see the anti-papist laws of the mother country applied in the province lock, stock, and barrel.

The split was certainly revealing not only in the passage of the Quebec Act but also in the later campaign for Catholic emancipation in Britain. To Burke the concept of toleration in Quebec was desirable as long as sufficient provisions existed for exempting Protestants from tithes and establishing the Church of England. He delivered a moving two-hour speech on the subject which maintained the ever-sacred consistency for the Rockinghams with regard to religion in the province since 1766.[36] In fact, Burke went a little further, advising the House to look closer to home on this issue: "There is but one healing, Catholic toleration in this House," he declared, "the thirsty earth of our own country is gaping and crying for that healing shower from heaven." Fox took a similarly conciliatory view of the question, his only worry being that the king was granted too great a discretion over the adjustment of who should and who should not pay tithes. He praised the House for supporting the spirit of this section in the bill, "growing wise enough, growing Christian enough, growing philosophic enough to hold out principles of toleration." In fact, if the pronouncements of Fox and Burke are taken together in this debate, they provide the very foundation for Sir George Savile's toleration bill of 1778 (Savile was also a Rockinghamite) and the stand of the whig party on Catholic emancipation thereafter.

Other speakers opposed to the bill in general found themselves unable to take this conciliatory line on the religious clauses. In Barré's view the time for equivocation had now passed. Confronted with the spectre of toleration for Catholicism in the territory he had fought to conquer for the Protestant crown of Britain, Barré's prejudicial temper burst forth. He confessed no belief in an act that favoured a religion which "had the power of persecuting other religions," and accused the government of harbouring a secret purpose in passing the act. "You mean to raise a popish army, to serve in the colonies of America," he declared, "from this time on all hope of peace in America will be destroyed." This speech was as firm a declaration of the popular or radical position as could be made. The gates of religious and racial bigotry had opened and several MPs willingly entered them. The traditional ogres of Catholicism, despotism, and evil French designs received a full airing in the debates that followed. On 8 June, for example, Thomas Townshend Jr told the House sarcastically that they should all attend with "white roses in our hats," so popish seemed the mood of MPs present.[37] Barré continued along this line by declaring quite openly, "this bill is popish from the beginning to the end." He then went a step further, acknowledging that there was only one hope left of amending the legislation and it lay with those seeking parliamentary seats in a forthcoming general election. In these remarks Barré laid out the ground for several campaigns during the election by lumping the ministry's policies on the Middlesex Election, America, and Quebec into one tyrannical conspiracy. "The public looking at the history of this Parliament," he said, "will see that by some papers found after their decease, there was a great reason to think they died in the profession of the Roman Catholic religion." The only accusation not thrown out during these debates was that the king was a papist, though it would certainly appear after the act of 1778. The opposition to religious toleration became desperate after 7 June because there was no broad support in parliament for a discriminatory policy in Quebec. In four divisions on the bill on 7, 8, and 10 June the minority totalled 31, 31, 40, and 21. The hard-liners stuck to their guns but by the evening of 10 June had become very frustrated indeed, no longer disguising their appeals for the public and press to support the strict whig, Protestant cause. The bill was "a plan of despotism" to Townshend, and, as George Dempster added, everyone should understand that "laziness, and precipitation, ignorance, and folly eternally attend despotic governments." This end to the debate must have been particularly galling to the Rockinghams, who counted Dempster among their flock. Several probably walked out in disgust, for the speech immediately preceded the minority of 21 votes to the government's 76.

This friction and division on the religious clauses coloured debate on the remainder of the act, relating to the absence of trials by jury in civil suits and how an appointed governing council for Quebec should be constituted. The debate on the former issue in committee on 10 June to some extent reflected a contemporary concern about the sanctity of juries in the wake of the activities of John Wilkes and his followers.[38] Few constitutional principles were closer to English hearts than a person's right to a trial by twelve of his peers, and on this point the opposition could at least unite. The government handled the case well, however, with Wedderburn pointing out that such institutions and procedures could not be applied willy-nilly to a French colonial society towards which MPs expressed so much ignorance and misplaced hostility. Furthermore, he added in conclusion, the amendment proposed by the opposition for jury trials involving French-speaking Canadians, and what became known as majority decisions, did not conform to the English system at all. They would, Wedderburn said, "Better be without a jury until they are fitted to receive such a jury."[39] Though this proved a strong point, and the minority rose to 40 votes, the government more than matched the effort again and its votes rose to 80.

After this debate the opposition gave up the ghost. Its speakers had been hoist by their own petard. Differing opinions, prejudices, and downright bigotry ruined any hope of a successful parliamentary campaign. By 7 June the effective opposition to the bill had been taken over by the popular press, which had been more or less invited to do so by Chatham's parliamentary followers. The political initiative had fallen away from the opposition at Westminster because certain MPs simply refused to adjust the ideological assumptions and traditions about the events of 1688–89 so ingrained in their minds. To those like Barré, Townshend, and Dempster, a conciliatory clause on Catholicism meant opening the gates to despotism. The other clauses, setting a threatening boundary to America, depriving the province of an assembly and even of trial by jury bore the basic fear out. It proved tiresome and worthless to fight the bill clause by clause, so the whole was castigated for what they believed it to be – a plan of popish despotism. These MPs had nothing to lose. The Rockinghams and independents refused to act with them, for there was a consensus among the social and political élites, including the bulk of the parliamentary classes, that favoured a special tolerant case being made for Quebec. And the precedent would, in turn, have far-reaching effects on domestic attitudes, politics, and policy on the religious element of this matter in the future. The point was underlined, and the battle-lines drawn, in Chatham's final outburst against the act as it passed the Lords on 17 June 1774. In a concluding tirade against the legislation, he maintained "that the dangerous innovations of this bill were at variance with all the safe-guards and barriers against the return of Popery and of popish influence, so wisely provided against by all the oaths of office and of trust from the constable up to members of both Houses, and even to the sovereign in his coronation oath. He pathetically expressed his fears that it might shake the affections and confidence of His Majesty's subjects in England and Ireland; and finally lose the hearts of all his Majesty's American subjects."[40] There was no alternative to governing seventy thousand or so French-speaking Catholics offered or spoken of. The speech simply represented a last, vain cry from a bruised patriot heart.

Thus the government managed to guide the act on to the statute books without serious pitfalls or difficulties; those awaited out of doors. Much has been written on the importance of this legislation to the development of a more benign imperial rule. Judgment on the policy in the past alternated between seeing the act as a piece of imperial statesmanship and seeing it as an instrument of arbitrary government.[41] More recently the view has fluctuated between three points: the French Canadian school, which examines the effect of British policy in general on the Society of New France; the economic determinism associated with the work of Ouellet; and finally Neatby's view that the act merely represented a ratification of local realities after the conquest.[42] The Quebec Act certainly contained some mix of all these factors, but there needs to be a revision on one crucial point. The act broke new ground not simply because of the novel pragmatic clauses affecting a new colonial government but also, more importantly, because of the domestic climate in which the policy had been formulated and passed. It is this British context to the legislation that rendered the actions of North's government into a truly radical departure from tradition. At root, the Quebec Act created a fissure in the rigid constitutional structure that had been established in Britain over the eighteenth century and which exercised such close control over its society and politics. The anger of those opposed to the act in parliament and the country at large did not arise simply because of distress at the mistreatment of three hundred or so English-speaking settlers in Quebec. Opposition grew from a broader understanding of what was at stake in the future now that a precedent had been set. In the carefully chosen words of warning from the *Middlesex Journal*: "the people seem roused from lethargy ... one would imagine that the days of James the Second were again revived, and the Pope, priests and popery, letting in by gatefulls upon us."[43] The fight to resist Catholic toleration, as with the Quebec Act, would eventually be lost, but not until the country had experienced a great deal more agony and bloodletting on this, the most vexatious of all constitutional problems in Hanoverian Britain.

Postscript

Between the passage of the Quebec Act and the effective date of its enactment on 1 May 1775, opponents of the legislation expended much energy in vain hope of repeal. What appeared a simple imperial issue in the early 1760s became a cause célèbre at the centre of a domestic political debate between North's government and the popular and parliamentary opposition. This was nowhere more evident than in the general election during the fall of 1774, and the controversy certainly warrants more attention than can be allowed here.[1] There existed various shades of opinion in the opposition to the act. At one extreme were the dissenting Protestant groups who attacked the religious and legal clauses of the act, which, in their view, established popery and despotism under the British crown. At the other lay high-church Anglicans, like Chatham and Walpole, who could not understand why the bishops in the House of Lords had sanctioned the action on Quebec. It had shown, in Walpole's words, that they "were too good courtiers and too bad Christians to vote *against* the bill."[2] For those supporting the act no such divisions emerged. There was an unerring philosophical and strategic rationale about the conciliatory policy towards Quebec that eventually proved irresistible. Nevertheless, for nine months or so, the opposition put up a gritty fight.

The essential point the radical politicians attempted to prove in their campaign was that a corrupt government had passed laws offensive to English liberties. The Coercive Acts and the Quebec legislation offered the most flagrant examples, and to avoid any further occurrences fundamental political reform at the centre should be enacted. The Quebec Act entered popular radical mythology. Those voting for it in parliament were condemned as enemies to liberty, and the *London Evening Post* printed a blacklist of MPs so that the electors preparing to vote in the 1774 general election knew where their representatives stood on the issue.[3] The repeal of the Quebec Act appeared as a central plank in the printed platform of several candidates putting up for election; Joseph Mawbey's address to the electors of Surrey carried the

148 The Imperial Challenge

message: "If I should be happy enough to be the object of your choice in the next [parliament], you may be assured I shall continue to vote for shortening the duration of parliaments; for a bill for the exclusion of Placemen and pensioners in the House of Commons, and for repealing the Quebec Bill, by which popery and French laws are established, not tolerated in that extensive country."[4]

The common factor in all these attacks was that they remained purely destructive in intent and scope. The role of Canada within the empire did not warrant discussion, nor was discussion necessary if the Quebec Act simply acted as a stick with which to beat the ministry. As seen in the parliamentary debates on the subject, constructive criticism of the legislation did take place, but it was not mirrored in the few pieces that appeared in the press. Even the one printed extract of a speech from Edmund Burke that appeared during the controversy merely reinforced the crude points made by the radicals against popery and French influence. "You are drawing a line between freedom and despotism," the *Public Advertizer* reported him as saying, and similar extracts from the speech appeared in the *Middlesex Journal*. This hardly did a man of Burke's capacity justice, yet it characterized the tone of the criticism against the act.[5]

The saving grace in the debate was the fact that the government bothered to reply to the enemies of its legislation. In contrast to the attacks on religious issues in 1769–70, ministers seemed to have been genuinely alarmed at the size and ferocity of the press campaign against the act. The pending general election made it imperative that critics should be answered, for ministers feared the opposition Campaign could affect returns in several constituencies. In the months that the controversy raged, pro-ministerial correspondents wrote many letters to the press, and at least three full-length pamphlets appeared justifying the legislation. These supporters of the legislation were assisted in their task by the more sober news journals, which viewed the Quebec legislation with less shock and horror. Not all the organs of the press sympathized with the radical writers and publishers like Thomas Hollis, Thomas Mortimer, and Caleb Fleming, who gave voice to their opinions in the *London Evening Post*, the *Political Register*, and the *Middlesex Journal*. An instructive comparison can be drawn from the way newspapers reported the City petition against the Quebec Act presented to the king on 24 June. Those elected to the committee had not minced their words when it came to outlining their basic objections to the legislation. At the centre of the problem was the omnipresent religious question, or, as it appeared in the petition, "the Roman Catholic religion which is known to be idolatrous and bloody."[6] The petition became an event of the utmost importance for the radicals. Each preliminary meeting that led up to its presentation to parliament warranted close scrutiny from the radical newspapers, with even an effort at headlines fulminating against popery and French influence.[7] The *Gentleman's Magazine* took a more circumspect view of these events. It published the mayor's petition in the June issue, but without editorial comment or mention of events preceding its presentation.[8] The *London Magazine* followed a similar line, adopting a stern attitude to the more extreme pieces published against the act. In August the journal concluded a review of one broadside entitled *An Appeal to the Public: stating and considering the objections to the Quebec Bill* with the advice: "We wish the writer to review coolly some other hasty strokes of his pen, and to promote union at home, whatever may be the fate of America."[9] In general, the supporters of the Quebec Act presented a far more skilled and erudite defence of their case than did the opposition. The government and its press sympathizers knew that many of the radicals and zealots used the Quebec legislation for their own domestic ends, and they came down hard on such motives. The letters of "NUMA" in 1774 contained a straightforward rebuttal of the accusations thrown out by opponents of the Quebec Act. In July, for example, the *Gentleman's Magazine* carried a letter from "NUMA" refuting the claim that the government sought "the *establishment*" of Catholicism in Canada.[10] "The bill in question is not a bill of *donative*, but of *confirmation*," he pointed out; "it does not give a single indulgence in spirituals to the Canadians; it barely *ratifies* what they were *previously* entitled to, and solely strengthens the public promise of the crown by the solemnity of an act of parliament." This carefully prepared argument looked a good deal more persuasive than the extremist views expressed by the religious zealots. It laid bare the technical weaknesses of the radical argument, and reflected the prevailing opinion among the government's legal officers. In fact, the concluding sentence of "NUMA"'s letter could well have come from Wedderburn's report on Quebec or even Mansfield's concluding remarks in the case of *Campbell and Hall* in 1774: "That in a newly ceded country, consisting almost entirely of papists, the popish religion is only tolerated under the declared supremacy of the English crown, agreeably to the rules of sound policy, the dictates of benevolence, and the plighted confidence of nations."

Where correspondents like "NUMA" sought to undermine the theoretical base of the act's opponents, others forced a more direct challenge by asking what else could be done. These letters are particularly worthy of note, for they reveal a progression in thought from the debate of 1760–63 about the value of Canada to the empire. These correspondents still adhered to the economic and strategic arguments for retaining Canada, and justified them by the evidence of the first decade of British rule. The interesting addition to the debate is an injection of emotive self-righteousness about Britain's responsibility to the conquered population. These writers argued that parliament could respond to this special imperial problem with a unique constitutional solution, firmly rooted in the free-born English tradition. "Columbus" stated the case most forcefully on the legal dispute, for instance, in his letters to the *Public Advertizer* in the summer of 1774. He believed that the future loyalty of the Canadians lay in Britain's inescapable duty to govern the colony justly. On 15 June he wrote:

Experience has evinced the necessity of restoring to our new subjects in that province those laws by which they were governed before the conquest, the most eminent men for wisdom and public knowledge . ... after many years of deliberation attention and mature consideration, have formed a code at once adapted to the desires and dispositions of the Canadians, and calculated to secure their affection to the mother country. If the intention and the use of laws are to make men happy, and at the same time to preserve a due subordination, the system of civil judicature for this province must fully answer all those valuable purposes.

This opinion directly reflected the view within the government's own ranks. As Henry Ellis commented to William Knox on 15 July: "As to the Quebec Law, to me it appears the most judicious, as well in point of equity as policy, that could possibly have been formed."[11]

Though there was a healthy mixture of rhetoric with the message to support the Quebec Act, the implication remained that Britain would have to change its attitude to the Canadians and their religion and culture, rather than the reverse. Supporters of the act canvassed this change with a moral conviction that no other choice existed but to adapt the British constitution to meet the specific needs of the Quebec people, in religious as well as legal matters. "A Canadian" stated the fact quite clearly in the enemy's own camp, the *Middlesex Journal*, during June 1774. "Canada is a conquered country," he observed "and if we wish to preserve the allegiance of these people, and the advantages arising from our conquest, it would by no means be conducive to the end desired to change the established religion of the country ... in this instance there is nothing more done than shewing indulgence which is generally shown to the conquered by the victor."[12]

In one respect or another, all these supporters of the act embodied some part of the unequivocal commitment to meeting the special needs of Quebec. In his speech to parliament at the close of the session in June 1774, the king himself paid tribute to the Canadian legislation, saying that "my assent is founded on the clearest principles of justice and humanity; and will, I doubt not have the best effects in quieting the minds and promoting the happiness of my Canadian subjects."[13] It was from this speech that William Knox moulded the most complete justification of the Quebec Act, in his pamphlet entitled *The Justice and Policy of the Late Act of Parliament for ... the Province of Quebec.* It had appeared in July 1774, less than a month after the act became law, and, though Knox said nothing original about the legislation itself, it is striking for the way he dealt empirically with the issues. He traced the background of the act, disposing of the imputation that it could be considered as one of the punitive measures against Boston. The merits of the religious, legal, and political clauses in the act were then discussed, including the boundary problem which created so much heat in parliament but so little in the press. In conclusion, Knox castigated opponents of the act, especially the Rockinghams, as opportunists who based their campaign on a misrepresentation of the facts and motives behind the government's action. With such impressive armoury in the press it is no surprise that the government came out of the debate unscathed. In parliament the legislation had passed with large majorities, and pro-ministerial writers quickly saw an opportunity to damn their attackers as an extremist minority. Parliamentary opponents of the Quebec Act became known as "the thirty-seven patriots" – no term of endearment but representative of the limited scope of their appeal.

In the context of an eighteenth-century political debate waged in the press it is unrealistic to expect more sophistication than was shown in these broadsides. Yet the lessons to be learned from this material should not be ignored. The press mirrored a developing argument over Quebec both before and after the conquest, an argument that progressed from the bitter disputes between the trading and territorial imperialists after the fall of New France to an airtight commitment on securing Quebec's position and loyalty under the British crown. The expansionists won this debate on the promised expectation of wealth and security throughout the whole Atlantic empire. These same expansionists stood their ground under attack in 1774, but the attack necessitated a more thorough and sophisticated analysis of British traditions and assumptions than was ever envisaged in 1759. These deliberations to justify the Quebec Act resulted in significant constitutional concessions in the development of imperial policy and very possibly domestic policy too. The issue of Catholic emancipation was an explosive issue in British domestic politics, and would remain so for the next fifty years. Yet here were a government and its supporters endorsing a civil and religious policy that no Catholic in Britain or in its most immediate Catholic domain, Ireland, enjoyed. It cannot be denied that the policy arose in part from the force of circumstance in Quebec society, but this does not wholly explain the unerring commitment to an equitable settlement of Canadian problems. Indeed, if a group of radicals existed in the parliamentary and press campaign of 1774, surely those who supported the Quebec Act and grasped the nettle of toleration should assume the title.

Notes

ABBREVIATIONS

BIHR *Bulletin of the Institute of Historical Research*
CHA *Canadian Historical Association*
CHR *Canadian Historical Review*
EHR *English Historical Review*
HJ *Historical Journal*
HMC Historical Manuscripts Commission
JAS *Journal of American Studies*
Parl. Hist. Parliamentary History of England from 1066 to 1803, ed.
W. Cobbett
TRHS *Transactions of the Royal Historical Society*
WMQ *The William and Mary Quarterly*, 3rd series

CHAPTER ONE

1 London, British Library, Additional Manuscripts 57820, fol. 165 (27 Aug. 1758). All citations of manuscript collections in the British Library will hereafter be prefixed with BL, followed by either Add. MSS or the name of the collection and then the call number.
2 *Gentleman's Magazine* 29:440. References to this and other contemporary magazines cited in the notes that follow refer to the bound volumes and then page numbers in a particular volume.
3 Lewis, ed., *Horace Walpole's Correspondence* 29:327 (hereafter cited as Walpole, *Letters*).
4 *London Gazette*, 24–17 Nov. 1759.
5 Sedgwick, ed., *Letters from Geo III to Bute*, 32 (9 Oct. 1759).
6 Schweizer and Brown, eds., *The Devonshire Diary: William Cavendish Fourth Duke of Devonshire Memoranda on State Affairs 1759–1762*, 109 (hereafter cited as *The Devonshire Diary*).

7 Schweizer, "The Seven Years' War: A System Perspective," in Black, ed., *The Origins of War in Early Modern Europe*, 225 n. 1.

8 Ibid., 248–51 and Mackay and Scott, *The Rise of the Great Powers*, chapter 6 *passim*.

9 See, for example, Middleton's study, *The Bells of Victory*.

10 Newman, ed., *Leicester House Politics 1750–60, from the Papers of John, Second Earl of Egmont*, 227 (hereafter cited as *Leicester House Politics*). For another perspective on the anti-war material, see also Peters, *Pitt and Popularity*, 177–87.

11 Spector, *English Literary Periodicals*, 89, and Schweizer, "The Bedford Motion and the House of Lords," *Parliamentary History Yearbook* 5 (1986):107–23.

12 BL Add. MSS 32906, fol. 97.

13 Strathpeffer, Cromartie Estate Office, Cromartie MSS Bundle 22.

14 Russell, ed., *Correspondence of John, Fourth Duke of Bedford, selected from the originals at Woburn Abbey*, 2:415, Newcastle to Bedford, 27 June 1760 (hereafter cited as *Bedford Correspondence*).

15 *British Magazine* 1 (1760):34.

16 For more detail on this see Lawson, *Grenville*, chapter 2.

17 Sedgwick, ed., *Letters from Geo. III to Bute*, 47.

18 Russell-Barker, ed., *Horace Walpole's Memoirs of the Reign of King George the Third* 1:106 (hereafter cited as Walpole, *Memoirs*).

19 Lords Address, 18 Nov. 1760, *Journals of the House of Lords* 30:10 (hereafter cited as *Lords Journals*).

20 The following account and quotations, except where noted, are taken from Chatham's papers deposited in London: Public Record Office 30/8/66, fols. 229–34. All references dealing with manuscripts in the London Public Record Office will hereafter be prefixed with PRO and then the call number.

21 *Journals of the House of Commons* 28:973 (hereafter cited as *Commons Journals*).

22 The most topical contemporary illustration of this theme was Samuel Foote's play *The Comisary*, which can be found in Foote, *The Dramatic Works of Samuel Foote*.

23 *London Magazine*, Feb. 1760, for example, contained an attactive map, and demand was such that "near twenty hands have been employed in colouring the said map, it has been impossible to keep constant supply." For a more fascinating illustration of how Quebec was exploited commercially, see Brewer, "Commercialization and Politics," in McKendrick, Brewer, and Plumb, *The Birth of a Consumer Society*, 197–265.

24 Lambert, ed., *House of Commons Sessional Papers of the Eighteenth Century*, vol. 2.

25 For the originators of the myth see, Beer, *British Colonial Policy 1754–1765*, 152–9; Alvord, *The Mississippi Valley in British Politics* 1:52–62. For the revisionist view see Namier, *England in the Age of the American Revolution*, 273–82; Sosin, *Whitehall and the Wilderness*, chapter 1, and Labaree and Willcox, eds., *The Papers of Benjamin Franklin* 9:47–100.

26 See, for example, Callwood, *Portrait of Canada*.

27 *A Letter to the People ...*, 47.

28 *The Interest of Great Britain ...*, 45. Labaree seems to prove beyond all doubt that Franklin wrote the piece in *The Papers of Benjamin Franklin* 9:54.

29 See, for example, *A detection of the false reasons and facts contained in the five letters entitled, Reasons for keeping Guadaloupe at a peace, preferable to Canada by a Member of Parliament*.

30 In particular, *Gentleman's Magazine* 30:24.

31 *British Magazine* 1:95.

32 *Gentleman's Magazine* 31:123–4.

33 Sosin, *Whitehall and the Wilderness*, 13.

34 *The Reasons ...*, 8.

35 Ibid., 32.

36 *British Magazine* 1:95.

37 Lawson, "Parliament and the First East India Inquiry, 1767," *Parliamentary History Yearbook* 1 (1982):99–114.

38 *The Reaons ...*, 31.

39 A report in the *Public Advertizer*, 8 Apr. 1774, ran: "Lord North's slip about Salem and Marblehead is compared to a similar one in the last reign by mistake to have related to Cape Breton; whereas the real truth was that upon first settling of Nova Scotia the late Duke of Newcastle unluckily called it a very fine island."

40 For more background on this, see Lawson, "'The Irishman's Prize': Views of Canada from the British Press 1760–1774," *HJ* 28, no. 3 (1985):575–96.

41 See, for example the standard accounts by Pares, *War and Trade in the West Indies, 1739–1763*, 596–612; Dorn, *Competition for Empire, 1740–1763*, 370–84; Corbett, *England in the Seven Years' War* 2:328–76; Gibson, *The British Empire before the American Revolution* 8:284–312; Rashed, *The Peace of Paris, passim*; Hotblack, "The Peace of Paris 1763," TRHS 2 (1908):235–67; and Hyam, "The Peace of Paris (1763)," in Hyam and Martin, eds., *Reappraisals in British Imperial History*, 21–43.

42 Ibid., 40.

43 Apart from *The Devonshire Diary*, 24–186, further revisions of traditional views can be found in Schwiezer, ed., *Lord Bute: Essays in Reinterpretation*; Schweizer, "William Pitt, Lord Bute and Peace Negotiations with France, May–September 1761," *Albion* 13, no. 3 (Fall, 1981):362–75; idem, "The Cabinet Crisis of August 1761: Unpublished Letters from the Bute and Bedford Manuscripts," *BIHR* 59, no. 140 (1986):225–9; and idem, "Lord Bute, Newcastle, Prussian and the Hague Overtures: A Re-Examination," *Albion* 9, no. 1 (Spring, 1977):72–97.

44 Bullion, "Securing the Peace: Lord Bute, the Plan for the Army, and the Origins of the American Revolution," in Schweizer, ed., *Lord Bute: Essays in Reinterpretation*, esp. 27–30.

45 Schweizer, "The Seven Years' War: A System Perspective," in Black, ed., *The*

Origins of War in Early Modern Europe, 248–51.

46 Hyam, "Peace of Paris (1763)," in Hyam and Martin, eds., *Reappraisals in British Imperial History*, 39.

47 Mackay and Scott, *The Rise of the Great Powers*, 199.

48 *The Devonshire Diary*, 25.

49 Ibid., 26. For a narrative overview of these events see Rashed, *Peace of Paris*, chapter II.

50 The Spanish experience and Spain's fears of British expansion in this period are explored in more detail by Brading, "Bourbon Spain and Its American Empire," in *The Cambridge History of Latin America* 1:389–434.

51 Cited in Eccles, "The Role of the American Colonies in Eighteenth-Century French Foreign Policy," in Eccles, *Essays on New France*, 146.

52 Ottawa, Canada: National Archives, Manuscript Groups, Montcalm to Berryer, Minister of Marine, 4 Apr. 1757, copy from the original in the Dartmouth Papers, MG 23, AI vol. 4:4883. All references that follow to manuscripts from the Canadian National Archives will be prefixed with MG only.

53 Eccles, *Essays on New France*, 147–8.

54 Entries in *The Devonshire Diary* for July and Aug. give examples of this realization:105, 113, and 121.

55 Taken from the copy in Oxford University: Rhodes House Library, North MSS. fol. 190.

56 *The Devonshire Diary*, 169.

57 PRO 30/29/1/14 fol. 526.

58 Walpole, *Letters* 21:497.

59 London: Bedford Estate Office, Bedford MSS 43, fol. 130 (22 Feb. 1761). All subsequent references to these manuscripts will be reduced to Bedford MSS and then the call number.

60 MG 21 Add. MSS 32922, fol. 451; the accounts and quotations that follow are taken from here.

61 The dates were finalized in cabinet on 16 June 1761; for more background on this see Rashed, *Peace of Paris*, 76–92.

62 Bedford MSS 44, fol. 90.

63 The most erudite exposition of Pitt's hawkish views on this point can be found in Liverpool's papers, BL Add. MSS 38336, fols. I–II. Though this manuscript is dated c. 1763, it was almost certainly written in 1761.

64 *Bedford Correspondence* 3:22–9.

65 *Leicester House Politics*, 215.

66 *Bedford Correspondence* 3:30–4 (12 July 1761).

67 Ibid., 36–9.

68 PRO 30/29/1/14 fols. 526–8; the quotations that follow are taken from here.

69 This was the description of Charles Jenkinson, Bute's secretary, in a letter to Grenville, a member of the "nominal" cabinet and treasurer of the Navy. Smith, ed., *The Grenville Papers: Being the Correspondence of Richard Grenville, Earl*

Temple, K.G., and the Right Hon. George Grenville, Their Friends and Contemporaries
1:379 (hereafter cited as the *Grenville Papers*).

70 Bedford MSS 43: fol. 280.

71 Walpole, *Letters* 21:537 (6 Oct. 1761).

72 Lawson, *Grenville*, chapter 4.

73 Albemarle, ed., *Memoirs of the Marquis of Rockingham and His Contemporaries* 1:45.

74 PRO 30/47/28, unfol., Hardwicke to Egremont, 30 Dec. 1761.

75 Apart from the Grenville papers cited below, the best unpublished documentation of the final stages of the peace are the Viry-Solar correspondence in the
Shelburne MSS in the Clements Library, Ann Arbor, Michigan (hereafter
Shelburne MSS), and the Astle MSS in the British Library. For the most complete published record see *The Devonshire Diary*, 154–86.

76 PRO 30/29/3/1, fols. 24–9; the quotation that follows is taken from here.

77 See BL Add. MSS 57834, fols. 9, 59, 62, 64, and Northamptonshire County
Record Office, Henley (Watford) Collection; Northington MSS envelope
B – Political Papers (1).

78 Mansfield's correspondence on the peace can be found in the Egremont
papers of 1762–63, PRO 30/4/29, unfol.

79 PRO 30/29/1/14, fo. 533 Bedford to Gower, 8 Nov. 1762. Other correspondence of
the negotiations can be found in *Bedford Correspondence* 3:88–97 and Bedford
MSS 45: fols. 98–236 and 46: fols. 12–184.

80 PRO 30/47/27, unfol.

81 Shortt and Doughty, *Constit. Docs.* 1:85.

82 PRO 30/47/27, unfol.

83 Shortt and Doughty, *Constit. Docs.* 1:86. It seems clear that, unlike Egremont,
Hardwick had read an official document probably drawn up in 1760 (though
dated before 1759), entitled "sur la limite de Louisiane .. pourr fixer lex limites
des la Louisiane du cote des colonies des Angloises et du Canada." It had been
circulating for some time and bore a strong resemblance to the eventual outcome of the peace settlement for Louisiana. BL Add. MSS 38332, fol. 170.

84 PRO 30/47/27, unfol.

85 Shortt and Doughty, *Constit Docs.* 1:86.

86 Phillimore, ed. *Memoirs and Correspondence of George, Lord Lyttelton* 2:638.

87 Chesterfield, ed. *Letters to His Son* 6:2449.

88 Bedford MSS 45: fol. 236.

89 See Peters, *Pitt and Popularity*, later chapters and Rea, *The English Press in
Politics*, chapter 1.

CHAPTER TWO

1 Thomas and Simmons, eds., *Proceedings and Debates* 1:441, 445.

2 A convention for the final adjustment of these bills was signed by Britain and
France on 31 March 1766 and ratified on 22 Apr. 1766. *London Gazette*, 29

March – 1 April 1766.

3 BL Add. MSS 27777, fols. 2–3 (23 May 1763), where this letter with comment can be found.

4 *Gentleman's Magazine* 33:496–50. The quotations that follow are taken from here.

5 Robert Clive, for example, realized this in his early career in India, and always took care to have his publicists in London. Lawson and Lenman, "Clive and the 'Black Jagir,'" *HJ* 26, no. 4 (1983):801–29.

6 Hay's article emphasizes this point exceptionally well. "The Meanings of Criminal Law in Quebec," in Knafla, ed., *Crime and Criminal Justice in Europe and Canada*, 77–81.

7 Burt, *Old Province of Quebec* 1:73.

8 26–8 Feb. 1767.

9 In McKendrick, Brewer, and Plumb, *The Birth of a Consumer Society*, 197–265. To see how this worked at a local practical level, consult Jenkins, "The Tory Tradition in Eighteenth-Century Cardiff," *Welsh History Review* 122 (1984):193–5.

10 20 Oct. 1763.

11 7 Dec. 1763.

12 Neatby, *Quebec*, 3.

13 MG 23, G II series I, vol. 3:35–9.

14 See, for example, Brunet, *French Canada and the Early Decades of British Rule*, 7.

15 Neatby, *Quebec*, chapter 3.

16 Ouellet, "The British Army of Occupation in the St. Lawrence Valley, 1760–74," in Ion and Prete, eds., *Armies of Occupation*, 17–54.

17 This and other historiographical controversies surrounding the conquest are neatly presented and summarized in Nish, ed., *The French Canadians, 1759–1766*, and Gagnon, *Quebec and Its Historians*.

18 BL Add. MSS 38332, fols. 152–69.

19 Of the two Paris editions of Charlevoix's work in 1744, one was in four volumes, the other in six. It appears that British bureaucrats used the six-volume edition, and the quotations that follow from the reports are taken from here.

20 Charlevoix, *Histoire* 5:125.

21 BL Add. MSS 38332, fols. 152–9; the quotations that follow are all taken from this source.

22 The original edition was first published in 1693, and it then ran throught four more editions. The last appeared in 1751 and was reissued as late as 1804.

23 For a similarly pessimistic vision of the future to the south see Barrow's discussion of other reports from this manuscript collection affecting America, "A Project for Imperial Reform: 'Hints Respecting the Settlement for our American Provinces,' 1763," *WMQ* 24 (1967):108–26.

24 There is an extremely good description of these structures in Thomas, *British*

Politics and the Stamp Act Crisis, chapter 3.

25 See, for example, in the North American context, Christie and Labaree, *Empire or Independence* and Pocock, *Three British Revolutions, 1641, 1688, 1776.*

26 Steele, *Politics of Colonial Policy: The Board of Trade*, especially chapter 6.

27 On the former, see Langford, *The First Rockingham Administration*, 255–8; on the latter, Thomas, *Lord North*, 75.

28 Shortt and Doughty, *Constit. Docs.* 1:93 and n.

29 See respectively Humphreys, "Lord Shelburne and the Proclamation of 1763," *EHR* 49 (1934):241–69 and Crane, "Hints Relative to the Division and Government of the Conquered and Newly Acquired Countries in America," *Mississippi Valley Historical Review* 8 (1921–22):367–73.

30 Again respectively, see Burt, *Old Province of Quebec* 1: chapters 1–5; Neatby, *Quebec*, chapters 1–3; and Marshall, "The Incorporation of Quebec in the British Empire, 1763-1774," in Platt and Skaggs, eds., *Of Mother Country and Plantations*, 43–50.

31 There is a useful summary of Ellis's career in *Dictionary of American Biography* 6:104–5.

32 Shortt and Doughty, *Constit. Docs.* 1:104.

33 From the Proclamation of 7 Oct. 1763, ibid., 120.

34 Humphreys, "Lord Shelburne and the Proclamation of 1763," *EHR* 49 (1934):258.

35 Marshall, "The Incorporation of Quebec in the British Empire 1763-1774," in Platt and Skaggs, eds., *Of Mother Country and Plantations*, 46.

36 For more on the controversies surrounding this issue, see Marshall, "Colonial Protest and Imperial Retrenchment: Indian Policy 1764-1768," *JAS* 5 (1971):1:17.

37 For further background on this see Fitzmaurice, *Life of William, Earl of Shelburne*, 1:chapter 4 (hereafter cited as *Fitzmaurice*).

38 For greater detail on Halifax at the Board of Trade see Başye, *The Lords Commissioners of Trade*, especially chapter 2; on his career in 1763 see Shy, *Toward Lexington*, 68–83, and Wickwire, *British Subministers and Colonial America*, 70–1 and 103–4.

39 Cited in *Fitzmaurice* 1:143.

40 Tomlinson, ed., *Additional Grenville Papers*, 318.

41 *Grenville Papers* 2:481.

42 The judgment is printed in Shortt and Doughty, *Constit. Docs.* 1:366–72, and a shorter summary can be found in Harlow and Madden, *British Colonial Docs.*, 78–9.

43 The sources that exist on Mansfield's career hardly do justice to these achievements. The three main studies available merely emphasize the need for a study of his political career: Holliday, *The life of William, late Earl of Mansfield*, Fifoot, *Lord Mansfield*, and Heward, *Lord Mansfield*.

44 Sedgwick, ed., *Letters from Geo. III to Bute*, 202.

45 Christie, "The Cabinet during the Grenville Administration, 1763–5," *EHR* 73

(1958):86–92 and Lawson, "Further Reflections on the Cabinet in the Early Years of George III's Reign," *BIHR* 57 (1984):237–40.

46 MG 23, A5. It is likely the report passed between Barrington and Shelburne more than once. Shelburne wrote marginal notes on this document, and their is a similar document amongst Shelburne's papers now on deposit in Ottawa, MG 23, A4, vol. 50. Another example of these sentiments being expressed at the highest level can be found in Egremont to Grenville, 11 March 1763, BL Add. MSS 57808, fol. 65.

47 *Journals of the Commissioners of the Board of Trade and Plantations 1704–1782* 70:401 (hereafter cited as *Board of Trade Journals*). The reports from the three governors of 1762 can be found in Shortt and Doughty, *Constit. Docs.* 1:37–69.

48 The former comment came in the article by Wallace, "The Beginnings of British Rule in Canada," *CHR* 6 (1925):208; the latter was made by Marshall, "The Incorporation of Quebec in the British Empire," in Platt and Skaggs, eds., *Of Mother Country and Plantations*, 45.

49 MG 23, G II, series I, vol. 2:122 (14 Apr. 1764).

50 Madden's essay certainly stresses this point well, "1066, 1776 and All That ... " in Flint and Williams, eds., *Perspectives of Empire*, 9–26.

51 These proved to be profound changes, causing an ideological rift between the way the American colonists and British politicians looked at the constitution. One of the most revealing studies of late on this ascept of Anglo-American relations, post-1688, is Reid, *In Defiance of the Law*, esp. chapter 5.

52 This is Brewer's terminology, *Party Ideology and Popular Politics*, v.

53 Shortt and Doughty, *Constit. Docs.* 1:126–32.

54 It was 10 August 1764 because a clause in the Treaty of Paris, dated 10 February 1763, had given those Canadians wishing to leave the province eighteen months to do so.

55 Strathpeffer, Cromartie Estate Office, Cromartie MSS bundle 12.

56 Ibid. (13 March 1762).

57 For more background on these connections and the importance to decision-making in 1763, see Lawson, *Grenville* chapter 5.

58 MG 23, G II, series I, vol. 2:25.

59 MG 23, G II, series I, vol. 2:16.

60 All the references to the Instructions that follow are taken from Shortt and Doughty, *Constit. Docs.* 1:132–49.

61 Burt, *Old Province of Quebec* 1:82.

CHAPTER THREE

1 MG 23, G II, series I, vol. 2:183.

2 Cited in Machin, *The Catholic Issue in British Politics*, 1.

3 Knox, *The Justice and Policy of the Late Act of Parliament for Making More Effectual Provision for the Government of the Province of Quebec*. Knox made much the same

point, though in a more oblique way, in *Extra-Official State Papers*, 150–1.

4 Ellesmere's views are contained in tracts reproduced by Knafla, *Law and Politics in Jacobean England*, 203–53. The case is summarized in *English Law Reports: King's Bench Division*, 6, 77:377–411.

5 Notes on this case can be found in Historical Manuscripts Commission, *Dartmouth*, 14th report, 2:548 (hereafter cited as HMC and then the name of the report). The decision was ratified in a case of 1722 (2 peere Williams, 75), and a memorandum was then drawn up by the Master of the Rolls itemizing the salient points in the judgment. See *English Law Reports: King's Bench Divison*, 6, 77:398 and n.

6 The tone of anti-papist legislation was set in the first years of William and Mary's reign. See the acts 1 W. & M., c. 8, 9, and 15.

7 BL Add. MSS 32982, fol. 26.

8 Shortt and Doughty, *Constit. Docs.* 1:86.

9 Shelburne MSS 64:553–9; all the quotations that follow are taken from here.

10 Hertford to Shelburne, 1 Feb. 1764. Shelburne MSS 38: item 38.

11 18 Geo. III, c. 60.

12 18 Geog. III, c. 61. The recent D.Phil. thesis by Haydon, "Anti-Catholicism in Eighteenth-Century England, c. 1714–1780," has helped rectify the situation somewhat. An interesting line of inquiry has been opened on this topic by Donovan, who argues for the military origins of the Catholic Relief Act of 1778. Though he pays little attention to the imperial background for this policy, he does trace changes in official thinking before 1778. See "The Military Origins of the Roman Catholic Relief Programme of 1778," *HJ*, 28, no. 1 (1985):79–102. Other work in progress by Tom Bartlett on the emanicipation issue in Anglo-Irish relations 1760–1830 may well reveal a fuller picture of the common impetus behind the legislation of the 1770s. I am grateful for Dr Bartlett's information on this issue.

13 For the religious clauses in the Commission and Instructions to Murray see the respective sections in Shortt and Doughty, *Constit. Docs.* 1:127–8 and 239–40. There is no doubt that pressure from anti-Catholic merchants and the Society for the Propagation of Christian Knowledge influenced decisions of this nature. I am grateful to Joanna Innes of Somerville College, Oxford for pointing this out to me, and allowing me to see her unpublished work on these matters.

14 This and the quotation that follow are taken from Murray to Lord Eglinton, 27 Oct. 1764, MG 123, G II, series I, vol. 2:171. Eglinton was a staunch favourite of George III and held the office of lord of the bedchamber.

15 Burt, *Old Province of Quebec*, 1:84–5.

16 MG 23, G II, series I, vol. 2:104 (22 March 1764).

17 Shortt and Doughty, *Constit. Docs.* 1:121.

18 *English Law Reports: King's Bench Division*, 6, 77:398.

19 Shortt and Doughty, *Constit. Docs.* 1:149–52.

20 There is an excellent copy of this document in Shelburne MSS 66:5-17, with the marginal notes, which are not reproduced in full by Shortt and Doughty, *Constit. Docs.* 1:149-52. The quotations used in the account that follows are taken from Shelburne's manuscript copy.

21 A fair picture of Murray's character comes through in the short biography by Browne in *Dictionary of Canadian Biography* 4:569-78, though I disagree with one or two points made therein.

22 These clauses of the Instructions can be found in the manuscript collections of all the leading politicians of the day: see, for example, Rockingham's copy in his papers deposited in Sheffield's City Library, Wentworth Woodhouse Muniments R62-2 and that of Newcastle in BL Add. MSS 32982, fols. 16-20. All subsequent references to the Wentworth Woodhouse Muniments in Sheffield will be prefixed WWM only.

23 Shortt and Doughty, *Constit. Docs.* 1:153-6; the quotations that follow are taken from here.

24 "Address of French Citizens to the King Regarding The Legal System." The report was read at the Board of Trade on 7 January 1765; *Board of Trade Journals* 72:134. For a similar address from the French jurors of Quebec see Shortt and Doughty, *Constit. Docs.* 1:156-61 and the reply to this in MG 23, AI vol. 4:4519-20.

25 *Board of Trade Journals* 70:427; a copy of the petition can be found in Shelburne MSS 66:1-4.

26 See, for example, the day's proceedings at the Board of Trade for 18 June 1764 and 27 Nov. 1764, *Journals* 71:72-5 and 113-16.

27 Murray sent letters of introduction to London for Cramahé to ensure that he saw the right people in power. MG 23, G II, series I, vol. 2:183 provides a sample of this. For more on Cramahé's career see *Dictionary of Canadian Biography* 4:787-93.

28 Printed in the *Quebec Gazette*, 4 July 1765; the quotation that follows is taken from here.

29 Murray's bitter complaints about being deprived of his military powers can be found in his letters to London of fall and winter 1764-65; see, for instances of this, MG 23, G II, series I, vol. 2:154-6, 164, and 192-3.

30 The MPS were Peregrine Cust (Bishop's Castle), Richard Glover (Weymouth and Melcombe Regis), Robert Harley (Droitwich), and Robert Ladbroke (London); for further information on their careers see Namier and Brooke, eds., *House of Commons* 2:291-3, 504-5, and 586, and 3:16 respectively.

31 Shortt and Doughty, *Constit. Docs.* 1:169.

32 The whole case was heard at the Board of Trade on 18 June 1765. *Journals* 72:185.

33 20 Oct. 1764 to Lords of Trade and Plantations, Nottingham University Library, Portland MSS, PWF 9705 (hereafter Portland MSS).

34 The petition can be found in Portland MSS, PWF 9704.

35 Shelburne MSS 64:217.

36 Ibid., 64:218.

37 BL King's MSS 213, fols. 116-17.

38 Shelburne MSS 64:217.

39 A good summary of the episode can be found in Neatby, *Quebec*, 38-40.

40 Edinburgh, Scotland: Scottish Record Office, GD 32/24/18. All references dealing with manuscripts in the Scottish Records Office will hereafter be prefixed with SRO.

41 PRO TI 434/136-7.

42 PRO 30/47/15, unfol., miscellaneous papers in the Egremont collection relating to the Peace of Paris.

43 BL Add. MSS 38335, fols. 118-19. For a contemporary account of British failures in the beaver trade, see Williams, ed., *Andrew Graham's Observations on Hudson's Bay*, 256-67.

44 PRO TI 430/54; a good copy of this document can also be found in Shelburne MSS 62:213.

45 MG 23, G II, series I, vol. 2:224-5. A rather idiosyncratic background to the revenue problem can be found in Balls, "Quebec, 1766-1774: The Financial Administration," *CHR* 41 (1960):203-14.

46 PRO 30/29/1/14, II Sept. 1764.

47 For more background on eighteenth-century Ireland and its administration see McDowell, *Ireland in the Age of Imperialism*, chapter I and 2 and Bartlett and Hayton, eds., *Penal Era and Golden Age, passim*.

48 Shelburne MSS 61:685.

49 Cramahé to Murray 12 Jan. 1765, MG 23, G II, series I, vol. 2:259. See also Murray to George Ross, 26 June 1764, MG 23, G II, series I, vol. 2:53.

50 *Grenville Papers* 2:476-7. Marshall asserts that after dealing with this problem, Grenville ignored Quebec matters ("The Incorporation of Quebec in the British Empire," in Platt and Skaggs, eds., *Of Mother Country and Plantations*, 50). There are, however, many sources disproving this: see, in particular, the letters exchanged between Grenville and Halifax on 21 Apr. 1765 (Tomlinson, ed., *Additional Grenville Papers*, 265) and Whately to Grenville on II Apr. 1765 (BL Add. MSS 57817A, fol. 23.

51 For the full plan see Shelburne MSS 66:19-31; and for discussion in council see *Acts of Privy Council: Unbound* 6:396-9.

52 MG 23, G II, series I, vol. 2:260.

53 *Acts of Privy Council: Colonial*: 4:719-20. This contradicts the statement in Burt (*Old Province of Quebec* I:III) that the Privy Council issued a public rebuke to Murray.

CHAPTER FOUR

1 Mountstuart: Isle of Bute, Scotland, Bute MSS, Loudoun Papers, bundle 6: undated 1765 (hereafter Bute MSS).

2 MG 23, G II, series I, vol. 3:248.

3 The decision to order Murray to prepare for his return was taken in September 1765; notice was sent to Quebec in October and his actual departure requested in April 1766. He left Quebec on 28 June 1766.

4 HMC *Dartmouth*, 11th report: 179.

5 Cited in Langford, *The First Rockingham Administration*, 255.

6 HMC *Dartmouth*, 11th report: 179.

7 Langford, *The First Rockingham Administration*, 255.

8 A good copy of this report can be found in Shelburne MSS 64:325-63.

9 Much secondary work has become available over the last twenty years documenting Rockingham's contact with the merchants. See, for example, Langford, *The First Rockingham Administration*, 119-24; O'Gorman, *The Rise of Party*, 139-55; and Thomas, *British Politics and the Stamp Act Crisis*, 146-50.

10 MG 23, G II, series I, vol. 3:179. The two quotations that follow are taken from here.

11 MG 23, G II, series I, vol. 3:187.

12 MG 23, G II, AI, vol. 4:4564-79. The account and quotations that follow are taken from this source.

13 MG 23, G II AI, vol. 4:4580-4606. The account and quotations that follow are taken from this source.

14 *Board of Trade Journals*, 72:173. A full copy of the report, though misdated 1766, can be found in Shelburne MSS 66:19-32.

15 WWM RI-497. •

16 Shelburne MSS 64:546.

17 *Acts of Privy Council: Colonial, Unbound* 6:396-9.

18 Shelburne MSS 66:23. The quotations that follow are also taken from this document, fols. 23 and 30.

19 This is from the earl of Hardwicke's account of the meeting, BL Add. MSS 35914, fol. 8. See also *Bedford Correspondence* 3:288-90.

20 *Board of Trade Journals* 72:183.

21 Shelburne MSS 64:541.

22 *Acts of Privy Council: Colonial, Unbound* 6:402.

23 *Acts of Privy Council: Colonial* 4:725.

24 PRO 30/29/3/2 fols. 172-3.

25 PRO 30/29/3/2 fools. 176-7.

26 Shelburne MSS 64:325-67 seems to bear this point out.

27 Shelburne MSS 66:35-8. Printed in Shortt and Doughty, *Constit. Docs.* 1:171-2.

28 *Board of Trade Journals* 72:194-6.

29 Shelburne MSS 66:35-8. The quotations that follow are taken from here.

30 Langford, ed., *The Writings and Speeches of Edmund Burke* 2:55.

31 *Acts of Privy Council: Colonial* 4:696.

32 Shelburne MSS 66:38.

33 Levesue, Lemoine, and Porlier to Henri Guinand, 27 Sept. 1765, MG 23, AI, vol. 4:4608. For other complaints see *Acts of Privy Council: Colonial* 6:404-5.

34 *Quebec Gazette*, 21 Feb. 1766.

35 Burt, *Old Province of Quebec* 1:112.

36 MG 23, AI, vol. 4:4639-41.

37 WWM R65-5d.

38 WWM R65-11.

39 WWM R1-497 and R65-3.

40 MG 23, GI.

41 Ibid.; see especially clause 23.

42 BL King's MSS 213 fol. 59.

43 WWM R1 — 502.

44 Fuller background information on Briand's appointment can be found in Neatby, *Quebec*, 107-17.

45 Ibid., 124.

46 Shelburne MSS 64:539-40.

47 Cited in Shortt and Doughty, *Constit. Docs.* 1:179.

48 Ibid., 181.

49 These themes are traced in Colley, "Apotheosis of George III," *Past and Present* 102 (1984): 94-129 and Lawson, "Parliament, the Constitution and Corn: The Embargo Crisis of 1766," *Parliamentary History Yearbook* 5 (1986):17-37.

50 Shelburne MSS 64:547. Shelburne's comments are worthy of note, for they underline the fact that Briand's appointment was finally under ministerial control. The process of his elevation to bishop was not, as is sometimes implied in accounts of these events, secretive or presented as a *fait accompli* in which ministers somehow colluded after the event.

51 *Acts of Privy Council: Colonial* 4:725-6 and WWM R62-13.

52 PRO TI 461/328-9 and WWM R62-12, from where the quotation is taken. The Treasury sent out the requisite orders on 26 Nov. 1765.

53 SRO RH 4/56.

54 In particular a rum duty, which in 1761 raised £8,000 (ibid.). This lucrative levy had to be withdrawn, however, because it was not an operative duty under the French regime.

55 BL Add. MSS 35638, fol. 43 (Maseres to Yorke, 15 Nov. 1766).

56 Thomas and Simmons, eds., *Proceedings and Debates* 2:360.

57 BL Add. MSS 35638, fol. 43.

58 *Acts of Privy Council: Colonial* 4:725.

59 MG 21, Add. MSS 35914, fols. 100-2.

60 The best accounts are in Humphrey and Morley Scott, "Lord Northington and the Laws of Canada," *CHR* 14 (1933):42-61, and Hay, "The Meanings of Criminal Law in Quebec" in Knafla, ed., *Crime and Criminal Justice in Europe and Canada*, 77-110.

61 *Acts of Privy Council: Colonial* 4:697. The quotation is from the summary in Shelburne MSS 64:539.

62 MG 23, AI, vol. 4:4634-5.

63 MG 21, Add. MSS 35915, fols. 20–45.

64 Humphrey and Morley Scott, "Lord Northington and the Laws of Canada," *CHR* 14 (1933):44, and Marshall, "The Incorporation of Quebec in the British Empire," in Platt and Skaggs, eds., *Of Mother Country and Plantations*, 52.

65 WWM RI–638 (30 June 1766).

66 This is from Yorke's copy in the Hardwicke MSS from the collection on deposit in Ottawa, MG 21, Add. MSS 35914, fol. 192, and forms the basis of the account that follows.

67 *Grenville Papers* 2:476–7.

68 Hay, "The Meanings of Criminal Law in Quebec," in Knafla, ed., *Crime and Criminal Justice in Europe and Canada*, 97–8.

69 Bateson, ed., *Narrative of the Changes in the Ministry*, 77.

70 *Acts of Privy Council: Colonial* 4:697–8.

71 MG 21, Add. MSS 355914, fol. 192.

72 Langford, *The First Rockingham Administration*, 256–7.

73 MG 21, Add. MSS 35914, fol. 192.

74 WWM RI–638.

75 MG 23, A8, "Richmond's Private Journal: Extract concering Canada."

76 Langford, ed., *Writings and Speeches of Edmund Burke* 2:56. This settlement was no small feat in itself. Richmond made the breakthrough on an embassy to Paris in the spring of 1766. His correspondence on the subject (PRO SP 78/269) bears witness to the intricacies of the subject and his own difficulties with speculators "endeavouring to profit of this opportunity" (ibid., fol. 198) – something the previous government had had to contend with. The final settlement was published by government order in pamphlet form that same year: *Convention for the Liquidation of the Canada Paper Money: Belonging to the Subjects of Great Britain, between the King of Great Britain and The Most Christian King* (ibid., fols. 251–9): an esoteric document to say the least, which only those speculating in Canada paper showed any interest in or understanding of. For further contemporary comment see BL Lansdowne MSS, no. 7222, fols. 70–5.

CHAPTER FIVE

1 Humphrey and Morley Scott, "Lord Northington and the Laws of Canada," *CHR* 14 (1933):49.

2 See, for example, Coupland, *The Quebec Act*, 41 – 68; Burt, *Old Province of Quebec* 1:115–159; and Neatby, *Quebec*, 87–106.

3 The revised perspective of Pitt's role in the Seven Years' War can be found in Middleton, *The Bells of Victory*, and Baxter's essay, "The Conduct of the Seven Years War," in Baxter, ed., *England's Rise to Greatness 1660–1763*, 335–48.

4 On Townshend's background in imperial policy see Namier and Brooke, *Charles Townshend*, early chapters.

5 Shelburne MSS 49:17, "Things to be considered of in North America" (Aug. 1766).

6 In particular, see Shy, *Toward Lexington, passim*, and Thomas, *British Politics and the Stamp Act Crisis, passim*.

7 Shelburne MSS 50:38.

8 West Suffolk County Record Office, Grafton MSS 435 (hereafter Grafton MSS).

9 Stewart Wallace, ed., *Maseres Letters*, 55 (19 Nov. 1767). See also Humphrey and Morley Scott, "Lord Northington and the Laws of Canada," *CHR* 14 (1933):49.

10 Grafton MSS 435.

11 East Suffolk County Record Office, Barrington MSS HA 174:1026/6c/4 (hereafter Barrington MSS) I am grateful to Dylan Jones for bringing this document to my attention.

12 This is certainly the implication in Humphrey and Morley Scott, "Lord Northington and the Laws of Canada," *CHR* 14 (1933):49.

13 This story can be followed in Mabane's letter to Murray, Shelburne MSS 64:439–49.

14 See the address in the 29 Sept. 1766 issue of the *Quebec Gazette*.

15 WWM R62-20.

16 Shelburne MSS 64:447.

17 For more detail on the internal politics and problems in the province at this time, see Burt, *Old Province of Quebec* 1: chapter 7 and Neatby, *Quebec*, chapter 7.

18 Shelburne MSS 62:297 .

19 Shelburne MSS 64:425–31; the account and quotation that follow are taken from here. For a resolution of the issue, see *Acts of Privy Council: Colonial, Unbound* 6:449–53.

20 The entry in the *Commons Journals* (30:192) for 27 Feb. 1765 contains only a general summary of an amendment "to exempt the colonies of *Quebec* and *Grenada* from the Double Stamp Duties upon writings, not in the English language." In the final statute, 5 George III c.12, however, it states that the exemption will last "until after the expiration of five years from the commencement of the said duties" (*Statutes at Large*).

21 Neatby, *Quebec*, 88. For more on the initial research into this subject see Kerr, "The Stamp Act in Quebec," *EHR* 47 (1932):648–51.

22 SRO RH 4/56. Carleton also commented on the divisiveness of the Stamp Act in the province, saying that the discontented merchants "first joined the colonists" in protesting at its enactment. Shelburne MSS 51:287 (25 Oct. 1766). More on this topic can be found in PRO, CO 42, vol. 3 fol. 344 and vol. 5 fol. 252.

23 Shortt and Doughty, *Constit. Docs.* 1:170, lists the London merchants to petition about an assembly in Quebec.

24 *Calendar of Home Office Papers* 2:32–3, 37, and 43. This consultative body was still active in Apr. 1769, consulting the duke of Richmond on the possibility of

a campaign in the Lords on their outstanding grievances (WWM RI-1180 and 1181); and also in 1770, as a letter of complaint in the *Gentleman's Magazine* (II:119-20) made clear. Those still holding unsettled bills presented a petition to the Commons on 18 May 1770, but found no resolution to the problem. The petition was ordered to lie on the table. Thomas and Simmons, eds., *Proceedings and Debates* 3:329-31.

25 This and the quotations that follow are taken from Carleton's reports to the Board of Trade in November and December; Shelburne MSS 51:294-9 and *Board of Trade Journals* 74:369.

26 They are printed in Shortt and Doughty, *Constit. Docs.* 1:172-4.

27 Barrington MSS, HA 174:1026/6c/4.

28 Shelburne MSS 64:413. Maseres expressed a similar view in a letter to Hardwicke, Add. MSS 35915, fol. 70.

29 *Acts of Privy Council: Colonial* 5:50-1.

30 12 Jan. 1767. The manuscript documentation actually tends to support this view too; see BL Add. MSS 35915, fols. 121-56.

31 Ouellet, "The British Army of Occupation in the St. Lawrence Valley, 1760-74," in Ion and Prete, eds., *Armies of Occupation*, 36-46.

32 Marshall, "Colonial Protest and Imperial Retrenchment: Indian Policy 1764-1768," *JAS* 5 (1971):1-17. For a good contemporary account of the problem see B. Frobisher's report on Indian trade in Shelburne MSS 50:350-3.

33 For an excellent account and summary of this topic in general see Marshall, "Imperial Regulation of American Indian Affairs 1763-1774" (Ph.D., Yale, 1959).

34 For these exchanges see Shelburne MSS 59:13-77; there is related material in WWM R65-1 and PRO 30/24/3/1.

35 MacCleane's views at this juncture can be found in Shelburne MSS 64:483-91.

36 Shelburne MSS 62:493.

37 Shelburne MSS 64:491.

38 Haydon, "Anti-Catholicism in Eighteenth-Century England, c. 1714-1780" (D.Phil., Oxford, 1985) explores these themes in more detail. I am also grateful to Joanna Innes for allowing me to see her unpublished manuscript on William Payne, an anti-papist informing constable in London of the 1760s and 1770s.

39 See, for example, O'Gorman, *The Rise of Party*, chapter 8 and Thomas, *British Politics and the Stamp Act Crisis*, chapters 15-16.

40 George III was outraged at the "highly improper step one of my family took" (Grafton MSS 498, 23 May 1767) and it certainly surprised many contemporary observers, like Horace Walpole, *Memoirs*, 3:34.

41 BL Add. MSS 32982, fol. 49. Newcastle's other letters whipping in Lords for these debates can be found in subsequent folios.

42 *Lords Journals* 31:628.

43 The division to end a committee on the Quebec matters was won by the

government 73 votes to 61, a very slim majority in the Upper House: Sainty and Dewar, eds., *House of Lords Record Office Occasional Publications: Divisions in the House of Lords*. The only regret for Richmond was Mansfield's absence from the chamber that day; see Richmond to Rockingham, 12 June 1767, wwm ri-797. For more on the general background to these debates see Thomas, *British Politics and the Stamp Act Crisis*, 331, 334–6.

44 bl Add. mss 33030, fol. 262.

45 This is quite evident from the duke of Bedford's own journal (Wright, ed., *Bedford Journal*, 597–602) and the activities of Richmond. Bedford only gave the go-ahead to Richmond a week before the motion on 20 May; see Portland mss, pwf 6313.

46 Walpole, *Memoirs* 3:35.

47 Grafton mss 499 (2 June 1767).

48 Walpole, *Memoirs* 3:35.

49 It was entitled "Strictures on the Conduct of two successive Administrations with Respect to the Civil and Religious Establishments in Canada and the Grenadines" and can be found in bound volume 4 of the *Political Register*, 257–73. All quotations that follow are taken from this source.

50 This alluded to the publication in 1769 of Edmund Burke's tract *Observations on a Late State of the Nation*, in which the only mention of Quebec was in relation to the Canada Bills question. There was no mention of Briand or Yorke's proposals.

51 See, for example, the letters of "Pliny Junior" in the issues of the *Public Advertizer* between Dec. 1769 and Apr. 1770.

52 Thomas, "Imperial Issues in the British Press, 1760–1782" (D.Phil., Oxford, 1983) explores these movements in detail.

53 For more on this see Gipson, vol. 10: *The Triumphant Empire: New Responsibilities within the Enlarged Empire 1763–1766*, chapter 10 and Lawson, "'The Irishman's Prize': Views of Canada from the British Press 1760–1774," *HJ* 28, no. 3 (1985):587–9. The legislation can be found in *Commons Journals* 32:971–2.

54 The most pertinent documentation with which to follow these developments are Shelburne mss 64:459–67, 471–82; 622:221; and 59:13–17.

55 Shortt and Doughty, *Constit. Docs.* 1:196.

56 The crucial decision-making role of the effective cabinet in the 1760s is explained in Christie, "The Cabinet during the Grenville Administration, 1763–65," *EHR* 73 (1958):86–92 and Lawson, "Further Reflections on the Cabinet in the Early Years of George iii's Reign," *BIHR* 57 (1984):237–40.

57 Shortt and Doughty, *Constit. Docs.* 1:199.

58 Rees, "The Political Career of Wills Hill, Earl of Hillsborough" (Ph.D., Wales, 1976):309.

59 Shortt and Doughty, *Constit. Docs.* 1:211, especially clause 2.

60 *Board of Trade Journals* 76:103.

61 *Acts of Privy Council: Colonial* 5:97.

62 The fullest record can be found in Kennedy and Lanctôt, *Report on the Laws of Quebec 1767–1770, passim.*

63 Cited in Rees, "The Political Career of Wills Hill, Earl of Hillsborough" (Ph.D., Wales, 1976):313.

64 *Acts of Privy Council: Colonial* 5:96.

65 PRO TI 465/362–5.

66 *Acts of Privy Council: Colonial* 5:96.

CHAPTER SIX

1 Thomas and Simmons, eds., *Proceedings and Debates* 3:351.

2 Morgann was certainly not consulted by the Board of Trade or asked to give any written evidence by any other governmental agency.

3 Ouellet, "The British Army of Occupation in the St. Lawrence Valley, 1760–74," in Ion and Prete, eds., *Armies of Occupation*, 26–8. The same point is made in a more general sense in Reynolds, *Guy Carleton*, chapter 5.

4 Shortt and Doughty, *Constit. Docs.* 1:280–90.

5 Thomas and Simmons, eds., *Proceedings and Debates* 3:281.

6 *Grenville Papers* 2:477.

7 There is more detail on this episode in Burt, *Old Province of Quebec* 1:158–9.

8 More on this can be found in PRO, CO 45 vol. 1 Quebec Council.

9 Shortt and Doughty, *Constit. Docs.* 1:291–2.

10 Ibid., 292.

11 *An Abstract of the Several Royal Edicts and Declarations, and Provincial Regulations and Ordinances, that were in force in the Province of Quebec in the time of the French Government; and of the Commissions of the several Governours-general and Intendants of the said Province, during the same Period.*

12 MG 23, AI vol. 3:3382.

13 This and the quotation that follow are taken from BL King's MSS 213, fols. 57–8. A similar concern with defence can be found in the Rev. William Gordon's letters to Dartmouth. One of 14 Oct. 1773, for example, warned that "Quebec is in a defenceless state ... was France to plan the surprise of it and unknown to the English to send a fleet against it, Canada would be instantly lost." HMC *Dartmouth*, 11th report, 341.

14 Thomas and Simmons, eds., *Proceedings and Debates* 3:351 (7 Dec. 1770).

15 This is excellently portrayed in Lenman's study, *The Jacobite Clans of the Great Glen, passim.*

16 For an explanation of this see Brewer, "Commercialization and Politics," in McKendrick, Brewer, and Plumb, *The Birth of a Consumer Society*, 197–265.

17 For more on general public interest in Quebec see Lawson, "'The Irishman's Prize': Views of Canada from the British Press 1760–1774," *HJ* 28, no. 3 (1985):575–96.

18 *Commons Journals* 32:341–4.

19 SRO GD 248/201/2/1/16 (26 Aug. 1772) and *Board of Trade Journals* 78:242–5.

20 MG 23 AI, vol. I:IIII.

21 Shortt and Doughty, *Constit. Docs.* 1:292–3.

22 *The Justice and Policy of the late ACT OF PARLIAMENT for Making more Effectual Provision for the Government of the Province of QUEBEC, asserted and proved; And the conduct of the Administration respecting that Province, stated and vindicated.*

23 HMC *Dartmouth*, 14th report, 2:561.

24 PRO 30/29/3/2, fol. 174.

25 It is true to say, however, that the English-speaking merchants in Quebec never came to occupy this position before 1774 as the documents published by Shortt and Doughty testify.

26 There is a good summary of this in Burt, *Old Province of Quebec* 1:161–4.

27 PRO 30/29/3/2, fol. 174.

28 MG 23, AI, vol. 4:4842.

29 *Acts of Privy Council: Colonial* 5:97.

30 PRO 30/29/3/2, fol. 174.

31 *Acts of Privy Council: Colonial, Unbound* 6:459–60 (18 Jan. 1768). The quotation that follows is also taken from this source.

32 Shortt and Doughty, *Constit. Docs.* 1:310–37. All the quotations that follow are taken from here. There is also a full draft copy of Marriott's report in BL Add. MSS 26052, fols. 1–c75.

33 MG 23 A7: Bk2/B22 + 2.

34 Shortt and Doughty, *Constit. Docs.* 1:305–10.

35 Namier and Brooke, eds. *The House of Commons* 3:618.

36 Shortt and Doughty, *Constit. Docs.* 2:296–305.

37 MG 23, A7. The quotations that follow are taken from this acccount and from Shortt and Doughty's composite report published in *Constit. Docs.* 1:296–301.

38 PRO TI 461/148–51.

39 *The Justice and Policy* ... , 1–21.

40 Burt used this expression in *Old Province of Quebec* 1:167.

41 Coupland, *Quebec Act*, 121; Burt, *Old Province of Quebec* 1:168–9, and Lanctôt, *Le Canada et la Révolution Américaine, 1774–1783*, 38.

42 The petitions are printed in Shortt and Doughty, *Constit. Docs.* 1:340–52.

43 MG 23, AI, vol. 4:4933.

44 MG 23, AI, vol. 4:4917.

45 HMC *Various (Knox)* 6:III.

CHAPTER SEVEN

1 For a convenient summary of these historiographical debates, see Bennett and Jaenen, eds., *Emerging Identities*, chapters 4–5.

2 The standard texts follow this pattern; see for example, Neatby, *The Quebec*

Act: Protest and Policy; Lanctôt, *Le Canada et la Révolution Américaine, 1774–1783*; and Brunet, *Les Canadiens après la conquête*.

3 A more general exposition of this theme can be found in Lawson, "The Missing Link: The Imperial Dimension in Understanding Hanoverian Britain," *HJ* 29, no. 3 (1986):747–51.

4 Wilmot, *Memoirs*, 166–7.

5 Cited in Donoughue, *British Politics and the American Revolution*, 122. For a similar view in the press at that time see the letter from Henry Middleton in the *Gentleman's Magazine* 44:615–17.

6 The style and character of North's government is evocatively portrayed in Thomas, *Lord North*, chapter 3.

7 Donoughue, *British Politics and the American Revolution*, 107. Similar sentiments can be found in Neatby, *Quebec*, 140 and Burt, *Old Province of Quebec* 1:169.

8 This trend has been encouraged by throwaway statements in contemporary diaries like Walpole. See Stuart, ed., *The Last Journals of Horace Walpole* 1:353, in which Walpole revealed: "Much was said too on the production of the bill so late in the session, when some years have been taken to concoct it" (hereafter cited as Walpole, *Last Journals*).

9 For background see Lawson, "Parliament and the First East India Inquiry, 1767," *Parliamentary History Yearbook* 1 (1982):99–114; and Bowen, "British Politics and the East India Company, 1767–1773" (Ph.D., Wales, 1986).

10 *Parl. Hist.* 17:1400 and 1407.

11 This is well put in Thomas, *The House of Commons in the Eighteenth Century*, chapter 6.

12 One observer commented on 14 June 1774 that "ten nights the House of Commons was kept till one o'clock in the morning successively": cited in Donoughue, *British Politics and the American Revolution*, 125.

13 WWM R81-178. In fairness, Walpole does note that Rockingham "spoke well" in debates on Quebec, but it is difficult to imagine what line he and Richmond, who Walpole says "disputed to the last," adopted in opposition. In fact there is reason to believe that Walpole confused opposition to the Coercive Acts in general with objections to the Quebec Act in particular. This is unfortunate, for Walpole's journal has the most extensive account available of activity in the Lords (*Last Journals* 1:345).

14 *Lords Journals* 31:628.

15 This was spotted by MPs led by Charles James Fox, and they eventually obliged the government to produce two pieces of legislation – the Quebec Act itself and the Quebec Revenue Act – to overcome this constitutional problem: Shortt and Doughty, *Constit. Docs.* 1:406.

16 The following account is based upon the Dartmouth manuscripts MG 23, AI, vol. 4:4990–5020 and 5039–55. Most, but not all, of this material is reprinted in Shortt and Doughty, *Constit. Docs.* 1:373–401, especially the footnotes.

17 Walpole, *Last Journals* 1:346. For more detail on the episode see Rees, "The

Political Career of Wills Hill, Earl of Hillsborough" (Ph.D., Wales, 1976):315–18.

18 This document is unsigned and undated in Dartmouth's manuscripts, but Shortt and Doughty rightly attribute it to Mansfield. See MG 23, AI, vol. 4:5009–14 and *Constit. Docs.* 1:386–8. The quotations that follow are taken from these identical sources.

19 The account that follows is indebted to the work of Thomas and Simmons, who have reproduced all extant sources for debates on the Quebec Act in the House of Commons in volumes four and five of their *Proceedings and Debates*. These volumes are now essential reading for any student of this period in Anglo-Canadian history.

20 Thomas, *Lord North*, 79.

21 These figures were gleaned from Namier and Brooke, eds., *House of Commons*, volumes 2 and 3. The nine opposed to the act were William Baker, Isaac Barré, Paul Feilde, Sir Adam Fergusson, Sir George Savile, George Johnstone, D.B. Olmius, Jacob Bouverie, and Constantine Phipps.

22 Pulteney spoke in the committee examining witnesses on 3 June, and Prescott in committee on 6 June.

23 Thomas and Simmons, eds., *Proceedings and Debates* 4:23. Rice spoke in committee on 2 June.

24 *Commons Journals* 34:788–93.

25 London: Corporation of London Record Office, Guildhall MSS Journal of Common Council 46, fol. 105. There were four MPS present at the meeting (Frederick Bull, John Glynn, Richard Oliver, and William Plomer), but only Glynn spoke forcefully against the Quebec Act in the Commons.

26 This was nowhere better seen than in the estimates of the Quebec population offered by the opposition in debate. They ranged from "14 million" to "20,000" souls.

27 Thomas and Simmons, eds., *Proceedings and Debates* 4:42.

28 Ibid., 45.

29 The account and quotations that follow are taken from Thomas and Simmons, eds., *Proceedings and Debates* 4:47–88.

30 Ibid., 144–52.

31 This and the quotation that follows are cited in Thomas, "The Beginning of Parliamentary Reporting in Newspapers," *EHR* 74 (1959):634. For an example of this contrast between what was said and reported during the Quebec Act debates see John Dunning's speech on 7 June in Thomas and Simmons, eds., *Proceedings and Debates* 4:46–7 and the report of that same speech in the *St. James' Chronicle*, 7–9 June 1774.

32 Thomas and Simmons, eds., *Proceedings and Debates* 4:167.

33 The following account and quotation are taken from the report of the debate of 6 June in ibid., 89–123.

34 The report appeared in the issue for 9 June 1774.

35 Clark, *English Society, 1688–1832, passim.*

36 The quotations by Burke, Fox, and Barré that follow are taken from the account of the debate of 7 June in Thomas and Simmons, eds., *Proceedings and Debates* 4:146–52.

37 Ibid., 160. The account, quotations, and division figures that follow are also taken from here: 161–7.

38 For this debate see the article by John Brewer, "The Wilkites and the Law, 1763–1774," in Brewer and Styles, eds., *An Ungovernable People*, 128–71.

39 Thomas and Simmons, eds., *Proceedings and Debates* 4:190–1.

40 *Parl. Hist.* 17:1404.

41 For the former view, see Coupland's 1925 study, *The Quebec Act*; for the latter, Martin, *Empire and Commonwealth*, published in 1929.

42 In addition to the examples cited in note 2 above, see Ouellet, *Economic and Social History of Quebec, 1760–1850*.

43 Issue for 14–16 June 1774.

POSTSCRIPT

1 At time of writing, however, David Milobar is researching the genesis of the 1791 Canada Act at London University, which will shed light on this matter.

2 *Last Journals* 1:355.

3 15 Oct. 1774.

4 From the text printed in the *Public Advertizer*, 18 Oct. 1774.

5 *Middlesex Journal*, 4–7 June 1774 and *Public Advertizer*, 9 June 1774.

6 London: Corporation of London Record Office, Guildhall MSS, Journal of Common Council 66, fol. 106.

7 *London Evening Post*, 14–16 June 1774.

8 44:247–8, June 1774.

9 *London Magazine* 7, Aug. 1774:398.

10 *Gentleman's Magazine* 44:311–12. All the quotations that follow are taken from here.

11 HMC *Various (Knox)* 6:112.

12 16–18 June 1774.

13 From the text printed in *Parl. Hist.* 17:1407.

Bibliography

PRIMARY SOURCES

Manuscript Material

Ann Arbor, Mich. William L. Clements Library
    Germain Manuscripts
    Knox Manuscripts
    Shelburne Manuscripts
East Suffolk, England: Country Record Office
    Barrington Manuscripts

Edinburgh, Scotland: Scottish Record Office
  GD 30/29/3/2
  GD 32/24/18
  RH 248/201/2/1/16
  RH 4/56
  RH 24/567
London: Bedford Estate Office
  Bedford Manuscripts
London: Corporation of London Record Office
  Guildhall Manuscripts
London: British Library
  King's Manuscripts
    213
  Lansdowne Manuscripts
    7222
  Additional Manuscripts
    18399B
  Additional Manuscripts
    26052
  Additional Manuscripts
    27777
  Wilkes Manuscripts
    30871, 30866
  Newcastle Manuscripts
    32906, 32982, 33028-30
  Astle Manuscripts
    34712-13
  Hardwicke Manuscripts
    35408, 35638, 35879, 35881, 35914-15
  Liverpool Manuscripts
    38332, 38335-6, 38340-2
  Auckland Manuscripts
    46490-1
  Egmont Manuscripts
    47132
  Grenville Manuscripts
    57808, 57817A, 57820, 57834
  Additional Manuscripts
    5877
London: Public Record Office
  Manuscript Collections
    30/8/66
    30/24/3/1

30/29/1/14
30/29/3/1-2
30/47/15
30/47/27-9
Treasury Papers
TI 430, 434, 461, 465
State Papers, Domestic
SP 78/269
Colonial Office Papers
CO 42/1/1-8/A-F
CO 42/13-14
CO 42/24-33
CO 44/1/1-64
CO 47/110
Colonial Office, Entry Books
CO 43/1-2/7-8/12-13
Colonial Office, Sessional Papers
CO 45/1-2-3
Mountstuart: Isle of Bute, Scotland
Bute Manuscripts, including the
Loudoun Papers
Northamptonshire, England: County Record Office
Northington Manuscripts
Nottingham, England: University of Nottingham Library
Portland Manuscripts
Ottawa, Canada: National Archives
Manuscript Groups
MG 5A, 5B
MG 8-EI
MG 21, Add. MSS 21661-21892
MG 21, Add. MSS 32895-32922
MG 21, Add. MSS 35914-15
MG 23, AI-2, A4-5, A8, AIO
MG 23, G II, series I
Oxford University: Rhodes House Library
North Manuscripts
Sheffield, England: Sheffield City Library
Wentworth Woodhouse Muniments
Strathpeffer: Ross-shire, Scotland, Cromartie Estate Office
Cromartie Manuscripts
West Suffolk, England: County Record Office
Grafton Manuscripts

Printed Material

OFFICIAL AND PARLIAMENTARY SOURCES

Acts of the Privy Council of England: Colonial and Unbound Series. 6 vols. London 1908–12.

Calendar of State Papers: Colonial Series. London 1888–1908. Vols. 5, 9, 17.

Calendar of State Papers: Domestic Series. London 1859. Vol. 3.

Calendar of Home Office Papers … 1760–75. 4 vols. London 1878–99.

Devonshire Diary. See Schweizer and Brown.

English Law Reports: King's Bench Division. 6, 77.

Great Britain. Parliament. Almon, J. *The Debates and Proceedings of the British House of Commons from 1743 to 1774.* 11 Vols. London 1766–75.

– Cobbett, W. *Parliamentary History of England from 1066 … to … 1803.* 36 vols. London 1806–20.

– *Journals of the House of Commons.* Vols. 27–35.

– *Journals of the House of Lords.* Vols. 29–35.

– Lambert, S., ed. *House of Commons Sessional Papers of the Eighteenth Century.* 145 vols. Wilmington, Delaware 1975.

– Sainty, J.C., and D. Dewar, eds. *House of Lords Record Office Occasional Publications: Divisions in the House of Lords: An Analytical List 1685 to 1857.* London: House of Lords Publications 1967.

– Thomas, P.D.G., ed. *The Parliamentary Diaries of Nathaniel Ryder 1764–7.* Camden Miscellany Royal Historical Society Publications, 4th series, vol. 7. London 1969.

– Thomas, P.D.G., and R. Simmons, eds. *Proceedings and Debates of the British Parliaments respecting North America 1754–83.* 5 vols. Millwood, New York 1982–87.

Harlow, V., and F. Madden, eds., *British Colonial Documents 1574–1834.* Oxford: Oxford University Press 1953.

Journals of the Commissioners of the Board of Trade and Plantations 1704–1782. 15 vols. London 1920–38.

Kennedy, W.P.C., and G. Lanctôt, eds. *Reports on the Laws of Quebec 1767–1770.* Ottawa: F.A. Acland 1931.

Schweizer, K.W., and P.D. Brown, eds. *The Devonshire Diary: William Cavendish Fourth Duke of Devonshire Memoranda on State of Affairs 1759–1762.* Camden Miscellany Royal Historical Society Publications, 4th series, vol. 27. London 1982.

Shortt, A., and A.G. Doughty, eds. *Documents Relating to the Constitutional History of Canada 1759–1791.* Vol. 1. Ottawa 1907.

Statutes at Large. Vols. 9–10. London 1771.

HISTORICAL MANUSCRIPT COMMISSION REPORTS

Dartmouth
Lothian
Stopford-Sackville

Various. Vol. 6 (*Knox*)

CORRESPONDENCE, MEMOIRS, AND CONTEMPORARY HISTORIES

Albemarle, George, earl of, ed. *Memoirs of the Marquis of Rockingham and His Contemporaries*. 2 vols. London 1852.

Almon, J. *Anecdotes of the Life of the Rt. Hon. William Pitt, Earl of Chatham*. 3 vols., sixth edition, London 1897.

Anson, Sir W.R., ed. *Autobiography and Political Correspondence of Augustus, Third Duke of Grafton, K.G.* London 1898.

Bateson, M., ed. *A Narrative of the Changes in the Ministry 1765–67, as told by the Duke of Newcastle in a series of letters to John White M.P.*, New York: Kraus Reprint 1965.

Bedford Correspondence. See Russell, J. Lord.

Bohn, H.G., ed. *The Works of Edmund Burke*. 8 vols. London: Bohn's British Classics, G. Bell and Sons 1853–89.

Cannon, J., ed. *The Letters of Junius*. Oxford: Oxford University Press 1978.

Carswell, J., and L.A. Dralle, eds., *The Political Journal of George Bubb Dobington*. Oxford: Oxford University Press 1965.

de Charlevoix, F.X. *Histoire et description général de la nouvelle France, avec le journal historique d'un voyage dans l'Amérique*. 6 vols. Paris 1744.

Chesterfield, Philip, earl of, ed. *Letters of Philip Dormer, Earl of Chesterfield, to His Son 1738–1768*. London 1890.

Child, Sir J. *New Discourse on Trade*. London 1752.

Copeland, T.W., ed. *The Correspondence of Edmund Burke*. 10 vols. Cambridge: Cambridge University Press 1958–78.

Dobson, J. *Chronological Annals of the War*. Oxford 1763.

Elliot, G.F.S., ed. *The Border Elliots and the Family of Minto*. Edinburgh 1897.

Fitzmaurice, Edmond, Lord. *Life of William, Earl of Shelburne, afterwards First Marquess of Landsowne*. 3 vols. London 1875–76.

Foote, S. *The Dramatic Works of Samuel Foote, Esq.; to which is prefixed a life of the author*. 2 vols. London 1809.

Fortescue, Sir J., ed. *The Correspondence of King George the Third from 1760 to 1783*. 6 vols. London: Macmillan 1927–28.

Grenville Papers. See Smith, W.J.

Ilchester, earl of, ed. *Henry Fox, First Lord Holland His Family and Relations*. 2 vols. London 1920.

Jesse, J.H., ed. *George Selwyn and his contemporaries; with memoirs and notes*. 4 vols. London 1843–44.

Jucker, N.S., ed. *The Jenkinson Papers, 1760–1766*. London: Macmillan 1949.

Labaree, L.W., and W.B. Wilcox, eds. *The Papers of Benjamin Franklin*. 23 vols. New Haven: Yale University Press 1961–83.

Langford, P., ed. *The Writings and Speeches of Edmund Burke*. Vol. 2, Oxford: Oxford University Press 1980.

LeicesterHouse Politics. See Newman, A.N.

Lewis, W.S., ed. *Horace Walpole's Correspondence*. 48 vols. New Haven: Yale University Press 1937–83.

Malmesbury, earl of, ed. *A Series of Letters of the First Earl of Malmesbury, his family and friends from 1745 to 1820*. 2 vols. London 1870.

Maseres Letters. See Stewart Wallace, W.

Mure, W., ed. *Selections from the Family Papers preserved at Caldwell*. 2 vols. Glasgow 1854.

Newman, A.N., ed. *Leicester House Politics 1750–60, from the Papers of John, Second Earl of Egmont*. Camden Miscellany Royal Historical Society Publications, 4th seris, vol. 7. London 1969.

Oswald, J., ed. *Memorials of the Public Life and Character of James Oswald of Dunnikier House*. Edinburgh 1825.

Phillimore, R.J., ed. *Memoirs and Correspondence of George, Lord Lyttelton from 1743 to 1773*. 2 vols. London 1845.

Russell, J. Lord, ed. *Correspondence of John, Fourth Duke of Bedford, selected from the originals at Woburn Abbey*. 3 vols. London 1842–46.

Russell-Barker, G.F., ed. *Horace Walpole's Memoirs of the Reign of King George the Third*. 4 vols. London 1894.

Sedgwick, R., ed. *Letters from George III to Lord Bute* 1756–66. London: HMSO 1939.

Smith, W.J., ed. *The Grenville Papers: Being the Correspondence of Richard Grenville, Earl Temple, K.G., and the Right Hon. George Grenville, Their Friends and Contemporaries*. 4 vols. London 1852–53.

Spencer, F., ed. *The Fourth Earl of Sandwich: Diplomatic Correspondence 1763–65*. Manchester: Manchester University Press 1961.

Stewart Wallace, W., ed. *The Maseres Letters 1766–68*. Toronto: University of Toronto Press 1919.

Stuart, A.F., ed. *The Last Journals of Horace Walpole during the Reign of George III*. 2 vols. London: J. Lane 1910.

Taylor, W.S., and J.H. Pringle, eds. *Correspondence of William Pitt, Earl of Chatham*. 4 vols. London 1838–40.

Tomlinson, J.R.G., ed. *The Additional Grenville Papers 1763–65*. Manchester: Manchester University Press 1962.

Walpole, H. *See* Lewis, W.S. (*Letters*); Russell-Barker, G.F. (*Memoirs*); Stuart, A.F. (*Last Journals*).

Wilmot, J. *Memoirs of the Life of the Right Honourable Sir John Eardley Wilmot, Knt., Late Lord Chief Justice of the Court of Common Pleas*. London 1811.

Wright, J., ed. *Sir Henry Cavendish's Debates of the House of Commons ... With an appendix covering the journal kept by the Duke of Bedord, known as the Bedford Journal*. 2 vols. London 1841–43.

Wyndham, M., ed. *Chronicles of the Eighteenth Century Founded on the Correspondence of Sir Thomas Lyttelton and his family*. 2 vols. London 1924.

Yorke, P.C., ed. *The Life and Correspondence of Philip Yorke, Earl of Hardwick, Lord High Chancellor of Great Britain*. Cambridge: Cambridge University Press 1913.

NEWSPAPERS AND MAGAZINES

The British Magazine
The Gentleman's Magazine
London Chronicle
London Evening Post
The London Gazette
The London Magazine
Middlesex Journal
Political Register
Public Advertizer
Quebec Gazette
St. James' Chronicle

PAMPHLETS

A detection of the false reasons and facts, contained in the five letters entitled, Reasons for keeping Guadaloupe at a peace, preferable to Canada by a Member of Parliament. London 1761.

A Letter to the People of England as to the Necessity of putting an immediate end to the War: and the Means of Obtaining an Advantageous Peace. London 1760.

The Reasons for keeping Guadaloupe at a Peace, preferable to Canada explained in five letters from a Gentleman in Guadaloupe to his Friend in London. London 1761.

Burke, E. *Observations on a Late State of the Nation.* London 1769.

Cugnet, F.H. *An Abstract of the Several Royal Edicts and Declarations, and Provincial Regulations and Ordinances ...* London 1772.

Franklin, B. *The Interest of Great Britain Considered with Regard to her Colonies and The Acquisitions of Canada and Guadaloupe.* London 1761.

Knox, W. *The Justice and Policy of the Late Act of Parliament for Making More Effectual Provision for the Government of the Province of Quebec.* London 1774.

– *Extra-Official State Papers Addressed to the Right Hon. Lord Rawdon.* London 1789.

Marriott, J. *A Plan of a code of laws for the Province of Quebec reported by the Advocate General, James Marriott.* London 1774.

Maseres, F. *An Account of the Proceedings of the British and Other Protestants of the Province of Quebec.* London 1775.

– *A Collection of Several Commissions ...* London 1775.

SECONDARY SOURCES

Books

Alvord, C.W. *The Mississippi Valley in British Politics.* 2 vols. Cleveland: Clark 1917.

Andrews, K.R., and P.E. Hair, eds. *The Westward Enterprize: English Activities in Ireland the Atlantic and America 1480 to 1650.* Liverpool: Liverpool University Press 1978.

Bartlett, T., and D. Hayton. *Penal Era and Golden Age: Essays in Irish History, 1690–1800.* Belfast: Ulster Historical Foundation 1979.

Basye, A.H. *The Lords Commissioners of Trade and Plantations commonly known as the Board of Trade 1748–1782.* New Haven: Yale University Press 1925.

Baxter, S., ed. *England's Rise to Greatness 1660–1763.* Berkeley: University of California Press 1983.

Beer, G.L. *British Colonial Policy 1754–1765.* New York: Macmillan 1907.

Bennett, P.W., and C.J. Jaenen, eds. *Emerging Identities: Selected Problems and Interpretations in Canadian History.* Scarborough, Canada: Prentice-Hall 1986.

Berger, C. *The Sense of Power: Studies in the Ideas of Canadian Imperialism.* Toronto: University of Toronto Press 1970.

Black, J., ed. *The Origins of War in Early Modern Europe.* Edinburgh: John Donald 1987.

Brewer, J. *Party Ideology and Popular Politics at the Accession of George III.* Cambridge: Cambridge University Press 1976.

Brewer, J., and J. Styles, eds. *An Ungovernable People.* London: Hutchinson 1983.

Brooke, J. *King George III.* London: Constable and Co. 1972.

– *The Chatham Administration 1766–1768.* London: Macmillan 1956.

Browning, R. *The Duke of Newcastle.* New Haven: Yale University Press 1975.

Brunet, M. *French Canada and the Early Decades of British Rule 1760–1791.* Ottawa: CHA Booklet 1963.

– *Les Canadiens après la conquête 1759–1775.* Montreal: Fides 1969.

Bumsted, J.M., ed. *Canadian History before Confederation: Essays and Interpretations.* 2nd ed. Toronto: University of Toronto Press 1979.

Burt, A.L. *Guy Carleton, Lord Dorchester, 1724–1808.* Ottawa: CHA Booklet 1960.

– *The Old Province of Quebec.* 2 vols., 2nd ed. Toronto: McClelland and Stewart 1968.

Callwood, J. *Portrait of Canada.* Garden City, New York: Doubleday 1981.

Cambridge History of Latin America. Ed. L. Bethell. Cambridge: Cambridge University Press 1986.

Careless, J.M.S., ed. *Colonists and Canadiens 1760–1867.* Toronto: Gage 1980.

de Charlevoix, F.X. *Histoire et description général de la nouvelle France, avec le journal historique d'un voyage dans l'Amérique.* 6 vols. Paris 1744.

Christie, I.R., and B.J. Labaree. *Empire or Independence, 1760–1776.* London: Phaidon 1976.

Clark, J.C.D. *English Society, 1688–1832.* Cambridge: Cambridge University Press 1985.

Coffin, V. *The Province of Quebec and the Early American Revolution.* Madison, Wisconsin: Wisconsin University Press 1896.

Corbett, J.S. *England in the Seven Years' War.* 2 vols., 2nd ed. London: Longman 1908.

Coupland, R. *The Quebec Act.* London: Oxford University Press 1925.

Creighton, D. *Dominion of the North: A History of Canada.* Toronto: Macmillan 1957.

Dictionary of American Biography. New York: Scribners 1928.

Dictionary of Canadian Biography. Toronto: University of Toronto Press 1966–

Dictionary of National Biography. London: Smith and Oxford University Press 1908.

Donoughue, B. *British Politics and the American Revolution: The Path to War 1773–1775.* London: Macmillan 1964.

Donovan, R.K. *No Popery and Radicalism: Opposition to Roman Catholic Relief in Scotland, 1778-1782*. New York: Garland Publishing 1987.

Dorn, W.L. *Competition for Empire 1740-1763*. New York: Harper and Row 1940.

Eccles, W.J. *France in America*. New York: Harper and Row 1972.

– *Essays on New France*. Toronto: Oxford University Press 1987

Fifoot, C.H.S. *Lord Mansfield*. Oxford: Clarendon Press 1936.

Flint, J.E., and G. Williams, eds. *Perspectives of Empire*. London: F. Cass 1975.

Foord, A.S. *His Majesty's Opposition, 1714-1830*. Oxford: Clarendon Press 1964.

Gagnon, S. *Quebec and Its Historians: The Twentieth Century*. Montreal: Harvest House Press 1985.

Gipson, L.H. *The British Empire before the American Revolution*. 14 vols. Vol. 10: *The Triumphant Empire*. New York: Knopf 1936-70.

Haffenden, P.S. *New England in the English Nation 1689-1713*. Oxford: Clarendon Press 1974.

Harlow, V.T. *The Founding of the Second British Empire: 1763-1793*. 2 vols. London: Longmans 1952, 1964.

Heward, E. *Lord Mansfield: A Biography of William Murray, 1st Earl of Mansfield 1705-93*. Chichester, England: B. Rose Press 1979.

Holliday, J. *The Life of William Murray, Late Earl of Mansfield*. London 1797.

Hough, F.B. *Journals of Major Robert Rogers*. Albany 1883.

Hyam, R. *Britain's Imperial Century 1815-1914: A Study in Empire Expansion*. New York: Harper and Row 1976.

Hyam, R., and G. Martin, eds. *Reappraisals in British Imperial History*. Toronto: Macmillan 1975.

Ion, A.H., and R.A. Prete, eds., *Armies of Occupation*. Waterloo, Canada: Wilfrid Laurier University Press 1984.

Knafla, L.A. *Law and Politics in Jacobean England: The Tracts of Lord Chancellor Ellesmere*. Cambridge: Cambridge University Press 1977.

Knafla, L.A., ed. *Crime and Criminal Justice in Europe and Canada*. Waterloo, Canada: Wilfrid Laurier University Press 1981.

Lanctôt, G. *Le Canada et la Révolution Américaine, 1774-1783*. Montreal 1965.

Langford, P. *The First Rockingham Administration 1765-1766*. London: Oxford University Press 1973.

Lawson, P. *George Grenville: A Political Life*. Oxford: Clarendon Press 1984.

Lenman, B. *The Jacobite Clans of the Great Glen 1650-1784*. London: Methuen 1984.

McDowell, R.B. *Ireland in the Age of Imperialism and Revolution, 1760-1801*. Oxford: Clarendon Press 1979.

Machin, G.I.T. *The Catholic Issue in British Politics, 1820 to 1830*. Oxford: Clarendon Press 1964.

MacKay, D. and H. Scott. *The Rise of the Great Powers, 1648-1815*. London: Longman 1983.

McKendrick, N.J. Brewer, and J.H. Plumb. *The Birth of a Consumer Society*. Bloomington: Indiana University Press 1982.

Maxwell, C.R. *The Census Tables for the French Colony of Louisiana from 1699 thru 1732*. Baltimore 1972.

Martin, C. *Empire and Commonwealth*. Oxford: Clarendon Press 1929.

Middleton, R. *The Bells of Victory: The Pitt-Newcastle Ministry and the Conduct of the Seven Years War 1757–1762*. Cambridge: Cambridge University Press 1985.

Morton, W.L. *The Kingdom of Canada: A General History from Earliest Times*. Toronto: McClelland and Stewart. 2nd ed. 1969.

Muise, D.A., ed. *A Reader's Guide to Canadian History, Beginnings to Confederation*. Vol. 1. Toronto: University of Toronto Press 1982.

Namier, L.B. *England in the Age of the American Revolution*. 2nd ed. London: Macmillan 1961.

Namier, L.B., and J. Brooke. *Charles Townshend*. London: Macmillan 1964.

Namier, Sir L.B., and J. Brooke, eds. *The House of Commons 1754–1790*. 3 vols. London: HMSO 1964.

Neatby, H. *The Quebec Act: Protest and Policy*. Scarborough, Canada: Prentice Hall 1972.

- *Quebec: The Revolutionary Age 1760–1791*. Toronto: McClelland and Stewart 1966.

Newman, A., ed. *The Parliamentary Lists of the Early Eighteenth Century: Their Compilation and Use*. Leicester: Leicester University Press 1973.

Newton, A.P., and E.A. Benians, ed. *History of the British Empire: Canada*. Cambridge: Cambridge University Press 1930.

Nish, C., ed. *The French Canadians, 1759–1766: Conquered? Half-Conquered? Liberated?* Vancouver: Copp Clark 1966.

O'Gorman, F. *The Rise of Party in England: The Rockingham Whigs 1760–1782*. London: Longman 1975.

Owen, J.B. *The Eighteenth Century 1714–1815*. Totowa, New Jersey: Rowman and Littlefield 1975.

Ouellet, F. *Economic and Social History of Quebec, 1760–1850*. Toronto: Gage 1980.

Pares, R. *War and Trade in the West Indies, 1739–1763*. Oxford: Clarendon Press 1936.

Parkman, F. *The Old Régime in Canada*. Toronto: George N. Morang and Co. 1901.

Peters, M. *Pitt and Popularity*. Oxford: Clarendon Press 1980.

Platt, V.B., and D.C. Skaggs, eds. *Of Mother Country and Plantations: Proceedings of the Twenty-seventh Conference in Early American History*. Bowling Green, Kentucky: Bowling Green State University Press 1971.

Pocock, J.G.A. *Three British Revolutions, 1641, 1688, 1776*. Princeton: Princeton University Press 1980.

Porter, B. *The Lion's Share: A Short History of British Imperialism 1850–1970*. London: Longman 1975.

Quinn, D.B. *England and the Discovery of America 1481–1620*. New York: Knopf 1974.

Ramsay, D. *Military Memoirs of Great Britain or a History of the War 1755–1763*. London 1779.

Rashed, Z.E. *The Peace of Paris, 1763*. Liverpool: Liverpool University Press 1951.

Rea, R.R. *The English Press in Politics, 1760–1774*. Lincoln: University of Nebraska Press 1963.

Reid, J.P. *In Defiance of the Law: the Standing-Army Controversy, the Two Constitutions, and the Coming of the American Revolution*. Chapel Hill: University of North Carolina Press 1981.

Reynolds, P.R. *Guy Carleton: A Biography*. Toronto: Gage 1980.

Richmond, H.V., *The Navy in the War of 1739–48*. 3 vols. Cambridge: Cambridge University Press 1920.

Schweizer, K.W., ed. *Lord Bute: Essays in Reinterpretation*. Leicester: Leicester University Press 1988.

Shy, J. *Toward Lexington: The Role of the British Army in the Coming of the American Revolution*. Princeton: Princeton University Press 1965.

Simmons, R., *The American Colonies: From Settlement to Independence*. London: Longman 1976.

Spector, R.D. *English Literary Periodicals and the Climate of Opinion during the Seven Years' War*. The Hague: Moulton and Co. 1966.

Sosin, J. *Whitehall and the Wilderness: The Middle West in British Colonial Policy 1760–1775*. Lincoln: University of Nebraska Press 1961.

Stanley, G.F.G. *New France, the Last Phase 1744–1760*. Toronto: McClelland and Stewart 1969.

Steele, I.K. *The English Atlantic, 1675–1740*. New York: Oxford University Press 1986.

– *Guerillas and Grenadiers: The Struggle for Canada, 1689–1760*. Toronto: Ryerson Press 1969.

– *Politics of Colonial Policy: The Board of Trade in Colonial Administration, 1696–1720*. Oxford: Clarendon Press 1968.

Thomas, P.D.G. *British Politics and the Stamp Act Crisis: The First Phase of the American Revolution 1763–1767*. Oxford: Clarendon Press 1975.

– *Lord North*. London: Allen Lane 1976.

– *The House of Commons in the Eighteenth Century*. Oxford: Clarendon Press 1971.

– *The Townshend Duties Crisis 1767–1773*. Oxford: Clarendon Press 1987.

Thomson, M.A. *The Secretaries of State 1681–1782*. London: F. Cass 1932.

Trudel, M. *Histoire de la Nouvelle-France*. Montreal 1963.

Webster, J.C. *The Journal of Jeffrey Amherst*. Toronto: Ryerson Press 1931.

Wickwire, F.B. *British Subministers and Colonial America 1763–1783*. Princeton: Princeton University Press 1966.

Williams, G., ed. *Andrew Graham's Observations on Hudson Bay 1761–91*. London: Publications of Hudson Bay Record Society 1969.

Winstanley, D.A. *Lord Chatham and the Whig Opposition*. Cambridge: Cambridge University Press 1912.

Articles

Balls, H.R. "Quebec, 1766–1774: The Financial Administration." *Canadian Historical Review*, 41 (1960): 203–14.

Barrow, T.C. "A Project for Imperial Reform: 'Hints Respecting the Settlement for our American Provinces,' 1763." *William and Mary Quarterly* 24 (1967): 108–26.

Baxter, S. "The Conduct of the Seven Years War." In *England's Rise to Greatness 1660–1763*, edited by S. Baxter. Berkeley: University of California Press 1983.

Brading, D.A. "Bourbon Spain and Its American Empire." In *The Cambridge History of Latin America*. vol. I, edited by L. Bethell. Cambridge: Cambridge University Press 1986.

Brewer, J. "Commercialization and Politics." In *The Birth of a Consumer Society*, edited by N. McKendrick, J. Brewer, and J.H. Plumb. Bloomington: Indiana University Press 1982.

– "The Misfortunes of Lord Bute: A Case Study of Eighteenth Century Political Argument and Public Opinion." *Historical Journal* 16, no. 1 (1973):3:43.

– "The Wilkites and the Law, 1763–1774." In *An Ungovernable People: The English and Their Law in the Seventeenth and Eighteenth Centuries*, edited by J. Brewer and J. Styles. London: Hutchinson 1983.

Bullion, J.L. "Securing the Peace: Lord Bute, the Plan for the Army, and the Origins of the American Revolution." In *Lord Bute: Essays in Re-interpretation*, edited by K.W. Schweizer. Leicester: Leicester University Press 1988.

Christie, I.R. "The Cabinet during the Grenville Administration, 1763–65." *English Historical Review* 73 (1958):86–92.

Colley, L. "The Apotheosis of George III: Loyalty, Royalty and the British Nation." *Past and Present* 102 (1984):94–129.

Crane, V.W. "Hints Relative to the Division and Government of the Conquered and Newly Acquired Countries in America." *Mississippi Valley Historical Review* 8 (1921–22):367–73.

Donovan, R.K. "The Military Origins of the Roman Catholic Relief Programme of 1778." *Historical Journal* 28 no. 1 (1985):79–102.

Eccles, W.J. "Forty Years Back." *William and Mary Quarterly* 41 (1984):409–21.

– "The Role of the American Colonies in Eighteenth-Century French Foreign Policy." In *Essays on New France*, edited by W.J. Eccles. Toronto: Oxford University Press 1987.

Frégault, G. "L'Empire britannique et la conquête du Canada (1700–13)." *Revue d'Histoire d'Amérique Française* 10 (1956):153–82.

Hay, D. "The Meanings of Criminal Law in Quebec 1764–1774." In *Crime and Criminal Justice in Europe and Canada*, edited by L.A. Knafla. Waterloo, Canada: Wilfrid Laurier University Press 1981.

Hotblack, K. "The Peace of Paris 1763." *Transactions of Royal Historical Society* 2 (1908):235–67.

Humphrey, R., and S. Morley Scott. "Lord Northington and the Laws of Canada." *Canadian Historical Review* 14(1933):42–61.

Humphreys, R.A. "Lord Shelburne and the Proclamation of 1763." *English Historical Review* 49 (1934):241–64.

Hyam, R. "The Peace of Paris (1763)." In *Reappraisals in British Imperial History*, edited by R. Hyam and G. Martin. Toronto: Macmillan 1975.

Jenkins, P. "The Tory Tradition in Eighteenth-Century Cardiff." *Welsh History Review* 122 (1984):180–96.

Johnson, R.R. "Charles McLean Andrews and the Invention of American Colonial History." *William and Mary Quarterly* 43 (1986):519–41.

Kerr, W. "The Stamp Act in Quebec." *English Historical Review* 47 (1932):648–51.

Langford, P. "The Rockingham Whigs and America, 1767–1773." In *Statesmen, Scholars and Merchants*, edited by A. Whiteman, J.S. Bromley, and P.G.M. Dickson. Oxford: Clarendon Press 1973.

Lawson, P. "Further Reflections on the Cabinet in the Early Years of George III's Reign." *Bulletin of the Institute of Historical Research* 57 (1984):237–40.

– "George Grenville and America – The Years of Opposition 1765–1770." *William and Mary Quarterly* 37 (1980):561–76.

– "Parliament and the First East India Inquiry, 1767." *Parliamentary History Yearbook* 1 (1982):99–114.

– "Parliament, the Constitution and Corn: The Embargo Crisis of 1766." *Parliamentary History Yearbook* 5 (1986):17–37.

– "'The Irishman's Prize': Views of Canada from the British Press 1760–1774." *Historical Journal* 28, no. 3 (1985):575–96.

– "The Missing Link: The Imperial Dimension in Understanding Hanoverian Britain." *Historical Journal* 29, no. 3 (1986):747–52.

Lawson, P., and B. Lenman. "Robert Clive, the 'Black Jagir' and British Politics." *Historical Journal* 26, no. 4 (1983):801–29.

Madden, F. "1066, 1776 and All That: The Relevance of English Medieval Experience of Empire to Later Imperial Constitutional Issues." In *Perspectives of Empire*, edited by J.E. Flint and G. Williams. London: F. Cass 1975.

Marshall, P. "Colonial Protest and Imperial Retrenchment: Indian Policy 1764–1768." *Journal of American Studies* 5 (1971):1–17.

Marshall, P. "The Incorporation of Quebec in the British Empire, 1763–1774. In *Of Mother Country and Plantations: Proceedings of the Twenty-seventh Conference in Early American History*, edited by V.B. Platt and D.C. Skaggs. Bowling Green, Kentucky: Bowling Green State University Press, 1971.

Middleton, R. "Pitt, Anson and the Admiralty, 1756–1761." *History* 55 (1970):189–98.

Ouellet, F. "The British Army of Occupation in the St. Lawrence Valley, 1760–74." In *Armies of Occupation*, edited by A.H. Ion and R.A. Prete. Waterloo, Canada: Wilfrid Laurier University Press 1984.

Schweizer, K.W. "Lord Bute and William Pitt's Resignation, 1761." *Canadian Journal of History* 15 (1973):112–21.

– "The Cabinet Crisis of August 1761: Unpublished Letters from the Bute and Bedford Manuscripts." *Bulletin of the Institute of Historical Research* 59, no. 140 (1986):225–9.

– "The Seven Years' War: A System Perspective." In *The Origins of War in Early Modern Europe*, edited by J. Black. Edinburgh: John Donald 1987.

– "William Pitt, Lord Bute and the Peace Negotiations with France, May–September 1761." *Albion* 13, no. 3 (Fall, 1981):362–75.

– "The Bedford Motion and the House of Lords." *Parliamentary History Yearbook* 5 (1986):107–23.

- "Lord Bute, Newcastle, Prussia, and the Hague Overtures: A Re-Examination." *Albion* 9, no. 1 (Spring, 1977):72–97.
Thomas, P.D.G. "The Beginning of Parliamentary Reporting in Newspapers." *English Historical Review* 74 (1959):623–36.
- "Charles Townshend and American Taxation in 1767." *English Historical Review* 83 (1968):33–51.
Tracy, N. "The Gunboat Diplomacy of the Government of George Grenville, 1764–1765." *Historical Journal* 17, no. 4 (1974):711–31.
Wallace, W.S. "The Beginnings of British Rule in Canada." *Canadian Historical Review* 6 (1925):208–21.

Unpublished Theses

Bowen, H.V. "British Politics and the East India Company, 1767–1773." Ph.D., Wales, 1986.
Haydon, C. "Anti-Catholicism in Eighteenth-Century England, c. 1714–1780." D.Phil., Oxford, 1985.
Lawson, P. "Faction in Politics: George Grenville and His Followers 1765–1770." Ph.D., Wales, 1980.
Lowe, W.C. "Politics in the House of Lords, 1760–1775." Ph.D., Emory University, Georgia, 1975.
Marshall, P. "Imperial Regulation of American Indian Affairs 1763–1774." Ph.D., Yale, 1959.
Rees, S. "The Political Career of Wills Hill, Earl of Hillsborough (1718–1793) with particular reference to His American Policy." Ph.D., Wales, 1976.
Thomas, P.J. "Imperial Issues in the British Press, 1760–1782." D.Phil., Oxford, 1983.
Tomlinson, J.R.G. "The Grenville Papers 1763–1765." M.A., Manchester, 1956.

Index